VOICES OF AMERICA

Growing Up Black in

NEW CASTLE COUNTY

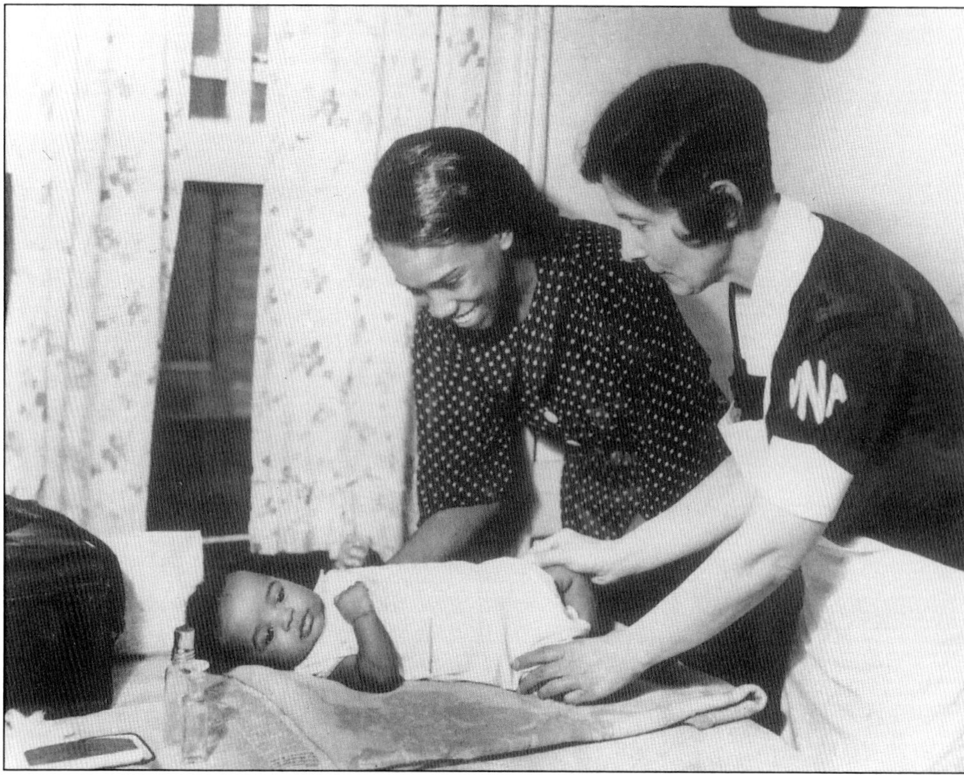

Virginia Cook Marks and Her Newborn Son Jimmy with a Visiting Nurse.

On the cover: ***Students in the Ezion Church Vacation Bible School (c. 1940).***

VOICES OF AMERICA

Growing Up Black in

NEW CASTLE COUNTY

Compiled by

Jeanne D. Nutter

ARCADIA PUBLISHING

ISBN 978-0-7385-0622-7

Published by Arcadia Publishing
Charleston, South Carolina

Printed in the United States of America

Library of Congress Catalog Card Number: 00-110681

For all general information contact Arcadia Publishing at:
Telephone 843-853-2070
Fax 843-853-0044
E-Mail sales@arcadiapublishing.com
For customer service and orders:
Toll-Free 1-888-313-2665

Visit us on the Internet at www.arcadiapublishing.com

This book is dedicated to my mother, Marie Nutter, whose smiles and pleasant disposition sustain me through the most difficult times.

I would like to thank the following individuals for their contributions to this project: Katherine Loraine Hamilton, Ventie Millis Williams, Marjorie Wright Scott, Elizabeth Anderson Hunt, Tobias Whitten, Charles Whitten M.D., Maurice Rouselle, Howard K. Toliver, William Pell Wallace, Olivia Jefferson Johnson, Mary Anne Wheeler Franklin Ph.D., William Webb, William Young, Katherine Young Hazeur, Joseph Young, Edward Loper Sr., Edith Elizabeth Faulkner Dickerson, Cora Pritchett Toliver, Robert J. Fleming Jr., Barbara Washam, Floyd W. Van Riper, Pastor Aretha Morton, Canon Lloyd Stuart Casson, Gladys Green Clark, Althea Unthank Harmon, Elizabeth Bungy Baylor, Dolores Twyman McCray, Leona Black Pinkett, Teal Taylor Petty, Eugene Charles Petty, Bernard Pinkett, Virginia Cook Marks, Richard Fleming, Reverend Clarence "Clyde" Herbert Knotts, Jean Quinn Lewis, Doris Lydia Camper Crommarte, Loretta Bruton, Jane Watson Mitchell, Retha Johnson Kelly, Bernice Jackson Anderson Hilton, Samuel Bernard Peterson, Jean Elizabeth Bolden Fleming, Elizabeth Peterson, Allan O. Wilson D.D.S., Clifton Alvin Lewis, Reverend Frank Gordon, Jeanne Boyer Parler, Robert George Harding, Helen Marie Harding Powell, Joseph Harmon, and William Jackson.

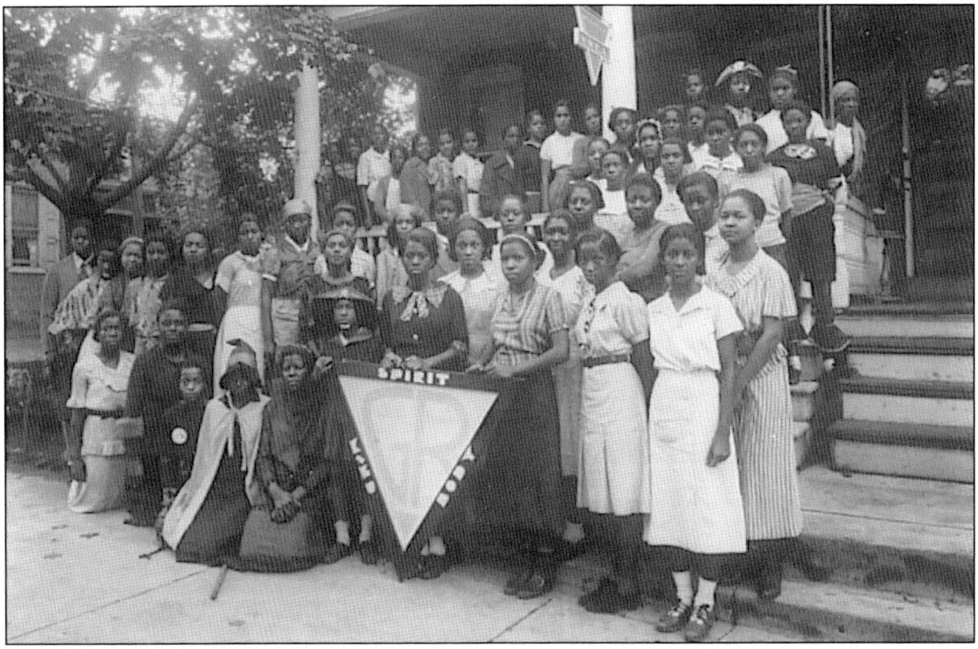

Members of the YWCA in October 1935. *(Courtesy of the Historical Society of Delaware [HSD].)*

Contents

Acknowledgments 6

Introduction 7

1. Wilmington 9

2. New Castle 71

3. Buttonwood 77

4. Belvedere, Newport, and Marshallton 87

5. Claymont 99

6. Christiana and Hockessin 105

7. Newark 111

8. Delaware City and Port Penn 117

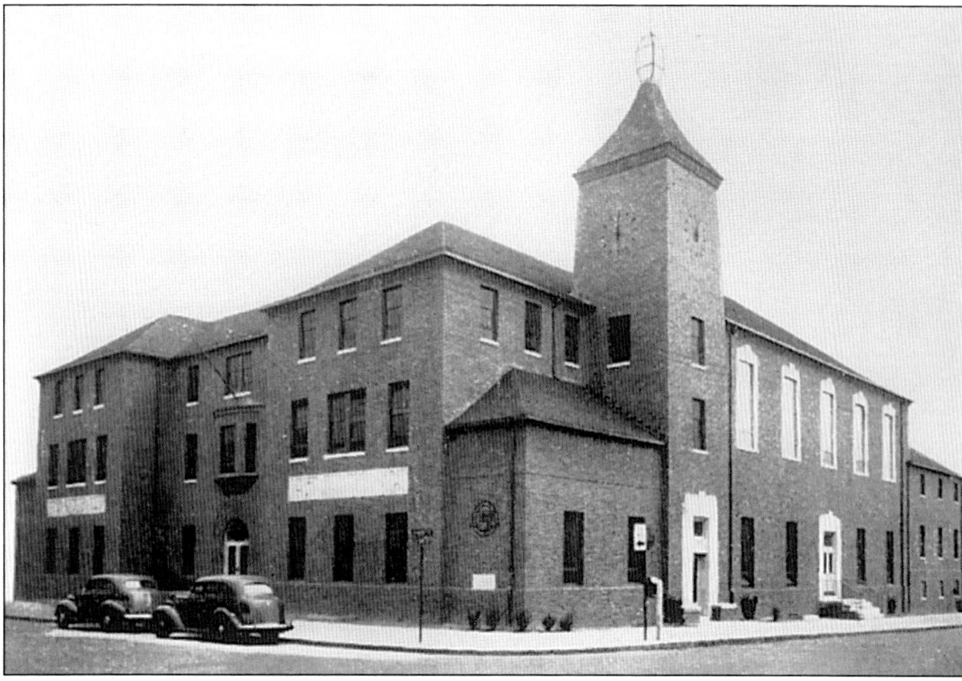

ACKNOWLEDGMENTS

This book developed as a result of my work with the Hagley Museum and Library. Over the past two years I have been collecting oral histories on film about African-American education in Delaware. During those interviews I realized there was much more information to be learned about the lives of people growing up in Delaware. I revisited many of my original interviewees and asked them for more detailed information about their childhoods. These interviews were broadened to include even more people who had lived in the northern section of the state. I owe a great debt to these individuals who trusted me with the intimate details of their lives as children. They shared with me their family relationships, their joys, sorrows, and disappointments. People were also very candid about race. I would like to thank each and every person who shared their stories with me.

There were many people who assisted in the production of this publication. Monica Williams, my assistant on this book and also my first publication, helped keep me organized and on track. I couldn't have done this without her. Lori English did a wonderfully professional job transcribing several of the interviews. Gerald Piotrowski and Eric Russell at Colourworks Photographic Services are a pleasure to work with, and they handled these images with care and respect. I value their aesthetic judgement. I also appreciate the help of individuals at various historical institutions. Jon Williams and Barbara Hall at the Hagley Museum and Library were always so generous with their time whenever I needed photographic images, and Ellen Rendle at the Historical Society of Delaware assisted me greatly in identifying early images of New Castle County.

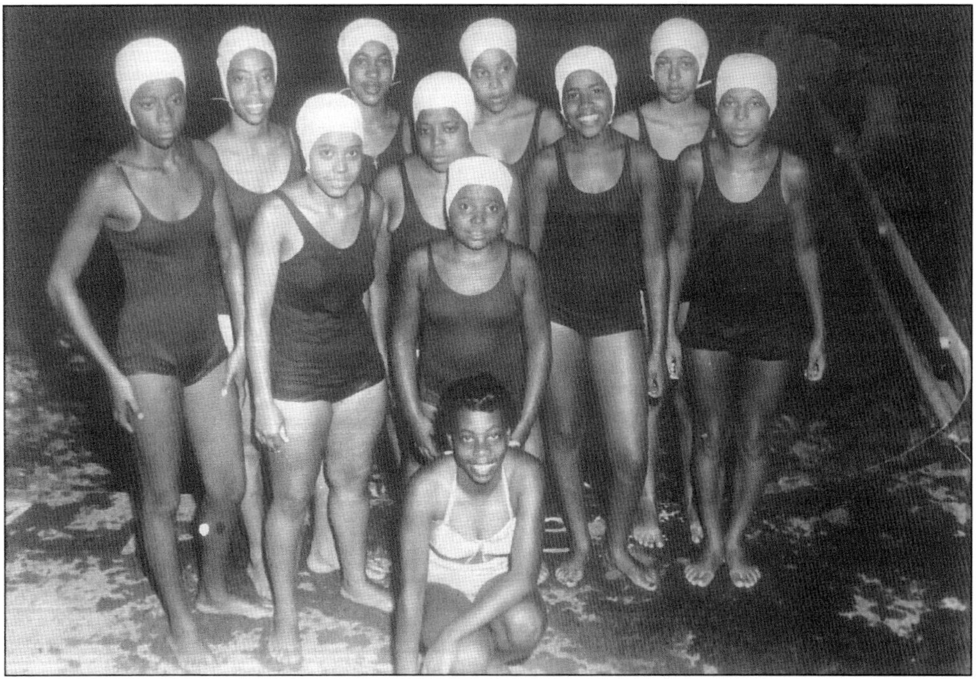

***The YWCA's Synchronized Swim Team.** (Courtesy of the estate of Gilbert H. Jackson.)*

Introduction

This book represents views of African-American life from the early 1900s through the 1950s. The majority of the interviews were conducted with individuals who grew up during the 1920s and 1930s, a time when the United States was defined by sharp racial divisions—especially in Delaware. The geographic area covered in this publication is the northern part of the state, known as New Castle County. Residents of this area talk about their communities, occupations of their parents or guardians, childhood activities and jobs, education, religious activities, and race relations.

The county was quite diverse in terms of living conditions. Some of the people you will meet here lived in urban areas, while others lived in small towns or very rural areas. Many families owned their own homes; others rented or were tenants on farms. The locale played a great part in shaping the experiences of these individuals regarding work, play, education, and race relations.

Many of the parents or guardians you will hear about within these pages worked as domestics or as skilled or unskilled laborers. But it is interesting to note that a number of family members worked for themselves or owned their own businesses. Several grandmothers were entrepreneurs, each operating her own store, boardinghouse, or employment agency. Many parents were professional educators, while others worked at trade occupations. Some were even trained in occupations that they could not later practice because of their race. One storyteller here notes that she learned very early that certain white-owned businesses hired only African Americans of a certain hue. No matter the situation most of the adults in the lives of those interviewed for this project were gainfully employed.

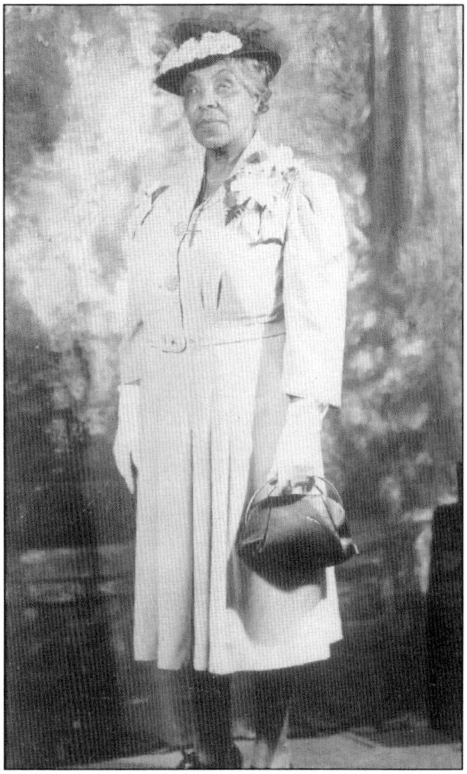

Maurice Rouselle's Grandmother Susan Edwards Rouselle.

Surprisingly enough, many of the games children play today were once played by their grandparents or great-grandparents. Children in the 1920s, 1930s, and 1940s played hopscotch, marbles, jump rope, monopoly, cards, football, basketball, and baseball.

School was a very positive experience for most people. Despite the fact that schools were segregated and the facilities were unequal, children appreciated their teachers and the sacrifices they made. The one element that all of the interviewees had in common was Howard High School, the only public high school in the state. The experience was a marvelous one for most. Traveling to school was often an arduous task. Students who lived outside the city had to travel by bus or milk train, which meant leaving home and school early. Many of these children could not participate in extracurricular activities; if they did, they had to hitchhike home.

Almost every family was involved in some kind of religious activity. Children attended church, Sunday school, vacation Bible school, and youth group activities. Many parents were leaders in the church. Children in both urban and rural locales remember August Quarterly, sponsored by the Mother AUMP Church. This was a time for celebration and meeting friends and relatives.

Like most American states of the period, Delaware was segregated. Blacks and whites did not worship in the same churches, eat in the same restaurants, sit together in movie theaters, or attend the same schools. And for the most part, blacks and whites did not socialize. Many of the comments you will read here regarding race referred to the inability of African-American children to have access to well-equipped playground facilities, baseball fields, and swimming pools. These children watched as their white counterparts played in facilities far superior to the ones they used. Many black children, especially the boys, did, however, play in the streets with their white neighbors, and this occurred frequently in Italian neighborhoods. The children who lived on "The Hill" tended to have good relations with their Italian neighbors, playing with them, eating with them, and developing relationships that lasted, in some cases, for over 50 years. These positive relationships were not limited to Italian neighborhoods, and there were instances of interracial activity in other neighborhoods. But there were also children who had no positive relations with the white community. All in all, children often negotiated the issue of race in their lives very differently than the adults around them. The poignant stories contained herein contain truths and lessons that remain relevant in our modern world as we continue to struggle with the issue of race.

Chapter 1
Wilmington

Katherine Lorraine Hamilton

I was born February 4, 1904, in Wilmington, Delaware. My father was from Smyrna, Delaware. My mother was from Chesterfield, Maryland. I don't know how they met. They had one child who died before I was born and that made me the oldest child. I had a sister Elizabeth. Well, I tell you the truth, we had good substantial food. But for breakfast my mother would have either oatmeal or rice and she always burned it. And we had to eat it burned or not. And of course we had homemade breads, biscuits, rolls. And we always met at suppertime—our family group. We always had our places. My father at the head, my mother at the foot, and my sister and I on either side. It was a lovely family. We had our ups and downs.

I was born in my grandmother's house on Third Street. Then they had a house on 921 Walnut Street. All my friends had porches. Then I got a house with a porch. Well, my grandfather was a preacher. My father worked for J.C. Wilson. He sold things like corn, beans, spinach. Stuff like that. And my mother was a professional dressmaker. If you came to her with material, she would design a dress for you. She worked for Raskob and F. Scott Fitzgerald. And C.J. Walker. The one who invented hair grease. She went to Drexel. They didn't want to take her but ... she sat and sat and finally they said, "Come on." I believe she was the first black to graduate from there. When I graduated from high school all I needed was the groom because I had the trousseau. I had a class day dress and a baccalaureate dress. I had a prom dress. I had a graduation dress. Commencement was at Wilmington High School. Of course it was a white school but they let us have it for commencement. Every other class wore black gowns and caps. We refused to wear them. The class of '21, there were 21 of us. The largest class that had ever come out of Howard High School at that time.

She [Alice Dunbar Nelson] was our sponsor, I guess you call it. She lived at

1204 French Street and the Gibbs at 916 French. Pauline Jones lived across the street. I can't remember that address ... next to the Monday Club. And, ah, once in a while, Elizabeth Stubbs who lived on the West Side came over and ... it was "The Gang" we called it. She had it in her cellar. She made that into a club for us. And we would meet there and we would have a piece to say or play the piano or do something. At Alice Dunbar Nelson's. She was just a person who liked children and we were about 10 or 12, I guess.

I've been a member of St. Matthew's since I was six years old. The Youngs were the backbone of the church. We had ... oh, the sweetest little church on Chippey Street. It was white and sort of had little colored pebbles on it. And most churches you went upstairs. We went downstairs. And we had a beautiful alter. Was there a choir?. Oh, yes. We had a choir. There was an incident. At Christmas time they entertained the children and they gave me a doll. We had to walk around the room for something and I would not put my doll down. I walked around with the hymnal in one hand and the doll on my arm! Another incident was when I was six. I was coming down the stairs one day. And I remember stopping, putting my hand on my hip, rolling my eyes, and saying "Sex! Sex!". That was naughty in those days. And I was caught saying it.

My uncle owned it [the National Theater] John Hopkins. Well, he was a black member of the city council. He was in the council for 40 years. Well, there was a door that begins and you walk into the box office, which Pauline Milburn took care of. It had a stage and Ethel Waters came and stayed at my grandmother's house. They would have little movies and then the show. Heavenly days, I saw so many. I went every day. It [movie] cost about a nickel. The highest it ever got was a quarter.

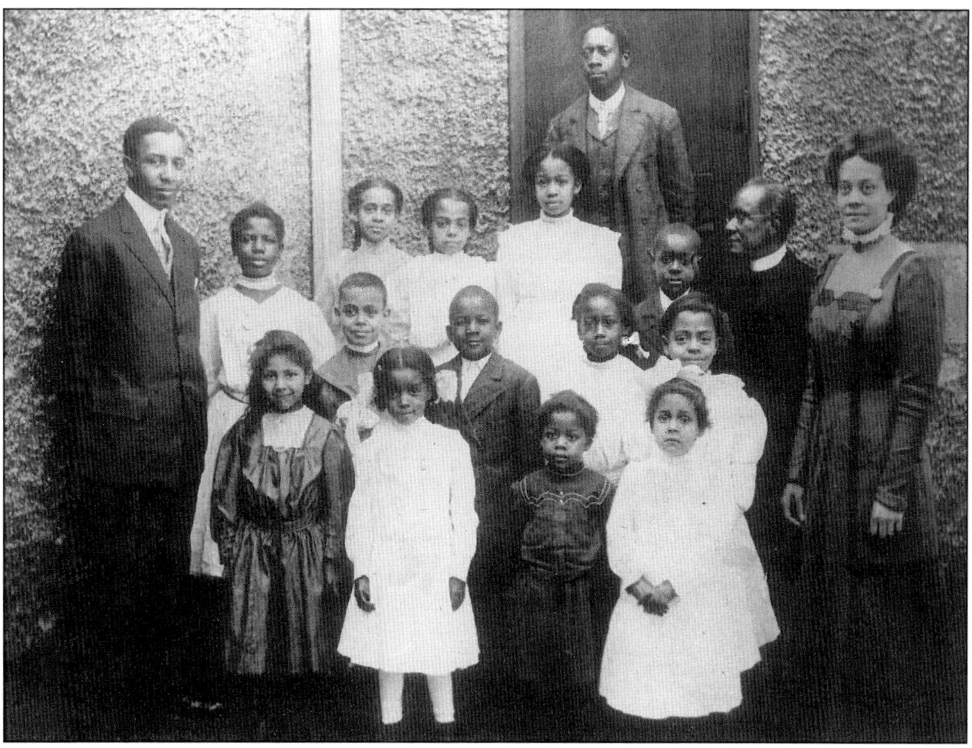

***St. Matthews Episcopal Church Sunday School with Teacher Alice Dunbar Nelson, c. 1910.** K. Lorraine Hamilton is in the front row (left) wearing a white dress.*

Oh, Christmas ... For a while in the early years we had to go to bed so Santa Claus could come but as we grew older we were allowed to help trim the tree. We had garlands of tinsel, white balls, and always had a tall pine ... not pine ... fir tree. I can't remember a Christmas without my fir tree. Even now, I get my fir tree.

Ventie Millis Williams

My father was William Millis and my mother was Mamie Millis. I grew up ... I think I was born over Eleventh Street Bridge, because I remember in later years coming back to Poplar Street. I was the oldest of four children. I started taking piano lessons when I was five years old. Wilmington was segregated but a white teacher would come to my house and teach me. That was unusual because Wilmington was segregated and I have thought recently ... that I wonder why she was around teaching. Her name was Mrs. Powell. And she came to your house and I had to practice before I went to school.

I went to #29 School at Ninth and Poplar. From there I went to Howard High School, which was at Tenth and Orange, and I played in all the musical things there. I played for everything. I graduated when I was 16 years old, I think, from Howard High School. I wanted to play the organ, so I would go up on the boat to Philadelphia and would take organ lessons from Mr. Hochster and come back on the boat. Wilmington Music School, which was prejudiced, opened up their school to Negroes. I was the first Negro to be in Wilmington Music School.

I do remember playing for a band, but I played with the orchestra ... I mean a four-piece band when I was 16. It was a trumpet, banjo, and I think a trumpet ... banjo ... and a saxophone. I think those were the instruments. And I used to go around with them and they would go down to Maryland to play. At age 16, I became the organist at St. Matthew's Episcopal Church. I also played piano for a five-piece band and the Shiloh Baptist Sunday School. After I graduated from high school, I found time to accompany the Treble Clef Trio (Helen Turner, Anna Grinnage and me), the Choir Celeste (that's a community chorus), and to play for Sunday afternoon services at Emily Bissell Hospital and the Episcopal Church.

My mother was a seamstress and she would make clothing or help mend clothing for people in the area. My father worked for an ice cream ... It wasn't a factory, it was just a small store right up from where we lived. It was called Cooper's Ice Cream.

I was always getting into trouble and sent to bed because I didn't obey my parents. I didn't think there was anything to do. There wasn't anything but to go to ... I think I went to Shiloh Sunday School. But there was no activity. Just practice the piano. There was no television, no radio,

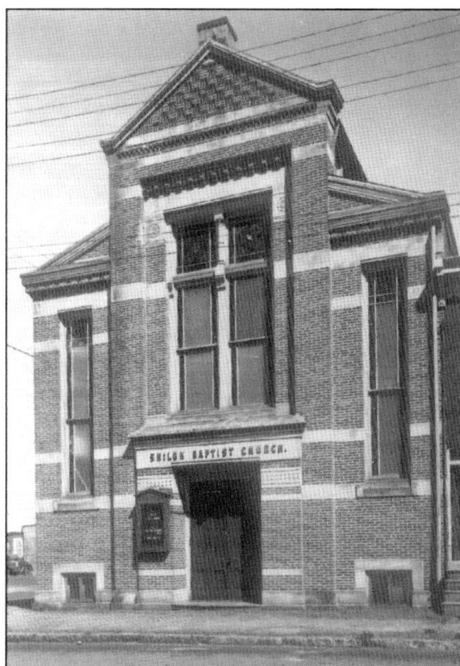

***Shiloh Baptist Church.** Ventie Millis Williams played for the Sunday school here. (Courtesy of the HSD.)*

so we just got into mischief. My mother would fix dinner, and put it on the table in the kitchen. I would go by and stick my fingers in the meat, or the pie. So I was sent to bed without anything to eat. Ninety years ago there wasn't anything exciting going on.

We had a prom because that was the thing my father took me to and brought me home. I didn't have any boyfriends to take me to the prom, I can tell you that. I think he took me and then he came for me and took me back home before we even got started!

Marjorie Wright Scott

I lived on Thirteenth Street between French and Walnut Street. And at that time it was called the Upper East Side. I was born in Philadelphia, but I was brought to Wilmington at a very early age, as a baby. And all of my growing up years were here in Wilmington. I went to #29 School, and when I left there, I went to Howard Junior High School and from Howard Junior High School to Senior High.

Well, my mother at one time worked for the Henry Canbys, which were rich people. And they had flour mills along the Brandywine River. And I wasn't born at that time while they were operating the flour mills, but she worked there for a while, and she would name me "Canby" after the lady. Her name was Marjorie Tatnall Canby, and my name is Marjorie Canby Wright. And my father's name was Wright. My grandmother lived four doors from us. And she was—what do you call them? My grandmother was a midwife, and she delivered many of the boys and girls in Wilmington. And my grandmother was just as much my mother as my mother was. And I can remember she used to say to us all the time "I want you to behave yourself because you know you are a Turner." And I often wondered what that meant, just because I am a Turner. Now I now what it meant. That she expected us not to bring shame to the name of Turner.

My uncle was one of the first mail carriers in Wilmington, my Uncle Patrick Turner. And who else? My Aunt Mahalia was a schoolteacher. My mother's twin sister, who lived in New York, she was in politics. And I had a uncle who lived in Philadelphia. He worked at the Philadelphia Naval Base. And my uncle's wife, Helen Turner, was a community activist. And she used to teach adults to read in the adult reading program in Wilmington. She did a lot of singing around the city and at the various churches. She belonged to the Episcopal Church, but she went to other churches to sing. She worked with children at the Girl's Industrial School at that time.

Well, most of the people were just about on the same level. They were very nice hard-working people. They didn't have big jobs, but most of them owned their own homes. Just about all of them who lived in that area of Thirteenth and French and down French Street. Mr. George Oscar Carrington lived down there. The Hollins, Dr. Hollins, who was a pharmacist at Ninth and French at the pharmacy on the corner there, and Elmer Lopeman and his wife.

And at that time the blocks were mixed black and white. But just about all of the people owned their homes in that area and that was the thing that many people didn't do at that time. But just about all those blocks were intact and people lived there for years.

We got along very well with them [white people]. I used to play with—there was an apartment house across the street from where I lived. And I remember I had a girlfriend named Audrey Murray, who was white. And we were very friendly, and we didn't have any arguments, and there were white people down French Street. Most of Walnut Street was black, but those

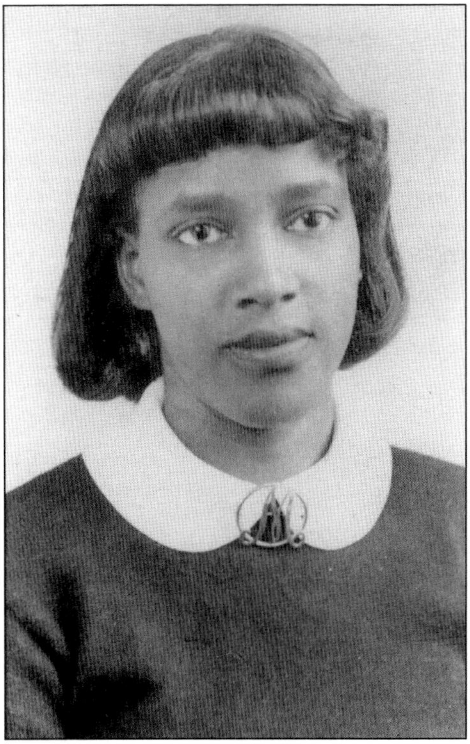

Marjorie Wright Scott as a Teenager.

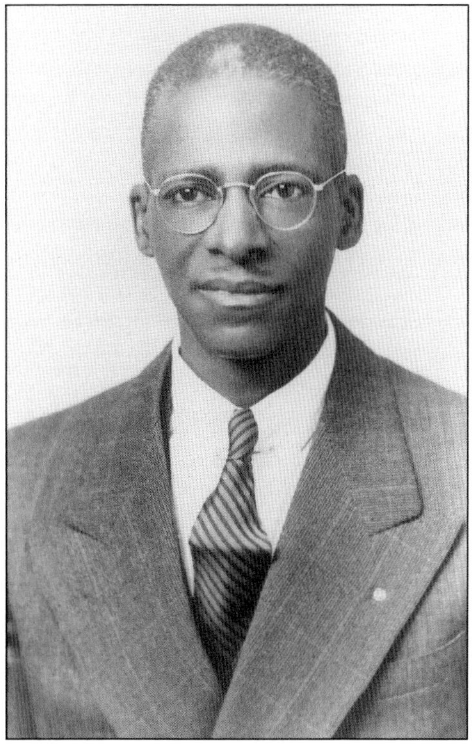

Marjorie's Uncle Patrick Turner. He was one of the first African-American mail carriers in Wilmington.

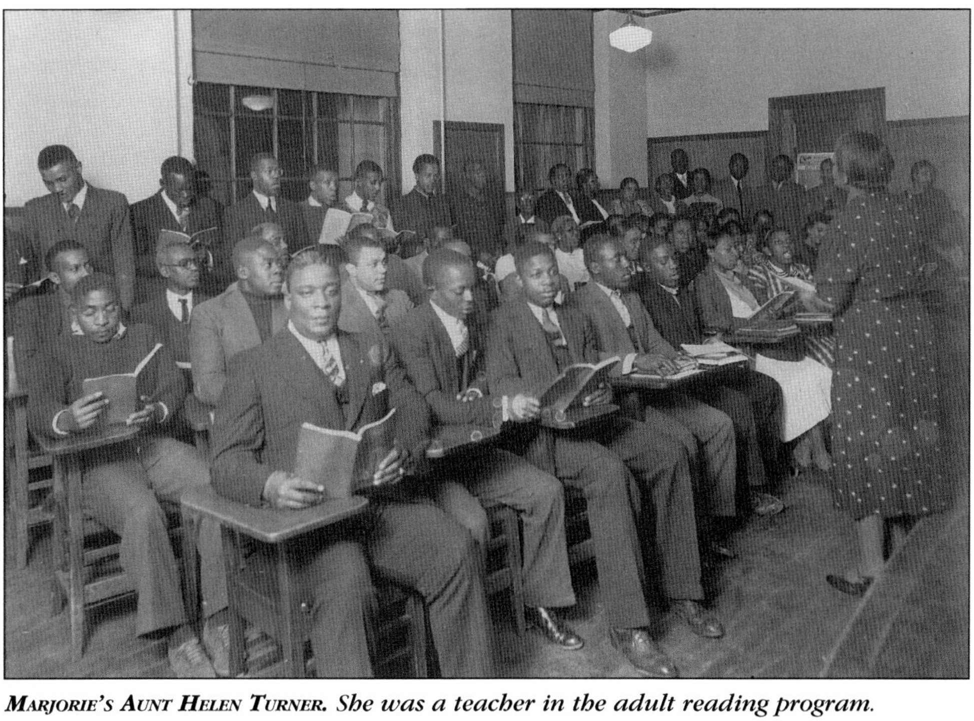

Marjorie's Aunt Helen Turner. She was a teacher in the adult reading program.

people too, Mr. Alonzo Shockley, who was a big member of Ezion Church, they owned their home. They had a beautiful home. Mr. Patrick Harris and his family and even Mrs. Pauline Milburn lived next door to the Harrises when I was a little girl down Walnut Street. She later moved up to Tenth and French Street. We skated up and down her alley, the children did. And then she used to chase us out of the alley. We had a doctor, Dr. Cuff, who was down Walnut Street. He was one of the early doctors. And he was a well-known family in Wilmington. His wife was a teacher at the Girl's Industrial School at that time. Eddie Jones and his wife, Mrs. Russ, David Russ's wife, they lived on Walnut Street . And Mr. Russ, a very handsome man, was a steward at the Monday Club, one of the early steward's at the Monday Club. All these people owned their own their property. There were Jewish stores, one at Thirteenth and Walnut and one at Kennebeck Street. The owners were very nice to black people. We never had any problems with them. They were very friendly at that time. "Slew" Jackson lived down the street in the next block from us, and he was at the 100 block of Thirteenth Street.

We played hopscotch in the street. There weren't that many cars and every time a car would come down the street, we would jump up on the sidewalk. And we played a game called "Scummy." We got down on all fours and shot a little disk in different numbers. We played hide and go seek. And we jumped a lot of rope. We had roller skates. We skated all up and down the street, right out in the middle of the street.

And the Clover Dairy was, down where Howard School is, at that time. And horses would come in the middle of the street. And as soon as we saw a horse, we would jump up on the pavement. I was always afraid of horses too. Well, that's about it. We used to go down to ... after the Howard School was built, we used to go down there. They had a playground down there. We played on the seesaws and the sliding boards and all the equipment, the swings they had down there.

Oh, we went to the movies every Saturday, the National Theater. That was the only one we could go to and it was crowded. Every Saturday we went to the National Theater to see the pictures, every Saturday. That was our entertainment. And every Friday night we would either go to Howard School to a dance or we had the YWCA, which was at Thirteenth and Tatnall Street, right on the corner in the house that Mrs. Slowe used to own. And we would go up there and jitterbug and was in—at that time we jitterbugged ourselves to death.

In the summertime, Ezion Church and Bethel Church had picnics up in—what's the name of that park? Oh, I can't think of that park that everybody went to. Shellpot Park and all the children looked forward to that. And our parents too, because grown ups went and children went. We had a special day to go. Black people couldn't even go any day. The days they set aside that's when we went to that park. And we had a picnic, and we stayed all day and rode on all the equipment in the park. We also went to the swimming pool. It was called "Kruse Pool," and we went there mostly—at least I did, in the afternoon. You could go in the mornings too. Mr. Wheeler was the instructor if you wanted to learn how to swim—Mr. Arthur Wheeler. There was a tennis court near the pool. In fact, the tennis court didn't start until they tore the pool down. That's what happened. And then the blacks used to go down there and play tennis. That was after the swimming pool was torn down. I don't know why they tore that swimming pool down, but they did.

And then we had a playground at Sixteenth and well, it was Cooper Street, I guess. They had a lot of equipment on it. And in the summertime we went to the playground. And people came up from Dover every summer.

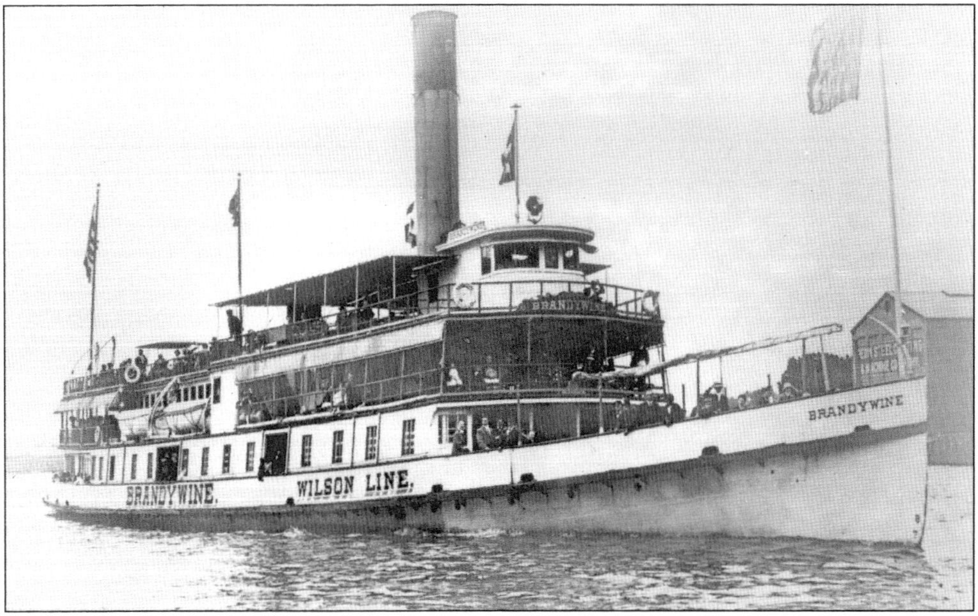

***The Wilson Line.** Marjorie Scott and her friends took this boat to Philadelphia to go to the theater or to see one of the big name bands. (Courtesy of the HSD.)*

We used to go up to Philadelphia to Market Street to shows at some of the theaters. They had big shows and they had big named bands. That was after we got to be teenagers. And we also used to have to ride up and down the Delaware River on the boat to Philadelphia for a quarter. That was the way we went to Philadelphia. We did not ride the train. We always rode the boat. We would get up early in the morning. Seven o'clock you go down to the wharf and get the boat to Philadelphia. And it went from Wilmington over to New Jersey and from New Jersey to Chester and from Chester on to Philadelphia. And that is what we did, and we used to take big baskets of food and sit on the boat and just have an outing. Oh, It was crowded all the time. That was our enjoyment that we did. We sat where we wanted to on the boat. In Wilmington if you could get on the conveyance, you sat where you wanted to sit. Of course, you couldn't go to the theater, so we didn't have that. But on the bus, on the buses—we called them trolleys—you could sit wherever you wanted. On the boat you could sit where you wanted....

It was mostly in the '30s that I can remember. We were only segregated in stores. You couldn't go to eat because I remember we used to go to the market down King Street every Saturday morning with my mother and we carried wicker baskets. And we always wanted to go down to the Woolworths down at Fifth and Market Street—Fifth and King. It ran from Market to King. And we always used to say, "Let's go in and have a soda." That was when we were real little. And my mother was saying, "Come on here." And we would walk right on past the store. And I was a little older when I realized that we couldn't go in and sit down. So she would go home and make something for us: sodas, snowballs. My mother was a cook and we always had a lot to eat. And we always had a lot of friends in the house.

There was a young man who lived down French Street. He was Irish and every now and then he would call us

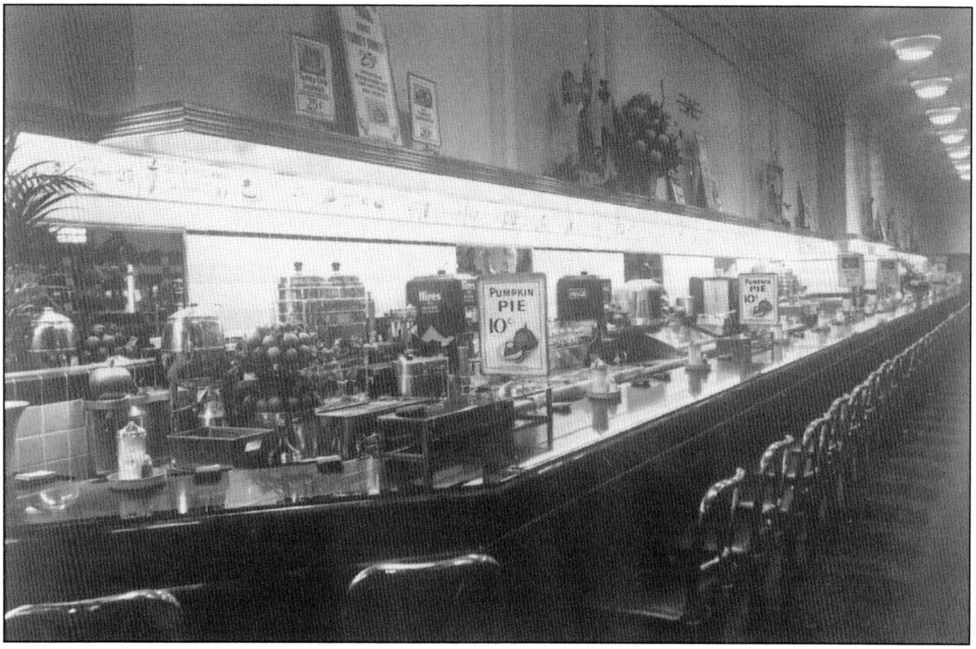

***The Woolworth's Lunch Counter.** Marjorie Scott and other African Americans were not allowed to eat here. (Courtesy of the HSD.)*

"Nigger" and we would chase him home. In fact, he lived next door to Thelma Henry—Thelma Lopeman. But we never really had any big fusses about race that I can remember. I didn't really become aware of that until I was much older. And then, of course. I wasn't just in my own area you know. It kind of spread out, and I met prejudice.

And I knew as a youngster we couldn't just go into the restaurants, but that was about the biggest thing. We could ride on the buses. I never had anybody asked me to go to the back door. That was the only other racial problem that we really had other than kids would call you "Nigger." And of course we all took care of that. That was the biggest thing I know. We had to stay in our own facilities. We had to do that so ... of course ... but other than that ... we got used to that. And we didn't even think about going to the bathroom. And we played with the white children, but they went to their church, and they went to their playground.

I do remember this: Kirkwood Park was designated as a white park and you couldn't swing, get in their swings. And I can remember that the teachers on the playground in the park would make us get up. They would chase us away. And we enjoyed getting into the swings, and they would say, "Go on! Get out of there! Get out of there!" And that was for a long time. I'd say for over a period of time. I can't remember when it started, but I had to be at least nine years old before I could go down there anyway. So I would say from nine years old until about fourteen when Kirkwood Park was designated as a white park. And then after a while as the white people started moving, then they turned it over to us. I remember going there right in the beginning, you know, it being a black park. We could always go through Rodney Square. We could go there and sit down if we cared to. I don't remember times that we couldn't. I don't remember any other park names—well, there was a park down Fourth Street, but

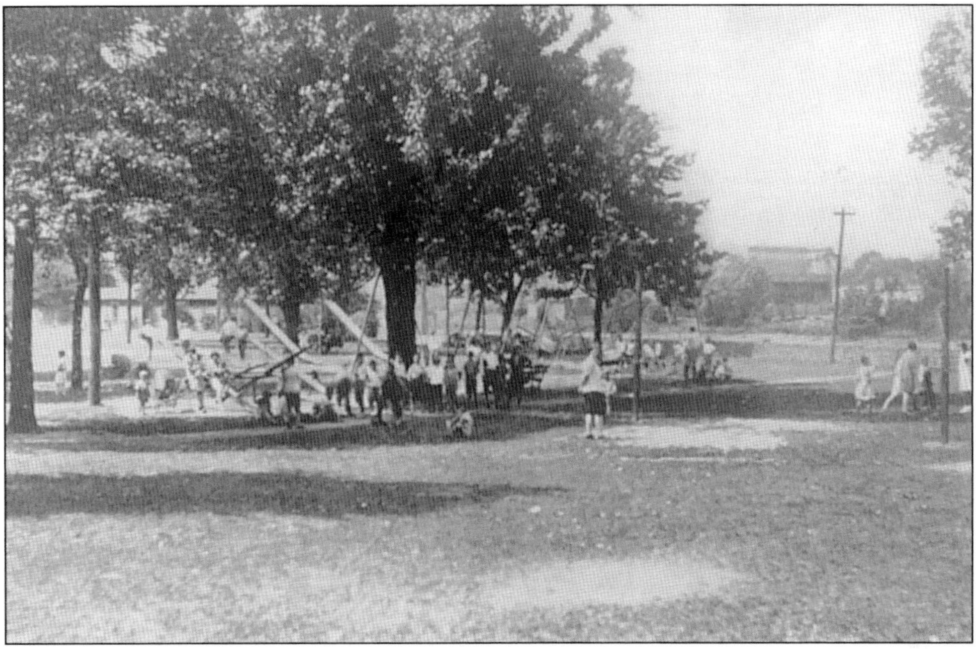

Kirkwood Park. *African-American children were not allowed to use the facilities here. (Courtesy of the HSD.)*

I didn't go down there because it was too far away. Kirkwood is the one I remember now. I think of that park now because I taught at Stubbs School, which is located in Kirkwood Park. And I used to look out the window and think to myself how I grew up and I couldn't even walk through that park because I was black.

Well, to me Christmas was a family time and my whole family would get together on Christmas. And in my own house, my mother—all she did was cook for it looked like a month. My mother and my grandmother made the best fruit cakes. There was a family named the Bushes, I believe, and the Biddles, and she used to make fruit cakes for them and the Spruances. And they would have her make these fruit cakes for a week. And then she would make fruit cakes at home. And they were really good fruit cakes. My grandmother and my mother made them. And sometimes I would help if I felt like I wanted to. And she made all kinds of cookies for the house, and we would decorate the house.

And the whole block— the whole block all around the area—there were lights that were on. People would do that, but we didn't light up our windows like they do now, only a few houses. And at that time we thought that was gaudy. Most people had wreaths in their windows and big red bows on the doors and on the windows. Only a few and as time went by, did you start seeing lights in windows. But they just had the doors so pretty just like in a picture. That's the way every house had a wreath and wreaths in the window. And they were live, and we bought them down King Street. You didn't go to the store and buy an artificial one. You bought live ones. It was the best holiday—it was really the best holiday.

Elizabeth Anderson Hunt

I was born here in Wilmington. My parents were Alice Benson and Thomas Anderson Jr. My mother finished Howard

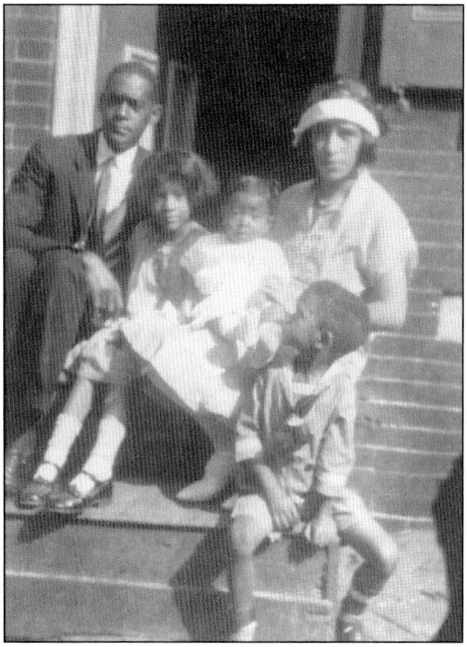

The Anderson Family on the Steps of Their Home in Wilmington. *From left to right are Thomas Anderson Jr., Elizabeth Anderson, Alice Benson Anderson holding Robert Anderson, and little Thomas Anderson.*

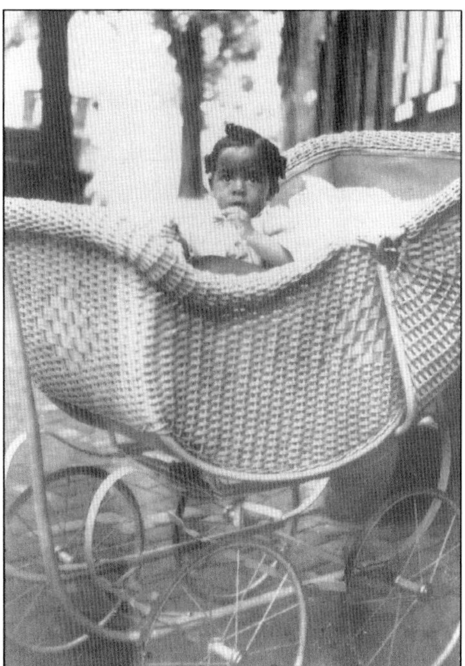

Elizabeth Anderson Hunt as an Infant.

High School and taught downstate or in Maryland, someplace. At that time you could teach right from high school. And my father finished Howard High School and went to Lincoln University. He was there in 1919. Taught school, mostly the rest of his life. He taught at Claflin College in Orangeburg, South Carolina, and at Tuskeegee Institute in Tuskeegee, Alabama. Some school I don't remember the name in Selma, Alabama, and then Howard High School—biology, botany, and general science.

I can remember living on Eleventh, between Eleventh and Twelfth on Walnut, the house is still there, and 1108 Poplar Street and 1325 Tatnall Street. On Walnut Street, I was pre-school age. It was across the street from a Morocco [leather] factory. It smelled bad. It was a rather intact little neighborhood, the block where I lived. Everybody knew everybody else. Everybody looked out for everybody else. I was happy there.

I've always gone to the library. Yes. And I did take piano lessons. The teacher was Miss Brooks. She lived in an apartment on Ninth Street and I took lessons from her. But before that, I took piano lessons when we lived in Tuskeegee. From what I have read since then, I think maybe Lionel Richie's grandmother taught me piano lessons in Tuskeegee.

It was a very close family. Stimulating! Studying to be somebody. I can remember even as children we would say "I'm going to be...". So my youngest brother was going to be a minister and my oldest brother was going to be a dentist. I was going to be a concert pianist. We were always intellectual in some way. We had activities right within our family and sometimes I would be giving a concert and my brother would be preaching a sermon, but we were always expected to do well and C's were not accepted. B's weren't very good either. You were expected to get all A's when you went to school. And I've never gotten over that.

I've taken courses to—later in life, and I said "I'm not going to get an A. I don't care what I get. I'm just going to take a course," and I'd end up making an A. I just couldn't do it. My mother was looking over my shoulder.

Well, I took college preparatory courses and had some of the best teachers anybody could ever have. At that time Howard High, I thought, was really wonderful and I never had any trouble keeping up with anybody afterwards. I had a good education. I have always been grateful for having gone to Howard at that time. When I was in college, I remember professors saying to me, "How do you know how to do that?" They were just amazed, you know, the things I could do and they'd say other people would have to be shown how to do certain things I knew. I said, "I learned that in high school." I had a very good education. I represented the school at conferences. I remember going to one in Pendle Hill, a Quaker institution that was in Wallingford, Pennsylvania, and staying with a Quaker family, and having to come back and report to the school about what the conference was all about. It was probably about unity between races, something along that order.

My aunt used to make these smocked dresses made of a material called pongee. They had a lot of smocked dresses, I can remember those little organdy dresses in the summertime. I always had a lot of clothes. But they weren't store-bought clothes. That's what I wanted, store-bought clothes. I can remember in Tuskeegee, I had so many clothes, I could change clothes two or three times a day. I did.

I lived with my mother's mother and father for many years, so I was close to them, and my father's mother and father lived out on "the Hill" and she would come in every Wednesday to the Farmer's Market and come down to the house and bring us eggs. She wanted to make sure we got fresh eggs every week. She would

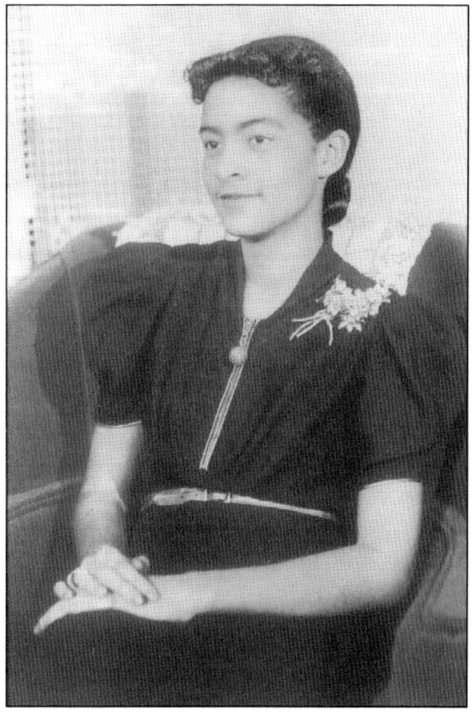

Elizabeth Anderson during Her Years at Howard High School.

bring eggs every week from the Farmer's Market. My father's father was a tinsmith. He had a shop in the back of his house. My grandmother was the one who talked and played with us. I can remember she made the best gravy I ever tasted, and root beer. She was a good cook. And so was my other grandmother. I can remember Sunday morning breakfast, veal cutlet, creamed potatoes, and homemade bread that was our Sunday breakfast. And my grandfather, my mother's father, was a chef, so he could cook anything. He was in great demand, as a person who roasted ox, pigs for organizations. His name was John Benson. He was very handy. He could do anything—carpentry, very versatile. He'd draw, paint, make posters, was a big Elk, more outgoing than the other grandfather. My grandmother was also active in the Elks.

He [my grandfather] built six houses which are still out there at Third and

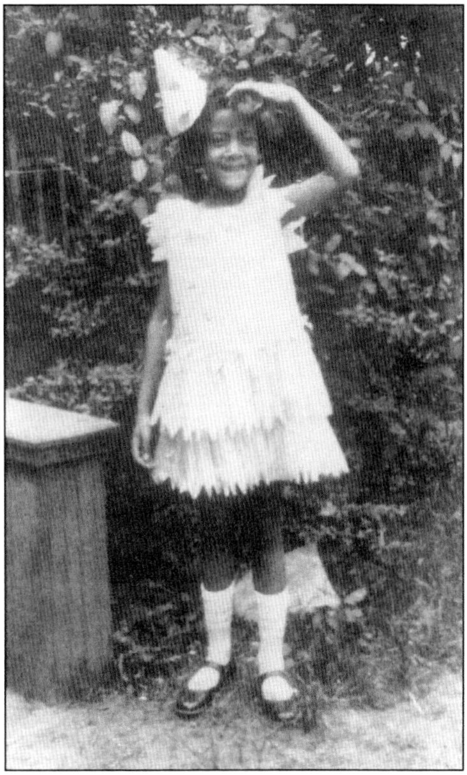

ELIZABETH ANDERSON, C. 1928, IN A FANCY DRESS MADE BY HER AUNT ANNA BENSON COMEGEYS.

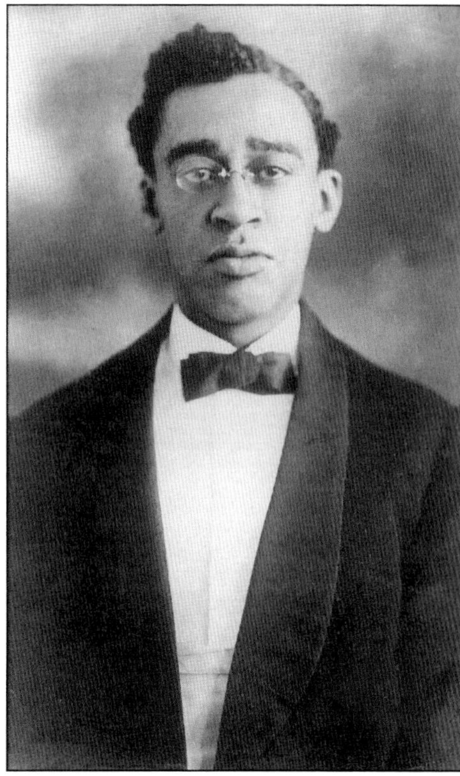

JOHN BENSON. Elizabeth's grandfather was a chef and an active member of the Elks.

Clayton Street. And, I remember my Uncle Perc saying that he was born in Princeton, New Jersey, and I don't know how he got here to Wilmington, but he was born in New Jersey. And he was a tinsmith. One time he had an exhibit of some kind at the Worlds Fair in Philadelphia. I don't know exactly what it was. But he made all kinds of things that were made of tin. He was a roofer when you had to have a tin roof.

Thomas Anderson Sr., his father was junior at one time, lived at Third and Clayton, which was almost like out in the country. Some relative of his, I don't know whether it was his uncle or cousin or somebody, owned a lot of property around what is now Fourth and Union Street and I'm told that at one time it was called Andersonville, cause he owned all that property out there.

My grandmother, my mother's mother, had a brother who was very fair and passed as white. I remember, when we visited him, we had to go at night because he was living in an apartment house down at Fourteenth and Walnut. I think the building is there now. Because he was passing, because we were not allowed in that building during the daytime, we had to go at night to see Uncle Zay.

I didn't have much contact with anybody [white]. When I went away to those conferences, I'd come in contact with white people. At that time everything was just closed. You went to school with black people and you socialized with black people. Just didn't come in contact with white people at all.

Tobias Whitten

My birth date is the tenth month, twenty-third day of 1928. I was born at 1011 Poplar Street, in the front bedroom by midwife. My parents are Mr. and Mrs. T. Emanuel Whitten. My mother's name is Emma Clarinda Carr. My birth certificate says legitimate ... colored and legitimate on my birth certificate. I was 18 months old when my daddy died so I have no remembrance of him whatsoever. I can basically remember everything else but that ... everybody but that.

My mother at that time ... She started teaching at the settlement. She was at the settlement, and well ... she sewed at night. She made slipcovers, and those type of things to help put some money in her pocket. Oh, she had time for everything, to educate, everything. She taught you everything that you knew or thought you knew or, and what you didn't want to know. My mother was very close to all of us. We were well raised and well loved and well cared for.

She knew everything. You could not fool her. She sent me to the store. I couldn't have been over 5 or 6 years old, and I bought a pack of cigarettes, and I went up in the bathroom and smoked a cigarette, and they saw all the smoke coming, and she wore me out. The thing about in the bathroom you couldn't duck. It wasn't big enough for you, so she could hit you from any angle ... You hit your head on the sink or tub or something. You got more abuse from trying to duck. But the worse part was ... the beatings never hurt. She'd sit down on the tub and talk, that what would make you cry. That would make you cry. When she finished talking to you, you had a good whippin.

She used to call me the owl. She said, "You sleep all day, and at night your eyes start opening up" but her last word as I was going out the door "I raised you, and I'm not raising anymore!".

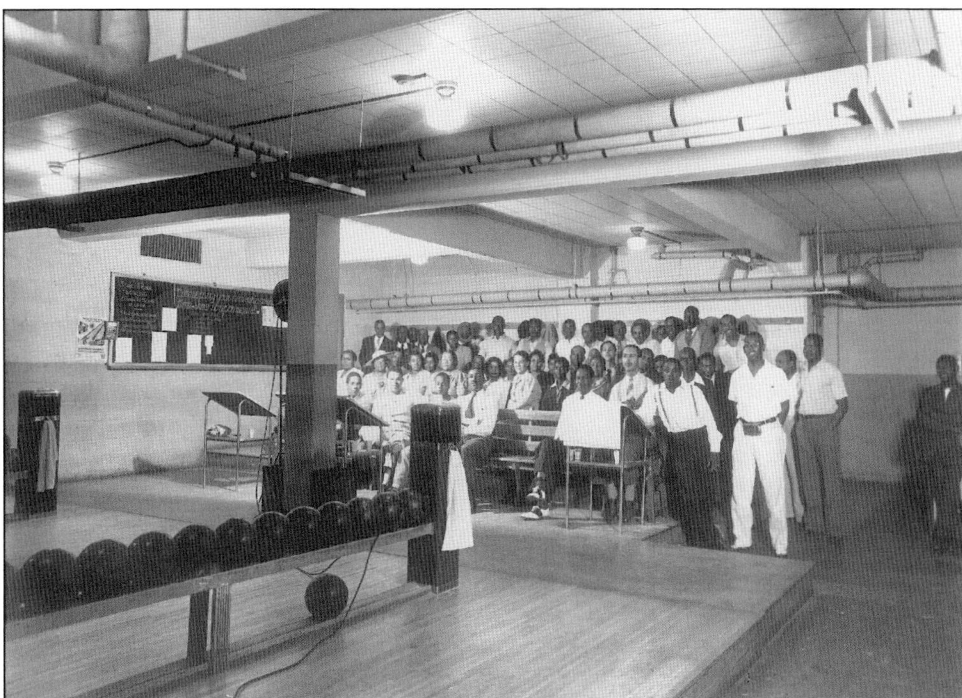

The Walnut Street "Y" Bowling Alley. Tobias Whitten worked here as a pin boy.

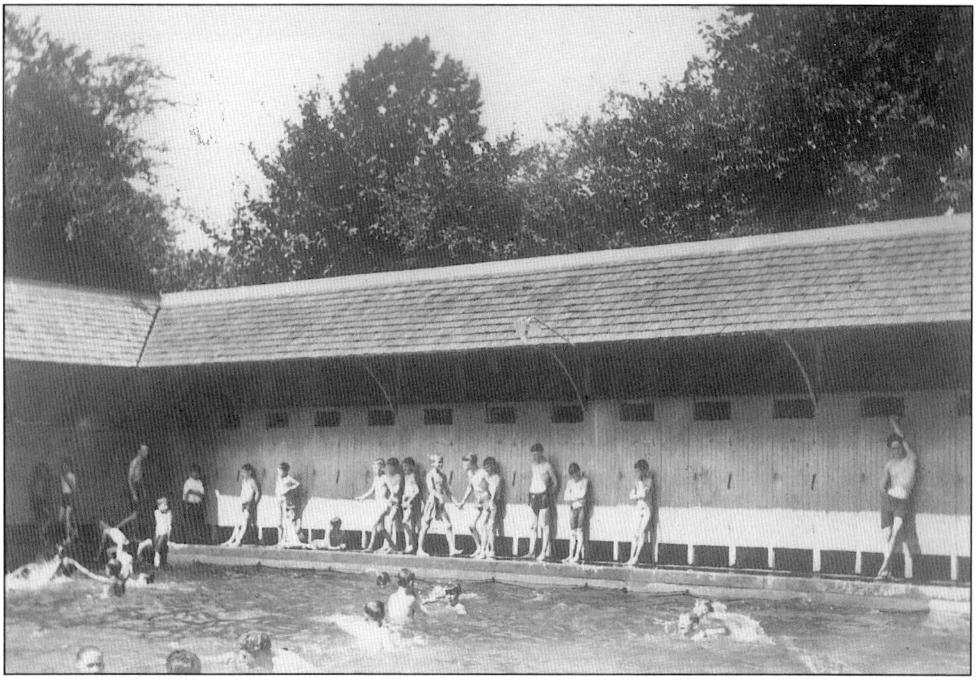

***The Swimming Pool at Kirkwood Park.** African-American children were not permitted to swim here. (Courtesy of the HSD.)*

And another thing you want to know about discipline, my mother taught at Ferris School. She taught white kids out there before it was allowed. Before it was allowed. The superintendent out there had her teaching white boys when it wasn't ... it was against the state law.

I don't remember the year that the plane fell at Eighth and ... Seventh and Poplar. Sonny Johnson got injured in that, and they couldn't find me. Fire engines and everybody went in. And for a couple of hours they couldn't find me, and they thought I was out there ... at the plane crash. Clarence Scott and I were playing Monopoly, and never moved. When I came out the house they were ready to kill me, but they saw me and I told them where I was, I was right across the street, and we never moved the whole time all that disturbance went on. We were playing Monopoly.

I was working at the bowling alley making 4¢ a line setting up pins. They charged 15¢, and the pin boy got 4¢ a game, and I wanted a bicycle. I got tired of what we called a tin lizzy. I wanted a balloon tire bicycle. So mother took me to Sears and Roebuck. I got a bike for $28.95, and I paid for it making 4¢ a game. Yeah, how long do you think it took me to pay for that bicycle?

Used to be a swimming pool down there [Kirkwood Park]. It was for whites only. We went in at night after the park guard left. Then you could go in. Yeah. Kirkwood Park they've had a swimming pool down there for years, but only for white kids.

Charles Whitten, M.D.

I had two brothers and a sister—Benjamin and Alice and Tobias Emanuel Jr., named after our father. My birth date is February 2, 1922. Well I had several early memories. I remember my father going into elementary school on a windy day walking behind him being protected from the wind going up the hill to #5 School. I remembered my father wore a vest with ... it had pennies in it, and he played the numbers every day.

We were very unfortunate that our father died. He had an insurance policy, but it lapsed. It lapsed. At that time that insurance policy was about $5,000, a lot of money. And it lapsed when he died. He died from pneumonia, and that was during the days when you had a nine-day crisis. You got well or you died. And I can remember the night before he died when we were supposed to be praying for him because it was a critical day. And the next morning when I woke up they had his body out in the back room. And it was covered and I pulled it back [the cover] and I recognized that he had died. But that was on the ninth day. I said his insurance policy had lapsed. And that made a big difference in our lives. We had a $5,000 insurance policy. And it lapsed.

I have to mention we had an aunt. My father's sister. Who was very, very important to us. She provided some help for us. When I went to college she paid my tuition. She paid my train fare. I commuted to the University of Pennsylvania. But she was very helpful to us you know through the years and that was real important.

In our neighborhood, my first and only contact with anyone my age that was white was when I went to the University of Pennsylvania. Because the only contact we had was the corner grocers.

My brother and I when we started working, bought a washing machine for her [mother]. And one time we bought a refrigerator for her, and she was very proud of this.. You know little jobs we were doing and so forth. We did a lot of

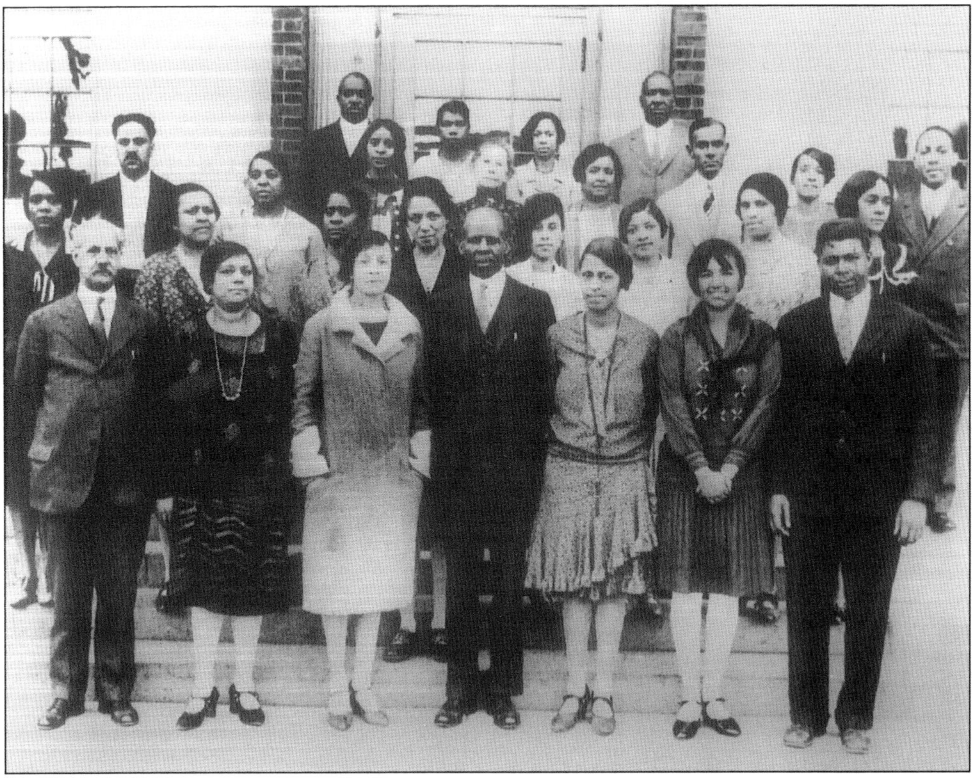

***Howard High School Faculty.** On the back row are Tobias and Charles Whitten's father, T. Emanuel Whitten, on the left, and their uncle George T. Whitten, on the right.*

shoveling snow, and some painting. And we saved money, and between shoveling snow and washing windows and that sort of thing in the neighborhood, we had paper routes. We both had paper routes. I remember buying that washing machine, and how proud my mother was. She was telling neighbors you know, "Look what my kids did for me." And so forth.

Let me tell you a couple of other things. Your bringing some of this back. We had August Quarterly. This was big enterprise for us. So we made the rootbeer early enough so it was easy to sell and so forth. Then one of Cliff Brown's brothers, Leon, and I, we sold fish from time to time. We'd go down to the market, buy fish, get a tub, put in ice and so forth and go through the neighborhood, "Fish oh fish!. Trout oh trout!". We had a great time with that. Made a few extra dollars.

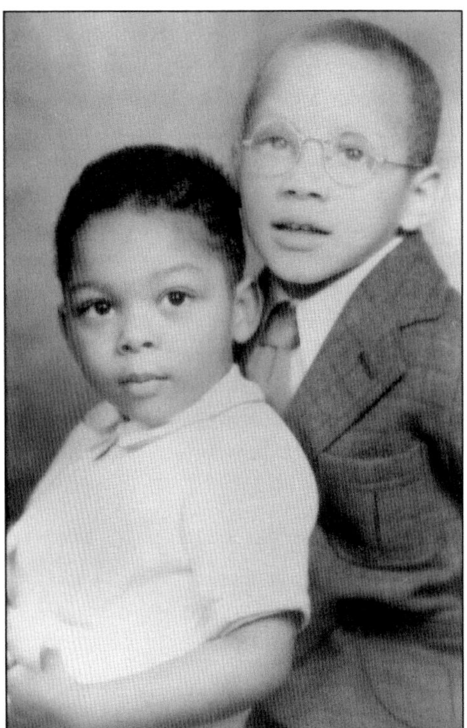

Maurice Rouselle and His Brother Charles Rodney Rouselle, c. 1937.

Maurice Rouselle

My grandmother related to me that she was holding me in her arms looking out of the window when apparently I mentioned in fact there was a bird in the sky. It was an airplane that was about to fall on the house. It may have just been the engine from the airplane. It was in approximately around 1932 because I was young. It was a stunt pilot. The pilot landed about a block away at Bancroft School. And the debris or the engine from the airplane fell into the house. Part of it was remodeled as a result of it. I was told that the airplane pilot was either flying from Blanca Airstrip on Airport Road or either the DuPont Field which is down on Airport Road which is [route] 273. It's where the present I guess Hare's Corner Post Office is. But back in those days, of course, it was all farms. As a matter of fact, where the airport is now, we used to ride down as kids and look at the cows. It used to be a farm. We used to go there on Sunday, my uncle used to just crank up the car, the old Ford. I remember cranking it up. We'd ride down on Sunday, in the rumble seat and just enjoy the times. That's my recollection of the airplane crash. Again I'm not certain. It had to have been 1932 or 33.

I grew up in a three-story house, 707 Poplar Street, with my mother, father, five cousins, two aunts, one uncle, and my grandmother and grandfather. It was fifteen or so, in the house. And we all had, you know, we'd lived on different levels of the house. Some of my recollections ... this was before refrigeration. And so my fondest memories were when we would have Thanksgiving dinners and my grandmother would take the turkey after Thanksgiving and put it under her bed with a damp cloth and save it until Sunday. Thanksgiving's on Thursday. I don't know why but the filling didn't turn. No one ever got sick. My grandmother was blind. That's why she kept it in her

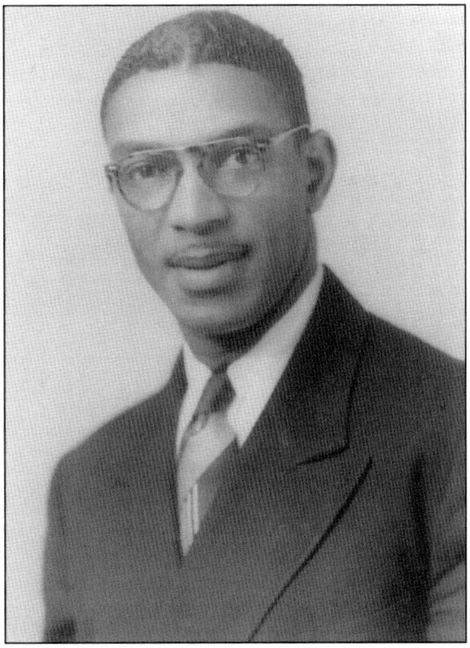

Maurice Rouselle's Father, Maurice Rouselle Jr.

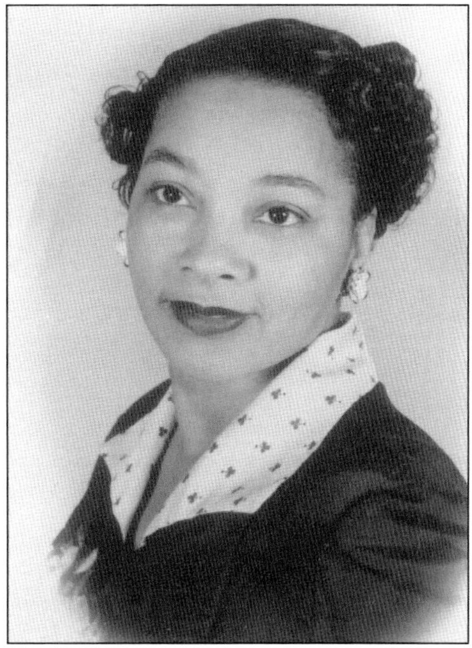

Maurice Rouselle's Mother, Lydia Camper Rouselle.

room. Everything stayed under her bed.

My grandmother at that time also had an employment agency. And she sent day workers out to clean the homes in Wilmington. And I remember, she used to charge $5 per day. I'm sorry, $5 to find employment, and many times the workers received $5 a day wages, and I was always amazed how my grandmother could count the money when the persons would pay her, you know, for securing employment. And how she could even dial the telephone, being blind. But I was amazed at it. But also that my grandfather's name was Maurice also, was highly involved in political process. He was a ward leader in Wilmington, as we called it in the old sixth ward. He was also a foreman over the Pullman Railroad and apparently there were not too many black foremen for the railroad. And I remember talking to a lot of men later on in life. They were telling me how they were appreciative they had gotten jobs especially during the Depression at Pullman. But my grandfather and a fellow by the name of Isaac Thornton, who had a funeral home at the 800 block of Popular Street, were highly involved in Democratic politics during the time when to be a Democrat was looked down upon. Many of the Negroes, as we called ourselves, in the thirties, were Republicans ... Of course this was how my dad probably got involved in politics later. But, I can recall myself when Roosevelt was going for his second term as president that it was the first time I voted by paper ballot. I don't know whether it counted or not. I had two aunts, Anita Rouselle and Constance Wongas, who were on the podium voting booths. Then it was part of St. Matthews Church at Seventh and Walnut Street. And they would allow me to cross off the Democrats and put in, in the little green box as I voted for President Roosevelt back in 1936 or 37. But I'll never forget that.

I lived one block from Bancroft Junior High, which was in the 700 Block of Walnut Street, which I was living at Seventh and

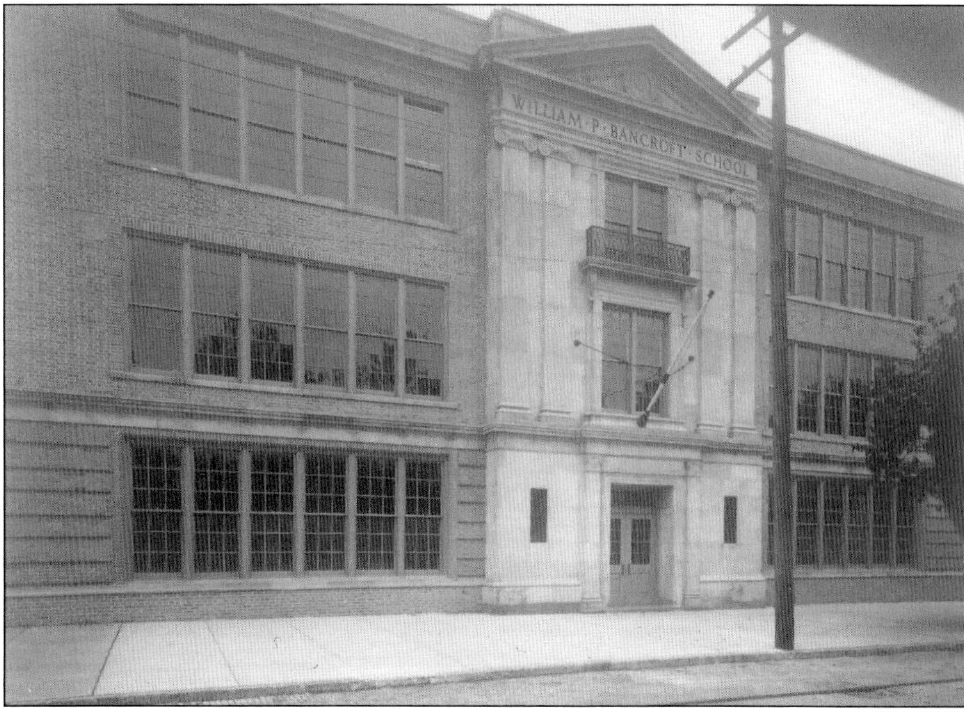

Bancroft School on the East Side. *It was segregated in the 1930s and 1940s, when Maurice Rouselle was a child. (Courtesy of the HSD.)*

Poplar. I know that the black kids that had to go to school, we weren't allowed to go to Bancroft. For what reason, I didn't know, other than the fact that Bancroft was an all-white junior high school. But some of my memories were that Bancroft school and People's Settlement, which is still there, both facilities. But People's Settlement had a baseball or a softball, or athletic field behind it, and it's still there; however, it's not an athletic field or a softball field. It's a parking lot now, but all the fellows growing up, the black guys, we used to go especially at night in the summer and we used to marvel at the playground or baseball field that had lights. All these white boys would be playing, playing softball and we were never able to understand why we couldn't get in to play softball with them. And I always marveled at that.

Also, in growing up at Seventh and Popular Street, Sam Chester's Market on one corner, we had a furniture store on the other corner. And I can just recall my grandmother sending me over to Sam Chester's and getting you know three eggs on the books. I know maybe I'd get a dill pickle and put that on the books. I don't know whenever the book got paid, but I used to always go to get on the book. I used to love to go over and they would send me over to get, we call it oleo, it was oleo margarine. It had a little color in it, and one of my chores was to mix up the oleo. This was before World War II. We used to sit up at nights, before it got dark, and watched the sparks coming from the Dravo Shipyard. Sitting on Popular Street we always marveled when the circus came to town because they would go up Spruce Street. But when the circus would leave on Sunday night, they would always come down Popular Street to go back to the train station. And I used to look out the third-floor window and all the kids would watch the elephants going down Popular Street. Popular Street was cobblestone in those days and it ran from Sixteenth Street right down to the train station. That was one of the amazing things we'd do—enjoyed sitting on the steps and lighting cattails in the summer. No one had air conditioning. Just sit out on the steps late at night. We just enjoyed our neighbors.

We had a corner lot at Eighth and Popular where we played marbles. All the fellows who lived around Seventh Street, Sixth Street, Walnut Street, Eighth Street to Taylor, up through Ninth, we'd call, I don't know why, we'd call ourselves the "Eighth Street Bears." I guess bears were tough in those days. We used to have a clubhouse that, it was an old barn on the westside of Walnut between Eighth and Ninth which was I guess located in the middle of the block. It was behind where the Hopkins Theater was, which in those days was called, I think it was the National Theater. It was the National Theater in those days and we used to go up there to play. We were considered kind of rough necks. We fought. We threw bricks We threw bottles, milk bottles off the steps at anybody especially the "Tenth Street Tigers." Even though we had to go across Tenth Street to go to school. Everybody has their territorial wars. I was an Eighth Street Bear. Very few of the Eighth Street Bears went away to further their education. Many of the Tenth Street Tigers did. The Tenth Street Tigers were a little more academically inclined than the Eighth Street Bears. When I moved to Ninth and Walnut Street, in '48, the Tenth Street Tigers embraced me. So I was both a Tenth Street Tiger and an Eighth Street Bear! So I got along with both groups. I don't know why they embraced me. I guess because I was living on Walnut Street as oppose to living on Tenth and Pine. Plus the fact that when I was in school I got on the athletic team. And most of the Tenth Street Tigers gravitated toward athletics. Most of the Eighth Street Bears, many of them that I knew, got in trouble. Some went to reform school. I guess about 15 years ago I saw one of the old Eighth Street Bears. I said "Man I haven't seen you in 25 years!" He said "That's about right." "Where have you been?" He was in prison for 25 years for murder. This was the Eighth Street Bears kind of thing. Even though all of the Eighth Street Bears, that I knew of—we all had parents. There was no such thing as a single parent home. But the neighborhood seemed to be much rougher. You didn't join it. You were just born into it by virtue of where you lived. If you were able to fight a little bit and run. It just happened that I ran for Howard High and Morgan State. I was pretty fast. I could outrun a lot of people. I can't say I could fight, but I could run. I remember that. And the Tenth Street

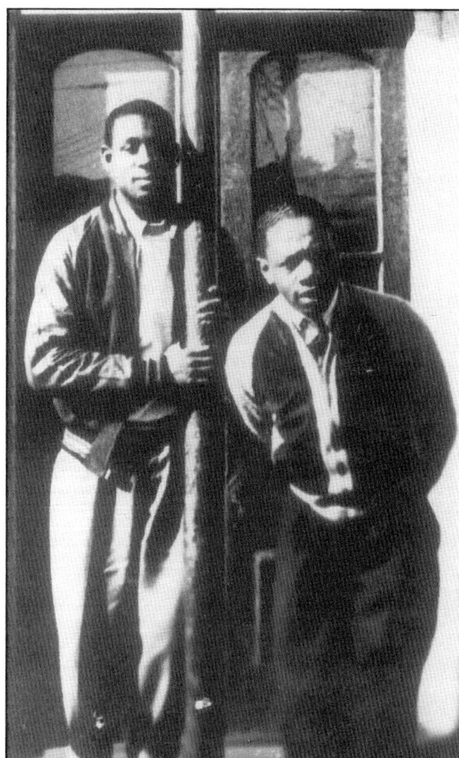

MEMBERS OF THE "TENTH STREET TIGERS." Gil Jackson is on the left. (Courtesy of the estate of Gilbert H. Jackson.)

Tigers were athletes—runners. And the Eighth Street Bears were battlers. We didn't carry switchblades but if Betty had a party on Friday and we weren't invited and you didn't let us in, we'd throw a brick through Betty's window. So the next time Betty has a party, we would be invited. Tenth Street Tigers didn't do things like that. They [our parents] didn't know.

HOWARD K. TOLIVER

I was born on June 7, 1920. I am the ninth child of Bessie and George Toliver. My father was a leather worker at J.E. Rhoads and Son. J.E. Rhoads was on Bancroft Parkway between Ninth and Eleventh Street. The factory is still there. He worked in the tannery and he stretched leather. They tanned cowhide

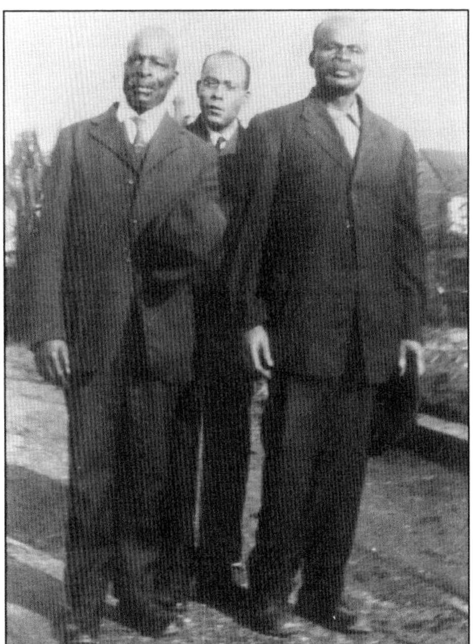

***HOWARD TOLIVER'S RELATIVES.** From left to right are his uncle Frank Toliver, a bootlegger; his father, George Toliver, who worked for Rhoads Leather Company; and his grandfather Charles H. Toliver, who was a businessman on the "Hill."*

for shoes. They stretched it. There were two stretching machines at Rhoads. The hides came from the tannery. In order to get the most production out of this hide, they put it on a stretching machine. They used clamps at one end and clamps at the other. They used air to stretch the leather—to get more shoes out of this particular leather. My father started working there when he was about 16 and I guess he was around 45 when he died. He had to stop working there because he went blind. My father got blind around 1929 or '30. There were ten of us living then. What happened was that he worked at the blind shop for a while then he didn't do anything after that. The blind shop used to make brooms there. He used to go downtown on Eighth Street. There used to be a shop below where Sallies [Salesianum High School] was. He used to go there. He would take my sister to school at #21 from Eighth and Union where we lived. He would come back and he would meet us at school and bring us home. We had a dog named "Jack" who did most of the leading. Jack would take him and bring him there. He just had a leash. He didn't have the thing they have now. Jack would take him down and bring him back. My mother was always working. She would see that we got off but then he would come get us. When Melissa was in the kindergarten he had to make two trips. See, he'd get her. He brought her to school. He'd come back at 12 o'clock and he and Melissa would pick me up. You see there is two years difference between my sister Melissa and I. My mother worked for A.D. Warner. She was a laundress. This was at 1005 North Broom Street. That's where the Warner's lived. It was a great big house. The house is still there. Great big enormous house. She would work about two days a week, maybe. Aunt Laura was the cook there at A.D. Warner's.

My brother's and sisters—Charles and Julia was a set of twins. Charles had a scholarship to Lincoln but he let my

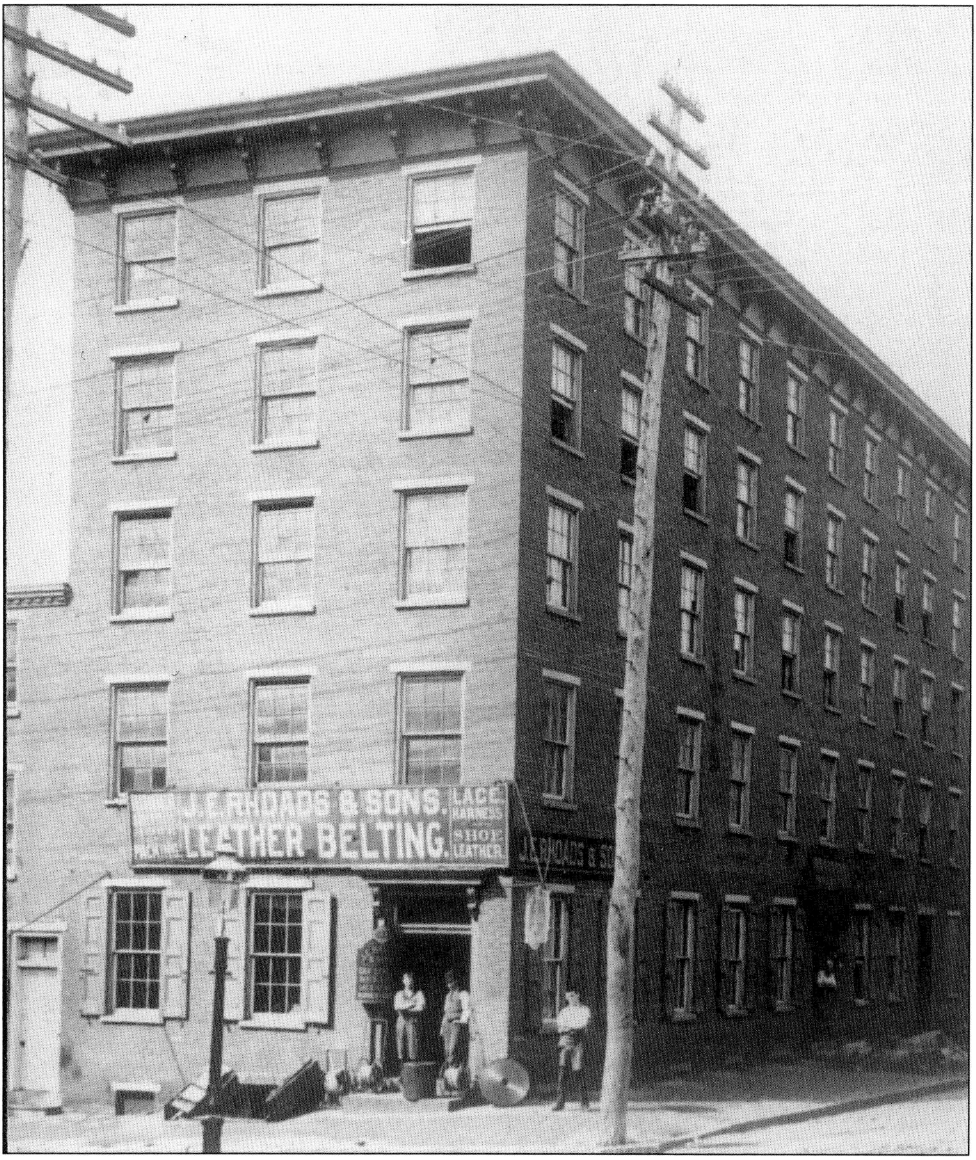

***THE J.E. RHOADS LEATHER COMPANY, WHERE HOWARD TOLIVER'S FATHER WORKED.** (Courtesy of the HSD.)*

sister go to Miner's Teacher's College. I guess it was around 1929 when she went to get a teaching certificate. They only had a three-year course there. She eventually went back and got the year so she had her degree. All of us finished high school—Howard High School. That was one of the things my mother was very proud of. She wanted us all to finish high school. We all did except one who died—she died when she was about 13 or 14, I think.

We lived on Eighth Street and we lived in an Italian neighborhood. The people there were really good to us. I had a sister named Margery who'd go their house and eat. I didn't do that too much but we had good neighbors. I got in one fight while I was there on Eighth Street. This boy called me "Nigger." That was fightin' words then. I bopped him along side his head and his nose bled. But that was the second day we were living there. Strangely enough, I didn't have any trouble with anybody else because I wasn't going to stand for any stuff. Eventually I got friendly with most of them. Most of the time I lived out on the "Hill." We played with them—played football with the Italians but couldn't go to school with them. We went to #21 and they went to ... I can't remember but it was at Ninth and Scott. I can't remember the number of the school but that is where they went. Then they closed it up and they built the Charles B. Lore School. Generally speaking, the neighborhood wasn't that bad. I played with them. I still have a good friend Anthony. We have been friends for a long time because we are the same age, graduated from high school at the same time. We went into the army at the same time—about the same time. He went to a white unit, I went to a black. I see him every once and awhile. Most of the people out there on the street where we lived between Lincoln and Union are dead. All the black people out there are dead. There's still one black family that lives there. But that's about all.

The "Hill" started at Clayton Street and ran down to Union. From Ninth Street down to Third Street. There were two sections. Delamore Place was one section and we lived at the other section. Most of the[black] people went to three churches at the time: Haven United Methodist Church, St. Peter's Methodist Church, Eighth Street Baptist, and there was one on Holland Street.

A lot of people say I'm just like my mother—looks and everything else, ways just like her. She could manipulate a penny. This is the truth. I'll tell you. Have I told you about the rag man? The rag man used to come up the alley. "Rag, oh! Rag, oh!." So my mother always had a bag of rags for him. This was during the Depression. Any how, she would have this grass sack bag with rags in it. So every time he'd come you'd get 2¢ a pound. Fifteen, twenty, or thirty pounds and she put stones in it. He knew what she was doing. He felt this way. My mother (this was during the Depression) was having a hard time. My brothers were in CC Camp. Alvin and George were in CC Camp. My mother was having a hard time. He knew the story. My mother knew he knew what she was doing. But she was a widow and she had all of these kids. After we moved away, I would see the man. He was still on the street, especially, after I'd come back from the war. He lived down there on Fourth and Church. He was a very nice man.

Thinking about the Depression, there were two places we'd go. We'd go to Huber's Bake Shop at Ninth and Union and the trucks would come with this day-old bread. We'd go in there and pay 2¢ a loaf. Maybe we'd buy three or four loaves. Don't tell me that it wasn't a lot of people who got it. Then down the street at Tenth and Union, there was a pretzel shop. There was a machine that makes them. The ones that dropped off—you could go in there and fill your bag up. They would take the whole ones. Take a bag in there and you'd get a whole bag full 'cause you had to pick them up off the floor. But they'd run of the machines. Nobody stepped on them but they couldn't use them because they had to have the good ones. There used to be a dairy on the opposite corner of Haven Church. You'd go in there. Mom would send us down there with a gallon jug. And get a gallon of milk. It was skim milk—but it was milk. Maybe for 10¢ we could get a whole gallon. The neighbors were good too. They looked out for one another.

I carried clothes for Mrs. Shelton. She washed for a family named Ledman. They lived at Holland and Clayton. I bought a wagon and I had to pick up the clothes on Monday morning, bring them to Mrs. Shelton at West Eighth Street in the 1800 block and when she was done, I'd take them back. I got 15¢ every time I took them. My mother, if you got 15¢, she wanted a dime. This was during the Depression. I got so slick. First I didn't know what the story was. So before I'd get home, I'd stop at the store and get me something—what I wanted. I'd get a pie for a nickel. She would take the dime anyhow. I have fond memories of my mother.

I started playing football when I was in the ninth grade. Mr. Naylor was the coach. I can remember the first time I went out for football. Most of the guys from the East Side played football but we had to walk in town and come back from out on the "Hill." I wasn't too crazy about it. So I decided to go out because Harold Braxton and I and Sonny Johnson were all in the same class. Mr. Naylor had been trying to get me to go out because my oldest brother played. So I go out there and get these raggety pants and I sort of like it because I played football with the boys on the "Hill." The football season my senior year a guy named Sparky Anderson (Mr. Naylor knew him from Lincoln) came down. He was forming an All Star team up in Philadelphia. So, Mr. Naylor said "I've got three guys who I think would help him." It was Joe Burton, Charles Webb, and I. The man came down from Philadelphia, picked us up after practice and took us up there to practice.

William Pell Wallace

My parents were Charles and Carsie Wallace. My father was born in Cecilton, Maryland. That's below Elkton. My mother was born in rural Virginia in a place called Delwynn, Virginia. From Delwynn, Virginia, my mother then went to Richmond and lived with her oldest brother and went to school. Her parents then sent her from Richmond up to Washington and she stayed at the Phyliss Wheatley YWCA and attended Dunbar high School. After she finished Dunbar High School she went to Miners Teachers College and graduated from there. As I said my father was born in Cecilton, Maryland, and received all of his formal schooling in Cecilton. Schools at that point only went to the eighth grade. Students who wanted to go to high school during that time, I believe had to go to Cambridge, Maryland, and live there with families. He couldn't do that, so his formal education ended after eighth grade. Mother taught a couple of years in Maryland after graduation and it was there that she met my father. After they were married, she found that it was not economically feasible for her to continue to work as a teacher and as a result mother and daddy went into doing private family work. Sometimes I would live with them, other times I didn't. I would stay with my grandparents. I can

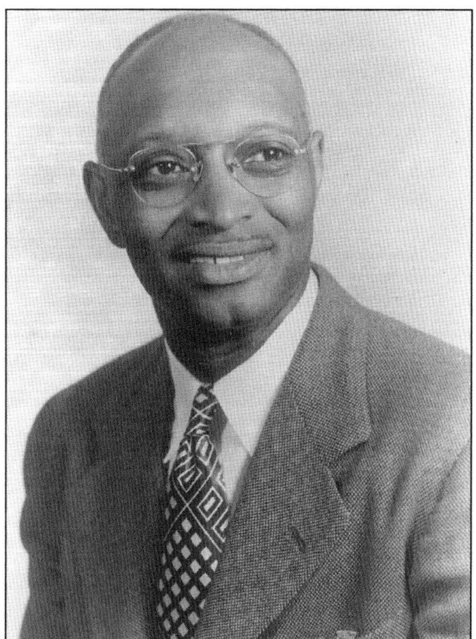

Charles Wallace, William Wallace's Father.

remember one year, spending a year in Philadelphia with a cousin and I didn't really live at home with my parents as a family until I started second grade.

I was born in Atlantic City, New Jersey, though I never lived there and my parents didn't live there. My parents explained that it was better for my mother if I was born in a hospital in Atlantic City. Segregation as we knew it was such that she did not want to go to a hospital in Maryland. She didn't want to go to a hospital in Wilmington, so she went to Atlantic City. She was admitted, I was born, and then we returned to Maryland. I was seven when I came to Wilmington.

We lived in Delamore Place. When I first went to Delamore Place we lived in the 200 block and I thought it was the best place you could possible have because we had an inside bathroom and we had a washroom. And that was a step forward, or maybe two steps forward from what it had been with my grandparents. Though I loved my grandparents and enjoyed myself being with them, they didn't have indoor plumbing.

I started at #21 School. Enjoyed schooling quite a bit. Enjoyed reading. I can remember my second grade teacher allowing me to bring books home so that I could finish reading. And that was a real privilege because students in the elementary grades were not suppose to bring books home. And she would stick it under my jacket and said to be sure to bring it back tomorrow.

It was a fun time living on "the Hill." There weren't many Afro-Americans out on "the Hill." Most of the black population was on the East Side but we had certain little streets that were relegated to Afro Americans on "the Hill." Delamore Place had six blocks and the first two blocks were relegated to Afro-Americans. If you went down in the 100 block, you didn't find as many Afro-Americans as you did in the 200 black. Above the 200 block ,you just didn't go.

We had Italians, Irish, Polish people. Generally, you got along with them. As youngsters, we played in the street, it was just that you knew you couldn't go to their schools. You couldn't go to their theaters. But when you were in the streets, you played and you knew their families and they knew yours and usually families got along very well. It was just that segregation which was the law at the time didn't allow you to get to know them any better or any differently.

My father stressed that you should not spend all that you make, no matter how much it was. That you should put some aside so you would have it for an emergency. That you should not use all of the money you've made to get things that you thought you wanted or thought you needed. And that you should have a good work ethic, and that is to go to work on time. Go regularly. Do what you're suppose to do, whether the person in charge was there or not. Be dependable, and if you can't be there to somehow let the person, your employer, know that you couldn't come and why you couldn't. And when he could expect you. Mother subscribed to the same thing. So they both were reinforcing each other on how you should govern yourself. When you went to work.

Well, they all stressed that you should respect your elders, that you should respect ladies. That you should tip your hat and give them a seat. Offer them a seat at least if you were sitting down. You should get up when they come in the room. All of the things which were good manners, which might not necessarily be thought of as good manners now. They were practice. There was also a great deal of instruction on table etiquette. And though we were poor, we knew how to sit at the table and how to use our silverware. And we knew when the table was set correctly because my parents did that for a living so it spilled out over to our home. And when we entertained and their friends who did the same type of work when they entertained, I mean, it was royal. It wasn't, you know, paper mat or things of that sort. They knew how to do and they did the same way they did when they were working, So my parents tried to expose me to worthwhile things and we would go to restaurants. There were no restaurants in Wilmington that we could go to other than, there was a restaurant at Eighth and Scott. Mr. and Mrs. Milburn had a little restaurant and my parents would take me there. The other times that we went to restaurants, we would go to Philadelphia and go to some of the nicer restaurants and I can't recall names now, that were owned by blacks, but they were very nice restaurants. And my father always said, "You know, you want to know how to act when you go in these places."

If you had a furnace in the cellar you were really "uptown" because the furnace sat usually about midway of the cellar. And in our house it wasn't central heat or anything because you simply had a big hole cut in the floor about 4-by-4 where the register and the heat rushed up out of that heater. Downstairs was fairly warm and comfortable, but upstairs we cut a hole in the ceiling and cut out another register so that the heat would go up. We burned coal, so you had to go down and take the ashes out. At night before you went to bed, you had to go down into the cellar and what they call "bank the furnace." Put coal on it and shake it so that it would burn slowly during the night. Hot water was the same thing. We didn't have gas hot water heaters, we had a little small coal stove and it was hooked to a water heater and that gave you hot water.

Sometimes I thought I spent more time at Eighth Street [Baptist] than the pastor. My mother was Baptist and my father was Methodist. Daddy belonged to Bethel, so I got to go to Eighth Street because it was easier for me to get over to Eighth Street than to Bethel. But they said that I had to be involved in the church and during that time, the church had lots of things going on so I went to Sunday school and then was church. Then you rushed back home and you had a little dinner. And you went back to three o'clock service, then you came home again and you had, what we called BYPU. It was Baptist Young People's Training Unit. And if I had somehow messed up during the week, my mother would tell me, "Maybe you better go on to night service." And most of the time I made night service because I was able to mess up during the week so bad. So I mean I just stayed at church. Then my mother said, I couldn't just go to church. I had to be involved with something at church, so I was an usher. Mr. Noel Banks used to play a saxophone. He was a very fine musician and he told me "You come on up to Eighth Street and bring that horn with you." So for years, Mr. Banks and

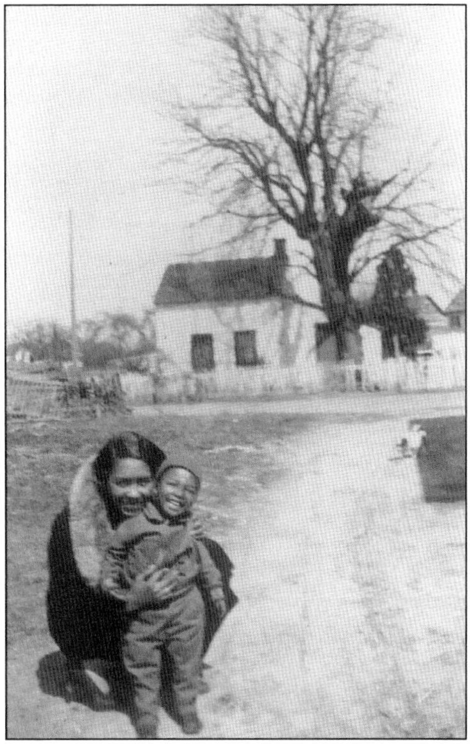

William Pell Wallace and His Mother, Carsie Wallace.

I would play at Sunday school and then we would play for the special events, you know, Christmas programs and Children's Day and all the 100 activities that we had. Since I was there all the time, the pastor didn't mind calling on me. He'd say "Wallace, do so and so and so and so." Then people in the church didn't mind saying to my mother, "Can your little boy do so and so?" So they always had me doing something in the church. You know if they wanted somebody to present the offering to the guest speaker, if they wanted somebody to give a welcome. If they had a lull in the program and they just wanted a filler. During the time I was in junior high school, poetry was important in the curriculum. And we had to memorize a lot of poems. And temporarily I could retain a lot of them. So it was not unusual that somebody would say, "William Wallace, come up here and speak." I would walk up and start reciting these poems that I had learned. So, yes I was involved in Eighth Street, as a youngster. And as I got older, I came back. I rejoined the usher board and I was a trustee for a number of years. So I spent most of my life at Eighth Street Church.

In the summer children used to wear sneaks. So I said, "Mother may I have a pair of sneaks?" And mother told me she didn't have the money to buy any sneaks. And I was still running out playing in my shoes so I was persistent. So I kept asking her, "May I have these sneaks?" So I had a pair of black boots. Use to be the kind that we wore in the wintertime. Boots that came up about this far. She said, "I'm going to make you some sneaks." So she took my boots and cut the tops off. Now, I don't have any boots and I don't have sneaks. The thing that really hurt me was the boots weren't good boots and they were made of compressed paper. So it wasn't leather coming up, it was compressed paper. And when you cut it, it was white inside and that white showed. So mother said, "Here, you have these just like sneaks. They come up over your ankles. Go outside." Well, I didn't want to go outside, so finally I put these sneaks on and I walked out. I was living up at the 200 block of Delamore Place and then I stepped out in the street there and Nooky Canon (God rest him, he's been dead for a long time), he said, "Boy what's that you have on your feet?" So I didn't want him to see it. So he said. "Hey come here, come see these!" So I started running and they chased me all the way up to Third and Delamore, up Third and Clayton, down across Clayton Park in there and they tackled me. And they were calling everybody "Hey! Come look at these things! What are these things you've got on your feet?" And they laughed at me for the rest of the summer.

Olivia Jefferson Johnson

When I was small, I lived at Eighth and Scott. My grandmother has a candy store there and I enjoyed working there because every now and then I would wait on some of the kids that came in from #11 School. Number 11 School was at Ninth and Scott. They called it Miss Irons' Candy Store. My grandmother was noted for making sticky apples. And that kept her busy all the time. Because they'd go to Miss Irons. She made the best sticky apples. So the kids would flock there after school and get a sticky apple. She made apples until there were no more apples. But I can't complain. My childhood days were very nice and I thought I was something. I'd take the kids in the summer and teach them at my grandmothers. I had a little school and I also taught then how to embroidery.

She was a beautiful lady. She'd do anything for anybody,. See she married, that was her second husband, if I'm not mistaken, and it was nice that he set her up in that business. The store was in the front, and we all lived in the back, and of course they had a second floor. Things weren't like they are now. We had to go outdoors for everything. But that's all right. It was a happy life. I didn't mind it at all. I had a lot of friends. And they were Italians. Up to this day, they say to me, "Oh, Olivia, how about the good ole days." Anytime they see you out there, they asked you go over to their house and get a bowl of spaghetti. And that's where I was living most of the time, in their homes. They were beautiful people.

We didn't have a bathroom or a toilet inside, so that, in those days people had to take a bath in the washtub upstairs in a big room. It was something.

Yes, I had three brothers and two sisters, and in all we were six. And by me being the oldest I got to the point, I told mother, "I'm tired of babysitting, Everyplace I go I had to take my brothers and sisters with me." The adventure was out to the zoo. We'd take a walk out there every Sunday, almost every Sunday, if not there, we would go to the B&O Station on Dupont Street and watch the trains come in and out.

Her [Olivia's mother's] name was Mary E. Jefferson and my father's name was Joseph H. Jefferson and he worked for Mac Brewer Company, a tobacco company, on Fourth Street between Shipley and Orange and he was the first black man that I know of as a shipping clerk. They did everything. They made cigarettes. But when a lot of those things came in, my father had to take them to be shipped out or taken out. Those days my father used to drive a horse and buggy on the outskirts of Wilmington to deliver these cigarettes or tobacco.

No, my mother did not work. She had her hands full with all us kids, trying to keep us up to the minute. She had no machine, but she made a lot of our clothes by hand. No machine. And as we had no

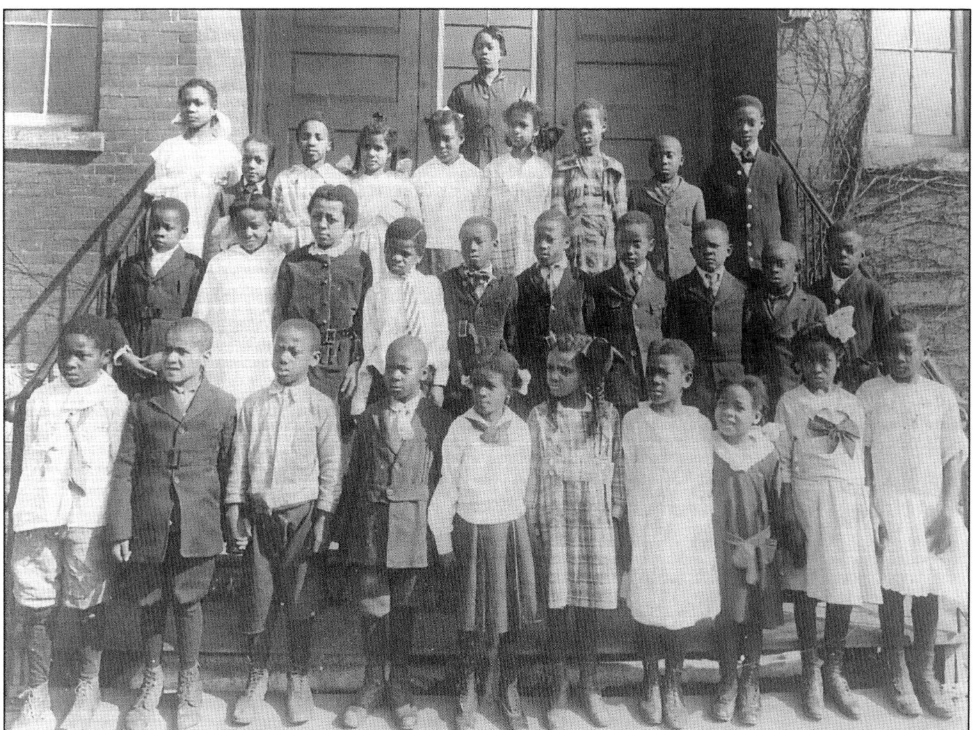

***Olivia Jefferson Johnson's School Picture.** Olivia (front row, fifth from the right) is wearing the dress she worked for and purchased at the Lippencott Company.*

machine, she would go and buy some of our things. She bought most of out things from Lippencott Company between Third and Fourth. She would always take us down there to get my clothes for school. And the dress I have on [in the picture] was ... I lost my dress on my way home from Lippencott. So my mother said, when I got home, "What happened?" I said I lost my dress. She said, "I think you better find yourself a little job to replace that dress." So I went to Lippencott Company. They didn't see it. They thought somebody stole it. When I was standing there waiting for the bus to come, a Jewish woman lived across the street from Lippencott. She said "Miss, would you like to make some money?" I said, "Doing what?" "Pressing my little girl's clothes." I went over there and made enough money to buy myself a dress. And mother was surprised when I came home with the dress.

I went to #5 School at the corner of Fifth and Scott. Mrs. James was our principal. Helen Starkey taught the second grade. Bertha Wilson taught the third grade and we had to go upstairs for the rest of the classes, the fourth, fifth, and sixth. And when we left, when I graduated from #21 School, we went to old Howard High School and I'm trying to remember who our first teacher was. We walked. We had to walk, there was a hill. We lived on the westside of the town. We had to walk from there down to Twelfth and Orange to school every day regardless of rain, hell, or what. And we made it going and coming. But we stuck together. Would be four, five, or six of us girls walking in there and it was a lot of fun.

Of course when you attend Howard High School, you had to take a cooking lesson. Mrs. Reed was the one who taught us how to cook, so every time we made something we had to go home and make it for our parents. We had Helen Anderson to teach us sewing. I had a green and white checked dress made with buttons all the way down the front and lace all around the collars and cuffs. "Oh, Miss Johnson, I'd like to put your dress on display. You made the prettiest dress of anybody in the class." So my dress was on display and then we went to Seth Harris. He taught us science. I know every year in September, we had to go in there and make this stuff. You couldn't stand the place. It was smelling so bad, and I started giggling. He'd say "Miss Johnson, I know your mother very well. I'm going to call her and tell her that you can't come back into this class unless you come with her." My mother went with me but I made out alright. I'd never forget as long as I live, how they were trying to get a new school. Our class was the first to graduate from the new Howard High School. It was beautiful and we enjoyed it very much because everything was convenient for us. Our class was very, very smart, but I'm glad that I lived long enough to experience all this in the year of 1929.

Mary Anne Wheeler Franklin

I was born February 24, 1921 and lived in Cambridge, Massachusetts, for four years. I went to visit my Aunt Eva, my mother's oldest sister who was teaching at Cheyney. As a little girl, I used to go back and forth. And they knew me like one of the family—like one of the students. I've been traveling ever since.

My mother was Madeline Ophelia Hall Wheeler-Brooks. My father died and she married again—Stephen Brooks, who was old man Averill Harriman's secretary. The year my brother was born 1926 we came to Delaware. We lived at Harry Lones' on DuPont Street. He had a barber shop. We lived on the second floor. There was an Italian grocery store right across the street on the corner. One night we didn't have any catsup and my father sent me to the grocery store for catsup. There was a big collie dog standing in my way. I would go

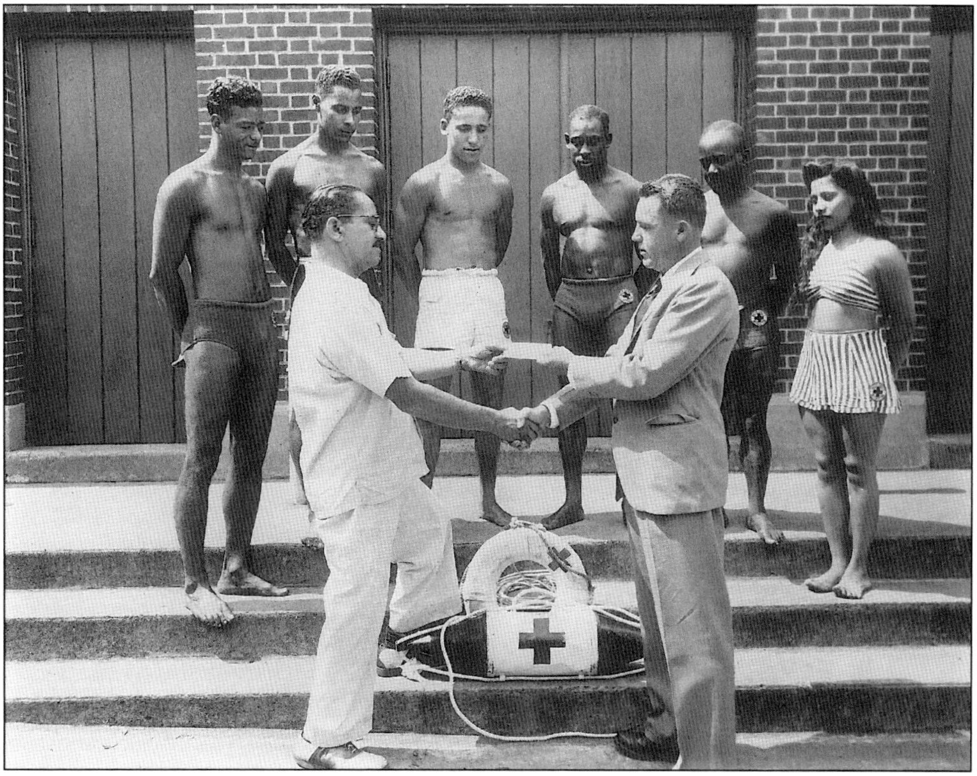

Mary Anne Wheeler Franklin and Her Brother Arthur Wheeler Jr. *The siblings (Arthur is in the white trunks) are receiving their Red Cross certification in this photograph. Their father, Arthur Wheeler Sr. (a Howard High School athletic coach), is the man in the foreground on the left.*

this way and the dog would go this way. I would go that way and the dog would go that way. Finally I looked the dog straight in the eye and I said "UHHHHHHGGGGGGGGGHHH!" And I got in the store.

My father was from Hartford, Connecticut. He was Arthur E. Wheeler Sr. And his father was a minister in the congregational church—First Congregational Church in Hartford, Connecticut, who was friendly with Dean Rockwell Harmon Potter of the Harvard Theological Seminary. My father's mother's was Mary Freeman Wheeler and she was the second black graduate of Oberlin College. That's not hearsay, I questioned it and they sent me the record. Evangeline Rachael Hall, my aunt, was the first black graduate of Radcliff College. She taught at Cheyney for 44 years and one semester in St. Louis. I think she graduated in 1901. Laura Wheeler Waring, who also taught at Cheyney and was my father's second oldest sister, was a very famous artist. She studied at the Philadelphia Museum of Fine Art and also at the Sorbonne in Paris. I used to go visit her. And whenever I would go visit her I would clean her house. I sat frequently with her when she had people sitting for her—W.E.B. du Bois, Marian Anderson, Jessie Fauset, in her home in Philadelphia on Forty-Third Street where her studio was. She did most of her landscape and other forms of art at Cheyney. Her husband was Walter E. Waring. He was of the Warings of Philadelphia. Walter was very fluent in languages. He was a professor in French, I think, and Italian and German at Lincoln University. And I went on their honeymoon with them. My Aunt Eva decided she wanted to go to Europe and she wanted a companion. She asked me if I would like to go. I didn't want to pass that up because I was eight years old. But my school didn't want me to go because I was going to miss two weeks of school. So my aunt said, "You don't have to worry about that." She was a professor of English and director of student teaching at Cheyney. "You won't have to worry about that. Any thing you want me to teach her, I'd be glad to. If you have any materials I will be glad to take them along." Every day: mornings—school, afternoons—touring. So they decided since she [Laura] had another fellowship, this time to Rome, that she and Walter would go to Rome and the four of us would meet in Paris. She and Walter had just been married. Somewhere around April or May 1929. I went to Europe when I was eight years old. Came back just before the stock market fell. We were in a terrible storm in September. So Walter, Laura, Eva and I spent about six weeks in Paris—going from Paris to other smaller municipalities—Flanders Field or Versailles or Switzerland or something. You know short trips, but always coming back to Paris as base. And sometimes they would go with us. Sometimes they would go in another direction because she may have an appointment with someone. But that's how they spent their honeymoon.

I got lost in Windsor Castle on the Windsor Castle tour. And if I have to say so myself, I was a pretty good looker! I had a nice wardrobe—nice clothing that my mother made. And Helen Anderson Webb, who was the home ec teacher at Howard, helped my mother make part of my wardrobe. She made gorgeous things. And we use to use hemstitching on the edges of ruffles and such. Somehow I was looking around and the tour had gone on in a different direction from where I was. Trying to find them, I wandered around to this huge massive room. Kind of dim light. I hadn't paid any attention to where I was. All of a sudden somebody said out of the dimness, "Oh little girl are you lost?" I am reported to have said, "No, I'm just looking for somebody." And he said, "Why don't you come over here and tell me who you are looking for and perhaps I can help you find them." So I did, being an obedient child. So he said, "Sit on my knee." So I did. Finally he got out of me who I was with and who I was looking for. And called somebody and had the tour people come get me. Guess whose knee I was sitting on? King George the V!!! But my aunt scolded me for getting lost from the tour. She said, "How dare you sit on the King's knee!" I said "Who's the king?" Didn't make any difference to me. I am American. "Who's the King?" But it was King George the VI.

When we got home after a very very rough trip, Laura and Walter came later. We went over on the Carmenian Cunard Line and came back on the *Acquitania*, a much smaller ship. And in the storm, they sat all of the children on the floor of the lounge on blankets. So that we wouldn't get hurt in a chair or something. They took all of the chairs and lined them along the wall and they were buttressed one against the other. So it was fun for us. We'd slid one way and come back and slide this way. But you couldn't go out doors. All of the exits were roped off. If you happened to look out there when a deck hand or somebody came in, you'd see the waves way above the ship. Because in those days they didn't have stabilizers. In the dining room they wet down the tablecloths so that the china wouldn't fall on the floor. So we finally steamed in to New York harbor. The fire boats were spraying water because they heard that we had come through that terrible storm. We then took the train to Wilmington after we got through customs. A lot of stuff we had sent because my aunt had bought a lot of brick-a-brack and momentos. Instead of carrying them, you could have them shipped but they came many, many, many weeks later. But eventually you have to pay duty. So we got through customs very easily. But they did want to charge her for my dresses. They claimed that they weren't worn. That we had bought them in Paris. My aunt said, "No, her mother made those with a friend." We got through customs. When I got home, my family had moved from West Sixth Street to Eighth Street during the summer.

William Webb

I was born in Wilmington, Delaware, at the Homeopathic Hospital or the Memorial Hospital. It was on Van Buren and that was August 10, on my mother's birthday, 1923. My father was a delivery man. He and his brother had horse-drawn carriages that used to deliver pharmaceutical products to different areas of the city. My mother worked in there also. I think she was the clean up lady around and they married in 1920 and there was six boys and eight girls. I am the third oldest, in fact, I'm the oldest of the fourteen right now.

I remember my grandmother, my mother's mother. She was, back in them days, we called it chambermaid at the Bellhaven Hotel down there in Rehoboth Beach. She was down there in the summer and she came to live with us in the winter, and my father's father, named Solomon Webb, lived in Harrington, Delaware, and he was a farmer, and during the fall of the years, he would go around, he and some other farmers in Harrington and kill hogs. That was their big thing, back there in them days, they would kill hogs, and distribute the meat and stuff to other members of the family.

I do remember August Quarterly. That was one of the big things in Wilmington. When we were at old Ezion at Nineteenth French Street, that was a big day for us. I was always there and people would be cooking and I would be in the kitchen helping to cook. Very seldom I would get a chance to see any of the services being rendered at that particular Sunday but it was rewarding and a very memorable day that comes back there in the thirties, forties, fifties, in the sixties. I don't know why the younger folks nowadays don't think too much of the August Quarterly. But it was people coming from Maryland, New Jersey, Pennsylvania, and New York for this one particular Sunday to worship and meet old friends. I was a child, but I was more the clean-up or the server. There were, chicken, pigs feet, hamburgers. And they had fish, and the food that us folks were brought up on pig feet, pig tails, reedbirds, and raised with barbeque ribs, potato salad, and sweet potato pies, apple pies. That was the big day on French Street.

This is a funny thing. My oldest sister and I at the time, we went to St. Joseph's School, used to be there at Eleventh and French. And I was there through the third grade and we would have to salute the flag and say a prayer at school time. After school, we had to go to the church for a dismissal and we had to read a verse. I came home one day and told my father that I wanted to join St. Joseph's Church. A couple of days later I was at #29 school. My father didn't want to think about joining a Catholic church since we were all Methodist.

You learned. And if you were doing something bad, the nuns would punish you. They have rules that they would introduce your hands to. They didn't try to kill you, but you learnt discipline by going to St. Joseph's School and the nuns didn't have no favorites, to my knowledge

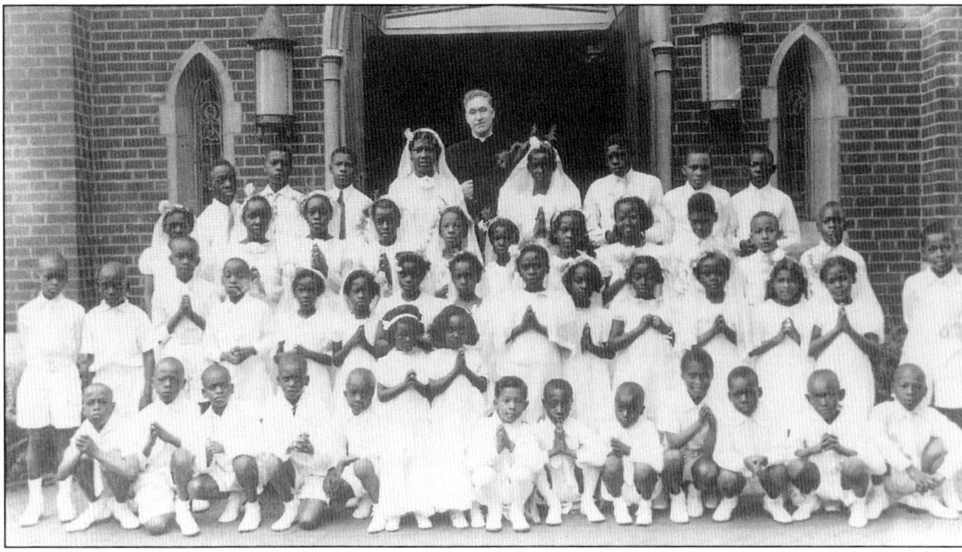

A Confirmation Class at St. Joseph's Catholic Church. (Courtesy Leroy Guines.)

in the classes I was in. You went there to learn, and if you learned, you were alright, if you didn't learn, well, that's on your part. But, we did learn something, being in the school.

On Fridays and Saturdays, there was a congregation of a few, Doc Hill, Lonnie Clark, Luce Clark, and Smut Johnson. We were all there finding out where the big party was going to be after the football game and if Coach Naylor came by and saw us there, we didn't get a chance to play. We had no business being out. We were supposed to be resting for the big game. But, I was in a play at the Y one year. It was called the *Pirates Umbrella* and it was real nice. I did a little skit. I called myself doing a Hawaiian dance. I love dancing and after a while I thought I was getting a little old for this kind of stuff, but the Y was headquarters. Played basketball there. Played table tennis. I wasn't much of a bowler. You had to be kind of good, and if you weren't, Miss Wilson wouldn't let you fool with that bowling alley. She was a head knocker. But, we learnt from Miss Wilson. And it was a wonderful place, the Y was a wonderful place back in those days.

William Young

I was born June 23, 1918. I was starting to think that what impressed me first was when I was about six or seven years of age, my father said, "I want to develop a newspaper route for you. A number of notable leaders in this locality first were newspaper boys. So I am going to start this paper route for you." At the time, we had living with us a student from Georgia, a secondary school student by the name of McGee. I want to put that in because my brother Joseph had remembered him, and I could understand because he was probably five. So what he [my father] did was to telephone people who he thought would be interested in the Sunday newspapers. In other words, by starting at the seventh block of Tatnall Street where there was Elmer Stubbs and there were three papers in the 800 block. My stop was at the home of a Dr. Stubbs and he brought four newspapers, and many of these were other newspapers, they were Philadelphia papers and New York papers. And then my next customers were in the 1100 block of Tatnall Street. There were six or seven white families who subscribed to Sunday newspapers. And coming down my next street was Twelfth Street, and from Twelfth and West and Twelfth and Tatnall I had three to four customers. And on Orange Street, the 1200 block of Orange Street, I had another six or eight customers. Then, from the block where Howard High School building was, I had about two customers. The bulk of my customers were in the 1200 block of Tatnall Street and I rose to go to pick up these papers at Second and Shipley Streets, at about 5 o'clock—it was still dark. That's one of the reasons my father asked that this young high school student who was staying at our place for his last senior year to accompany me. Because we had to go to Second and Shipley to pick up these [newspapers] in the dark. In fact, there was not light until we walked back up to Second and Shipley to Seventh and Tatnall where I served my first customer who was a realtor, Elmer Stubbs.

[I carried the papers] in a wagon. I had 208 papers. The wagons then were massive, they were built heavier. I don't see that kind of wagon today. So that when I had gotten to my home here and served all the people surrounding me at Thirteenth and Tatnall, I ate breakfast. And at that point, I picked up my younger brother Joseph, and then we went out on Madison Street to the 800 block of Madison Street, where my elementary school principal was, and we served the house there at 838 Madison. And then we went to Seventh Street, West Seventh Street, we took papers to Mr. George Whitten, who was a teacher in industrial arts at the Howard High School, and he lived at 707 West Seventh Street. And then moving up Seventh Street to Seventh and Monroe Street in that order, the Anderson family, the family of Dr. Leon P. Anderson. And we served there and the house next door, I think it was Clark. So when my paper route was at its highest in terms of numbers of papers, it was 208 papers, I didn't have 208 customers. Many of the people who bought Sunday papers bought three. Especially people who had larger families, they bought three or four papers. These were all black people.

Much of my time as the eldest child of five children was spent in work. I served newspapers; I transported ice. I bought ice—25 pounds for 15¢ or something. People in the neighborhood, since I had a wagon, would call on me to transport their ice because they needed it every day. Sometimes they made it last a day or two. But there were a few who bought 50 pounds of ice, which was 25¢. In fact, in order to keep their food from spoiling it was necessary to buy a block of ice, and you bought ice daily. I picked it [the block of ice] up with tongs, or some of the people would come out with papers to wrap the ice in and take it into their homes. But I had tongs to carry.

And imagine that the ice box might have been 4 foot, 4 foot oblong, and there were two sections. You had the ice section on the left, where you put the ice. There was a rack to put it on, and people were very careful not to open doors. Then on the right you had a door where there were sections for the food. And then you had a pan underneath to catch the melting ice, (and that you'd have to do periodically). I'd say ice for a day. You received 5¢ for transporting a 25-pound block of ice. You would receive 10¢ for a 50 pound block of ice. So that having a wagon, and I say not too many children had wagons. But since I was serving newspapers, the people said, "Well I need you to get the ice from the ice man, Isaac."

The next job I had was writing letters for elderly people of the neighborhood who may not have been able to write. And I wrote to their relatives, these letters which they would talk with me. And I would put down what I wanted to put down. I got the gist of it, see, and then in my own words I would write the main points of what they were saying and always keeping everything positive.

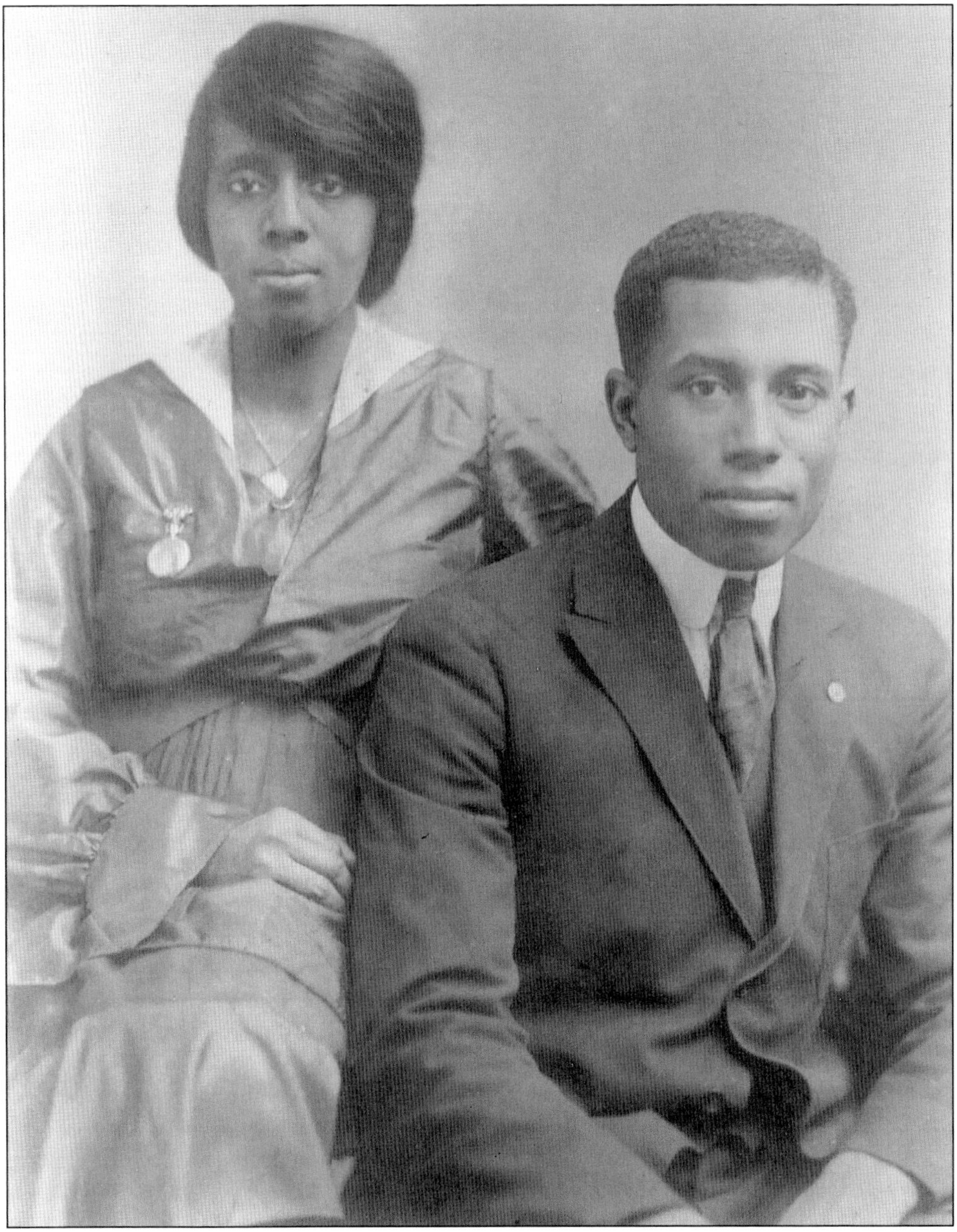

William Young's Parents, Alephia Young and William S. Young.

I wouldn't write anything tragic. So I did that, and I'd get about 15¢ a letter.

I served as the delivery boy for a lady who baked goods. The finest—I never tasted anything like that. Her name was Mrs. Ella Turner who lived at 1217 Tatnall. The one I purchased my house from. Now she made bread, rolls, and pies for the Junior League of Wilmington. You know, the Junior League, these were the affluent people. They had, the Junior League of Wilmington, a store on Ninth Street between Tatnall and West. It was directly in the center, so that I could go

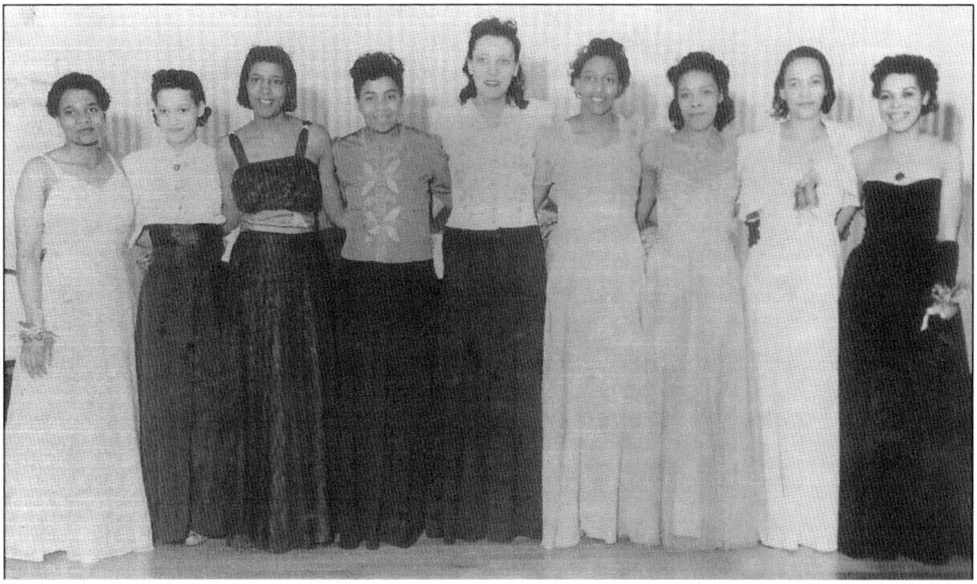

***Members of the Wil-O-Se (Willing Loyal Service) Club and Friends of William Young and the Spiders Club.** From left to right are Alice Cunningham, Virginia Holmes, Marjorie Wright, Gertrude Henry, Julia Vaughn, Sarah Wright, Tyvolia Gooden, Dorothea Harris, and Eldora Church.*

today to the very place. So the Junior League served home made baked goods from several people, because walking into the store you'd see all kinds of baked goods. And that was the job that paid me $1 a week. And that was the best. That was the first real job I had.

The Spiders Club was organized in 1932. As a group, we were friendly and used to visit churches for religious services and to become acquainted with the promising young ladies in those churches. Now, the key church was Ezion Methodist Church where Elizabeth's aunts and some of the others were active members. So when we were about tenth graders at the time—I was tenth grade, a grade ahead of many of the other Spiders. They were in the Class of '35, but I was in the Class of '34, so I was older than them at the time. So, Ms. Gertrude Henry, a teacher in the elementary school—the #5 School, was interested in teaching the boys, who befriended the WIL-O-SE girls, how to dance, so that on Friday nights following going to the movies, we'd return to her house on East Twelfth Street and she along with Ms. Benson, Betty Hunt's aunt, came over to teach the boys, who were there, how to do the Fox Trot and Two Step and how to waltz. We convened each Friday night over a period of months in order to learn.

Katherine Young Hazeur

I'm Katherine Young Hazeur. Born in the front bedroom of a house at 1232 Tatnall Street on December 13, 1923. My immediate neighborhood was quite mixed, but the fringe on the corner and four blocks down, it was really the black neighborhood. It held the black high school, the black church—Shiloh Baptist, the black barbers, the Masonics, the Odd Fellows, all of those organizations were in that section of town, and you will not find one of them there now. You think of it as center city. Not only was it my neighborhood, but my mother was born on Thirteenth Street between Market and Orange. That's where you find the Hercules Tower. My grandparents had a stable where he loaned horses to the city to pick up trash, and he also moved around Twelfth Street. So it was a very close knit community of blacks. Now the street I was on, initially my father was the first black, and I'll never forget too the day after he bought the house, the realtor came over, and offered him $500 if he would sell it back to them. The neighbors weren't so happy about him buying the house, and not only that, the neighbors on either side and on the back ... on Mondays—which was wash day—would just as soon as my mother hung out her wash they would get together and shake their dust mops out. So my mother became very articulate in many ways to let

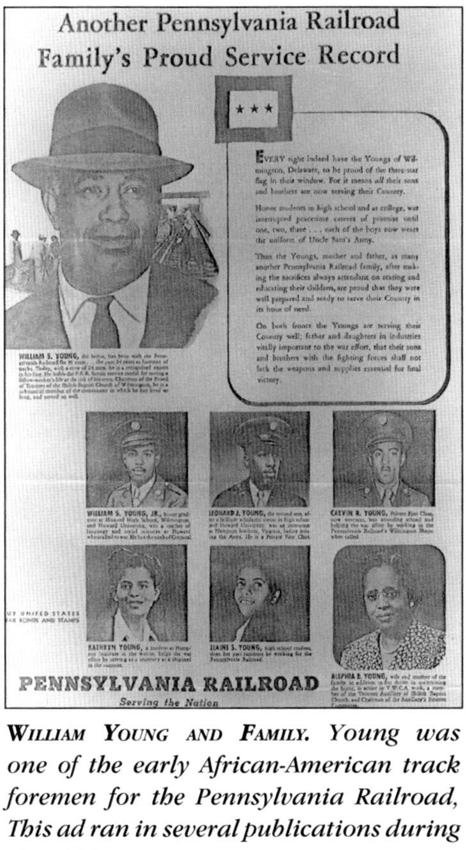

William Young and Family. *Young was one of the early African-American track foremen for the Pennsylvania Railroad, This ad ran in several publications during the 1930s.*

them know what she thought about them. But most of the whites seemed not to have been offended by us, and we weren't bosomy folk, but they were cordial. At the bottom of Tatnall Street on Fourteenth Street was the president of a bank, the owner of a gas company, a number of influential folk including the Bishop. The Episcopal Bishop's stead was down there, and so the Bishop and his folk would pass by. Many of the girls who were secretaries in the Dupont Building lived in those three-story houses as renters, and they were friendly, so when I grew up my feelings about race weren't strongly anything, because most of the people I had contact with were very cordial.

My father was Track Foreman of the Pennsylvania Railroad, and he met a boatload of Italian immigrants back in 1918. So he was conversant with the Italian language. They were very fond of my father and he was equally fond of them, and so on holidays they really treated us royally. And so I was very, very fond of most of the men.

Now I lived two blocks from #24 School which was on the bridge, Washington Street Bridge, but I went to #29 School which was about eight or ten blocks east of my house. Twice a day I would meet the white children who lived down on Thirteenth and on the East Side coming to the West Side to go to school, while I was leaving the West Side going to the East Side to school. If I had a crowd, the whites walked in the street. If they had a crowd, we walked in the street. We weren't mean to each other, but we could irritate each other, but that was sort of the extent of my knowledge of racism.

I think we had the only telephone on my street, and I think my grandparents had the only telephone on their street. So all through the day we had neighborly visits of persons who just wanted to use the telephone, and they were very nice. They would leave you a nickel or some

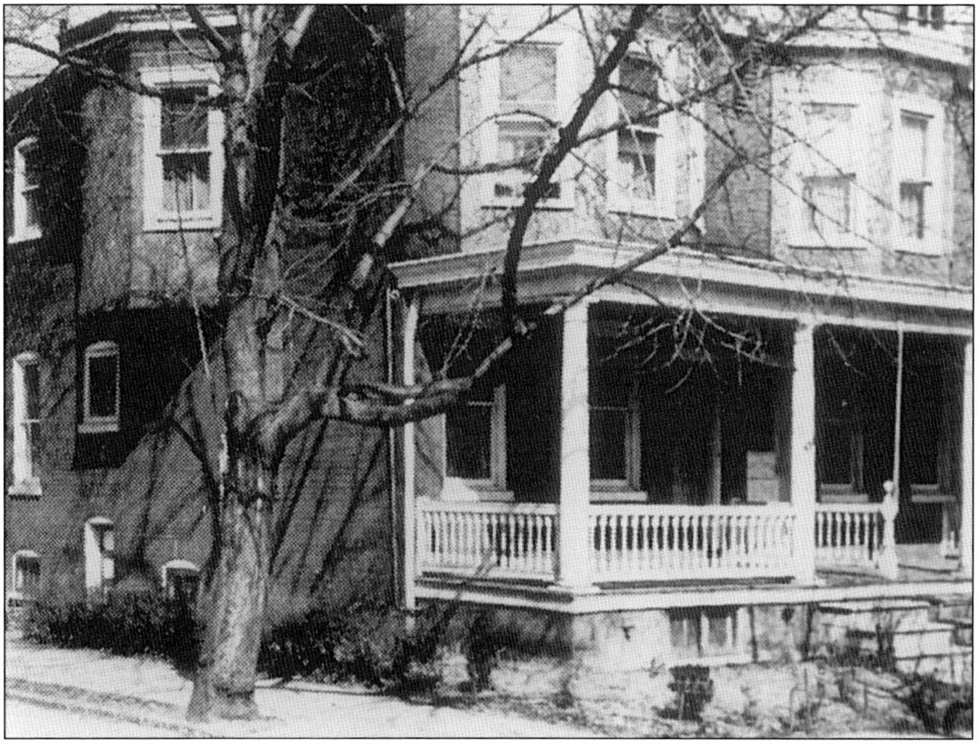

The Slowe's Home, Later the YWCA.

little something as a way of saying thank you. So my mother had a lot of company. She knew all the news of the street, and life was pretty nice.

There were about three big families—the Simms, the Bruces, and the Andersons. Now the Gardners were there, but there were just two of those girls, and my family, so that we could find enough to play with. Principal Johnson lived on my street for a while, and then moved out to the suburbs, but they would come back occasionally. On my street were the Slowe sisters, and one of the sisters was a dean at Howard University. She was one of the initial members of Alpha Kappa Alpha Sorority. Next door to me was a woman named Sarah Strickland. Sarah Strickland was the guidance teacher at Howard, and people today know her as one of the founders of the Links. So I grew up close to two of the founders of nationally known clubs.

Later the Slowes died, and their house was turned into a Women's Y, and that came about through a lady by the name of Clara Gilbert. Clara Gilbert was the nanny for Mrs. E. Paul Dupont, and Mrs. Dupont was good to her, and good to all of the things that Clara was interested in, and so she helped. I think her money helped Clara Gilbert, who went up and down the street one day soliciting pledges for a Women's Y. Well that kind of thing was unheard of at that time, so everybody was willing to participate, and for many years the Y was kind of a social center. They had meetings, and clubs, and teas. All kinds of good things so we were exposed to things that were a good part of our growing up. By virtue of the fact that we were in the midst of many who taught school, one of the things that you grew up knowing was that a college education was important. And even though you may not have known how you were going to get there, you sort of knew that you were going to college. And so bury your head in books and prepare yourself. So I think growing up on Tatnall Street was a boon to us, and even now when I go by, I look at 1232 because the people there keep it in such fine shape. One day I'm going to knock on the door and ask can I go in to see the front bedroom.

My father grew up on Shellpot. That was North Market Street amidst all of the farms, the Talleys, the Weldons, all those names of roads up there were farms when we grew up. And he lived on a little block. There was just a few blacks in that neighborhood, and they worked for those farmers.

I attest my fear of heights to the fact that we went to the Playhouse in the Dupont Building. But we had to go up the fire escapes to the gallery, and having gone up those fire escapes once, I had declared that never, ever again. You know the wind was at the bottom kind of moving the fire escape and you were going up, up, up, and it was the most unpleasant experience I'd ever had.

In the city of Wilmington when you were growing up, the top jobs black women could have were waiting tables at the Hob Tea Room, and operating the elevators at the Hotel Dupont. At that time, however, there was an intracultural thing going on, because you had to be a certain color. So when you looked in the mirror at yourself, you knew that you couldn't be a waitress, and you couldn't run the elevator, and the only other thing that you could be was a teacher, but you had to go to college to be the teacher. So it became very clear to me at a very young age that I was going to be a teacher.

Parents shielded you away from the things that were offensive and offending, and so I suspect that there was a great more going on, but your parents never sat down and discussed them. Now they always put in your mind, "You're somebody. You're going to be somebody. You're going to have to work to be that somebody," but they never spoke in terms of race.

Joseph Young

I was born in my grandmother's house at 110 West Twelfth Street, Wilmington. And I have been informed more recently that the midwife, Miss Bessie Henry—I believe it was—delivered most of my mother's babies at home. And the lady had to be supplied with a bottle of whiskey. And the whiskey was to rub the babies down after they were born. But she put the whiskey in her mouth to warm it up, and nobody knows whether she swallowed it or not.

The house where we were born, my grandmother's house, was one of the last houses demolished when the DuPont Company expanded. And they were really trying to get the blacks out of that neighborhood when they expanded their operations, or office building. And eventually, now, there is a garage where our house once stood—three-story garage. My father purchased a house at 1232 Tatnall Street which was just around the corner from my grandmother's. And I understand they moved in there when I was about two years of age. And we grew up on Tatnall Street. And there were a lot of families with a lot of children. My mother eventually had five children. There were several families with four or five children. So we always had kids to play with. And what I remember mostly is going to school. When my father purchased the house on Tatnall Street, I believe we were the first black family to move in that block, 1200 block, of Tatnall Street. And because of racism at that time, he delayed moving in until he had some, more or less, satisfaction that he could move in without being molested. But, I believe at one point they were even two Ku Klux Klan members marching up Tatnall—sort of put fear into anyone who moved into that block.

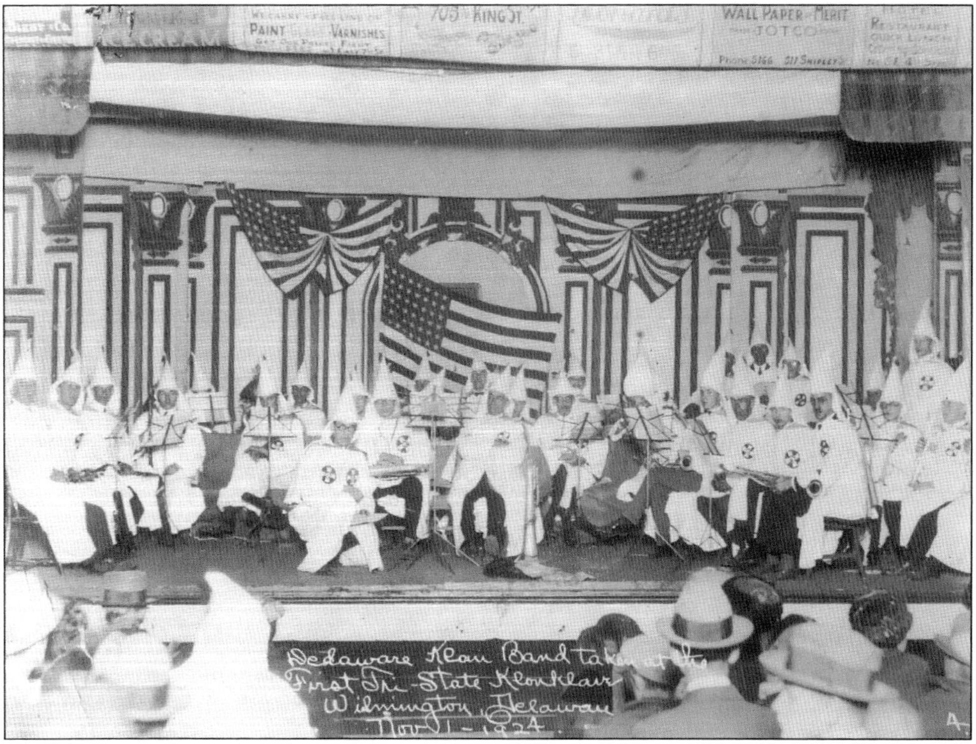

The Delaware Ku Klux Klan Band on November 1, 1924, at the Tri-State Klanklave. *(Courtesy of the HSD.)*

My earliest remembrance is mainly when I started school at age five. I went to #5 School for kindergarten. And I remember my aunt, my mother's brother's wife, who took us to Dr. Elbert to have a vaccination before we could enter school. And I ran down the hill from Tenth Street, from King Street, to French Street, and I fell and I skinned my knees. So, before I could get my vaccination, the doctor had to patch up my knee. After kindergarten, I went to #29 School, which was a block away, and I went to first, second, third, fourth, fifth, and sixth grade in #29 School. The one experience I had at #29 School that I remember vividly was having the job of taking the school banking money to the Artisans Savings Bank every week. Once a week many children were encouraged to save 5¢ or 10¢ a week. And they could bank that money at school. And they had a little bank book that would be written in. And at lunch time, the principal of the school would recruit me to carry the money in a canvas bag, with a lock on it, to the Artisans Savings Bank, which was on Fifth and Market Street. So I would walk down to Artisans Savings Bank, turn this bag in, then I'd get an empty bag to bring back to the school. And that was my job every week. I often wonder why I was selected, but I believe it was because many of the teachers and the principal knew my parents, and I assume they trusted me with the money.

After elementary school, I went to Howard High School for the seventh and eighth grade of junior high school. And while in junior high school, I took industrial arts, which included several experiences in workshop training, metal work, electricity, mechanical drawing, sheet metal, and something else. I was interested in those courses, and I wasn't

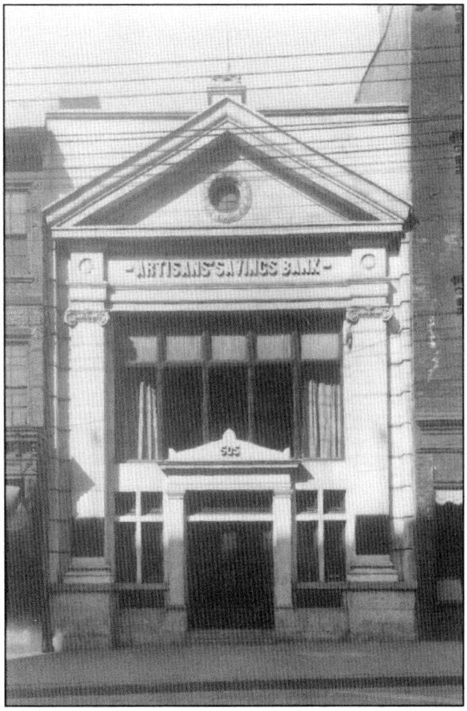

THE ARTISANS SAVINGS BANK. Leonard Young deposited #29 School's money at this location. (Courtesy of HSD.)

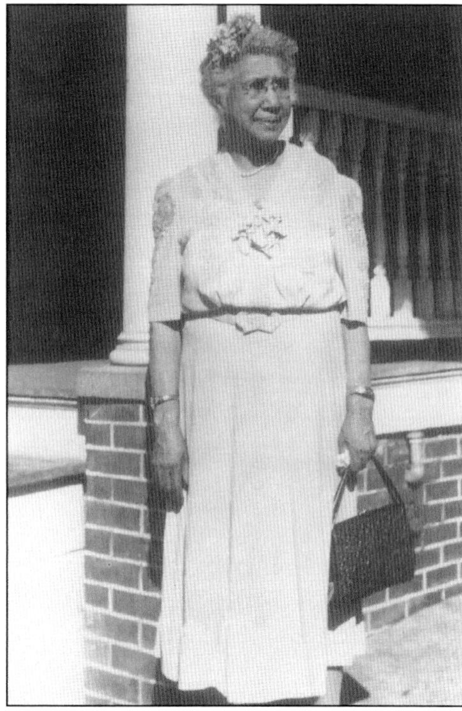

LEONARD YOUNG'S GRANDMOTHER, MARY SUSAN PAIGE COOPER. She operated a boarding-house.

so academically inclined for the academic courses, but I didn't have any failing grades. Then after junior high school, we had to decide which track we were going to follow: the college preparatory program, or vocational courses. And in consultation with the principal of the school, and because my brother was such an outstanding student, he assumed that I didn't have the academic skills, so he recommended that I follow the vocational program, which meant you just took the basic courses and shop courses. So I ended up with four years of shop training, woodworking mainly. And when I got near the end, ready for graduation, I had been visiting my brother at the university, and I decided I wanted to go to the university. But after talking with him, he found out that I didn't have enough courses to qualify for university entrance. So, then my shop teacher got involved, Mr. Eddie Fleming, and he suggested that I should try to apply to Hampton Institute, where I could work my way through school. And while at Hampton I could catch up on my high school deficiencies. So I applied to Hampton Institute in Virginia in 1937, and I was accepted for the work training program. So from 1937 to 1938 I was a work student. We worked 6-7 hours a day and then we went to school at night to finish high school courses. And after one year of the work study, then I was prepared to enter my first year of college. But back in high school, I had a few problems there because the principal—every time he saw me—kept asking me if I was Bill Young's brother. He knew I was Bill Young's brother. I don't think he liked some of the boys I used to go around with. He considered them trouble makers. So, several times I got in difficulty because I was with the wrong gang. Then some of my close friends in high school, we worked together, took some of the same courses, and did our lessons together. Yet, they got A's and B's and I got C's and D's. So we had a problem with some families getting priorities because of their light skin and light color—they got better grades. And they were pushed forward so they got the A's and B's, and yet I was doing the same work and the best I could get was a C. But that was heartbreaking when I was in school. But I learned to live with it.

I had to go to my grandmother's house because her ten-room house, now without children, now had two or three boarders. She had a couple of people staying there, and then some people would come in just to get a meal. And she would serve them dinner. So, everyday I'd have to got to the store, which was in the neighborhood, and do the shopping for a pound of butter, and a package of bacon, and a dozen eggs, and that type of thing. And then every Saturday morning, we'd go down to the King Street market with the wagon, and she would buy these large bushel baskets of potatoes, or tomatoes, or fruits in season. And she did a lot of canning. But also because she had large quantities of things, which was not common for many families, some of the neighbors would knock on our door, and she would sell them one tomato or two potatoes. And she would charge them for that. So she made money off buying wholesale. Then as it was nearing the end of my high school years, I got a job working in a pharmacy on Delaware Avenue. It was the only so-called professional pharmacy in the city of Wilmington. The pharmacy was Mr. Brown's Apothecary. That's what it was called, 43 Delaware Avenue. And I used to have to deliver medicine—during the school week I would work there from 4 o'clock to 8 o'clock at night. And on weekends, I would work all day Saturdays and Sundays. And delivering medicine all over the city of Wilmington, which at the time, was not as large as it is today. But many times we would have to go to the supply house at Second and Market to get things that he didn't have in stock. So maybe once or twice a day, I had to ride from Delaware Avenue down to Second and Market and back to Delaware Avenue with whatever he had to purchase. Then we would have to take medicine to the two or three hospitals in town. But one of the disgusting experiences I had was, many times we had to deliver medicine to the Du Pont Hotel. And the hotel would not permit me to enter the door. So the doorman would take the medicine into the desk, collect the fee for the medicine, bring it out to me at the door, and then I would take it [the fee] back to the store. So that was one of my disgusting experiences. And I almost promised at that time I would never go into the Du Pont Hotel.

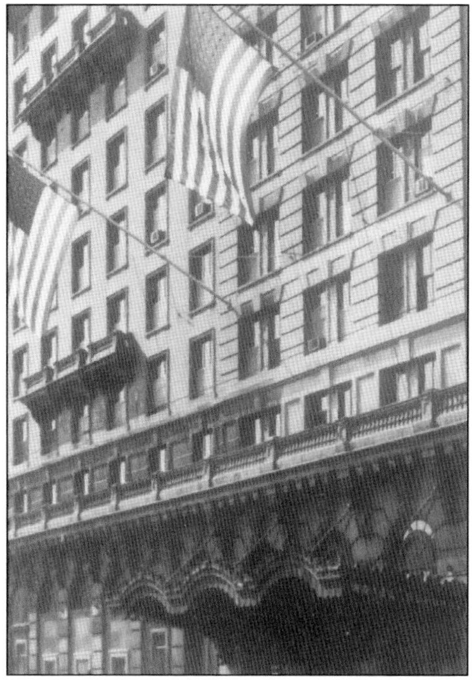

The Hotel Du Pont. *Leonard Young delivered prescriptions for Brown's Apothecary to this address. (Courtesy of HSD.)*

When I had the chance to get this job at the pharmacy, I had to have a bicycle. So my parents purchased a bicycle for me at one of the stores on King Street. Hurly-Powell I think it was. I had to pay this dollar down and a dollar a week for 29 weeks, or something. Many times we were late paying the payment, so that added interest charges and what not. So by the time the bicycle was paid for, I think we paid for it twice. While working at the pharmacy, Mr. Brown developed a liking for me. And when I was about to graduate from high school, he tried to encourage me to stay and continue working with him, he would teach me how to fill prescriptions. And maybe one day I could take the test and get a pharmacy license. He didn't see the need for me to [go to college], he didn't think that was necessary. He probably thought I would never make it in college. But there was a substitute—an assistant pharmacist there, a young fellow. And he used to work at night because the pharmacy was on call from nine at night to nine in the morning. They had a doorbell, and the people called up, or the hospitals called up and they needed medicine. They could have prescriptions filled. And he would corner me privately and he would tell me, "Mr. Brown is trying to discourage you from going to college. But if you have an opportunity to go to college, you should go." And he never had an opportunity like that himself, so he said, "If you can go, go on to college. It would be better for you." So he gave me a very nice leaving gift when I left to go to college. The leaving gift he gave me was a slide rule, which at the time, I didn't even know what it was. But it was a fancy thing for calculating all kinds of measurements. But while I was in college, at one point we had to use a slide rule to calculate math problems. So it came in handy. But a slide rule, in those early days, was very important for people in engineering.

Edward Loper Sr.

I was born in Wilmington, Delaware, in the section of town that was called Frogtown. Frogtown was on the other side of the Brandywine River from what is called Kirkwood Park. In that neighborhood, blacks lived on Heald Street, Fourteenth Street, Thirteenth Street, and Thatcher Street. Whites lived in the rest of the neighborhood. Back there, they had one section in that neighborhood that is called Gander Hill and that was on the other side of the railroad tracks and where today there is a prison in the section named Gander Hill Prison. The Italians lived on Twelfth Street for the most part. Some lived in other sections. The Swedish lived on Heald Street between Tenth and Twelfth. Some blacks lived on the other side of Heald Street. One of them was a woman who was a political person for the black community named Nora. And people used to call her Miss Nora. In the black section, during those times., blacks were moving from the South to the North, and since they were having a hard time getting settled, the people who had been in the neighborhood for a long while used to look down their noses at these black people who were moving in. They thought that they were going to mess up the neighborhood. It turns out that those people made contributions to the neighborhood as they got settled in and became more where they lived in single houses. At the beginning, whole families would live in one house, with rooms for each family.

When I was born they were deciding to have a playground for the neighborhood. So a man named Mr. Paige, he was a one-armed man, he took a little tree and carved it into a pole to put the flag on because the war had just ended and soldiers were coming home and the flag was very, very important. The fact is for years I used to make sure to hang the flag in our window every flag day, because I was so proud of the flag. Later on, I found out the flag didn't really matter to us because we were, we were left out. At that time, we were very, very proud. So when the playground was dedicated, they had a young man climb up the pole to hook up the flag onto the rope so it would show. They had a string tied to the flag and the flag was folded all up with dozens and dozens of little tiny flags, about 3-inches long. When they pulled the pulley, the flags all flooded down all over the place and everybody was happy. This was the first playground in the neighborhood. Of course they built another on the other side of the street, which was the white playground and of course it had real equipment that kids could play with. And the black people had to make swings themselves and all the other things they used in the playground—sand boxes and such. So I grew up in that kind of neighborhood.

The people who lived in the neighborhood, they were not absolutely in love with each other, but they tolerated each other. That tolerating of each other lasted until after the Second World War and the men came home from the war. Then suddenly the whites decided to move out and they were moving out one behind the other. They would come up to you if you were black and say, "I don't really like to leave this neighborhood because it's such a nice neighborhood, but I want to get a better education for my children." That was an excuse they used to get out of the neighborhood and make you feel as though they really weren't trying to get away from you.

My parents were part of the people who had been in the neighborhood for a long while. My grandmother was sort of a community leader. Her name was Hannah Jane Bratcher. And so she helped to run the neighborhood, sort of. She married a man named Richard Govens. And so in our house my grandmother did nice things. Her girlfriend died and my grandmother took her children and raised them. Even after my Aunt Ethel, who I called my aunt, one of the people my grandmother helped to raise, even after she had children, my grandmother always helped her out with money. My mother's name was Marian Eletta Loper. Her father and my grandmother separated about five years after they were married. My grandfather moved to New York and changed his name to Emmanuel Lopez. He did the same thing a lot of people did to stop from getting treated so much as black people. They thought that being Spanish would make a difference. They didn't know that the Spanish were going to have just as bad a time as the blacks.

My mother had me when she was about 17 years old. She and my father stopped associating with each other by the time she was 20. At that time, there used to be a Ma Rainey show that used to

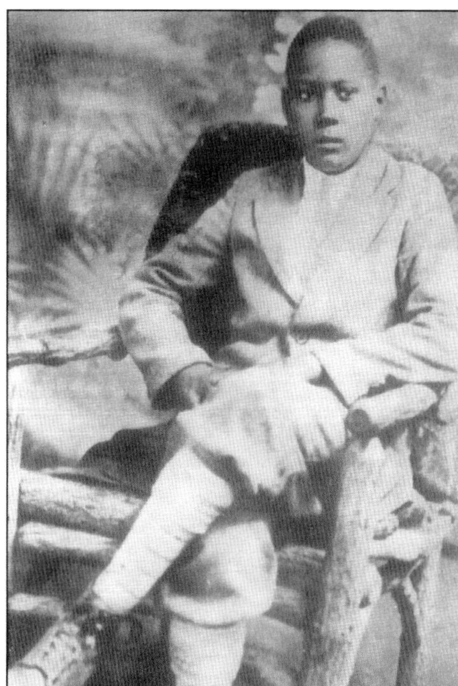

Twelve-Year-Old Edward Loper Years at Shellpot Park.

come to Delaware. They had this show. It would come in and it would have dancing, singing, and comedians. They had this show to come and it was in the form of a tent show. They set the tent up on Vandever Avenue where there was a large open lot in the neighborhood. A young man named Reese Scott met my mother and they seemed to have fallen in love enough that he decided not to leave when the show left. He at that time was a buck dancer. Now buck dancers is not the term they use today. We call them tap dancers, but that's what he did for a living. So he stayed in Wilmington and married my mother. The fact is that when he first arrived and met my mother he couldn't read or write his own name, so he got involved with the church and decided he wanted to read the bible. So he went to a lady named Henrietta Gray, who had been a former school teacher. So after going to Miss Gray and learning how to start to read and write, my father decided to enter night school at Howard High School. Now this was 1927 and the reason I know is 1927 was the year they had the sesquicentennial in Philadelphia. They also had the Ben Franklin Bridge built and opened that year. They had the Gene Tooney-Jack Dempsey fight that year. So my father, step-father, went to school and he learned to read and write. Later he became a local minister who went and preached in the AUMP Churches in rural areas around Wilmington. So, eventually he and my mother were given the church in Merchantsville, New Jersey. The church was not doing very well. So he stayed at that church for about seven or eight years. He did so well with this church, they had a church in Washington, D.C., named St Marks Church at Fourth and I Streets Southeast. So he took over that church and it was empty. People didn't go there. And as he got there, he took that church and made it into the most popular of the AUMP system. By this time he was doing his own typing. He eventually was quite a smart man, and he became well educated. The fact is, they had a problem with the churches. It was taken to the United States Supreme Court and he was the one that spoke at the hearings and he was honored for that. So I was very lucky to have a man of that type who had become my step-father. Today I think of him as my father, because my father didn't do anything for me. I would talk to him once in a while. I think he was fairly smart. He wasn't much of a father.

When I was about 12 or 13, there was a place called Shellpot Park. Shellpot Park was about three blocks north of Lea Boulevard on Market Street. There was a steep hill and Shellpot Park was at the bottom of that steep hill. Shellpot Park was an amusement park similar to the ones they have today and it was opened to whites all the year around. But they had one week that they would let colored people come to that park. Well, when that week would be on, black people would flock to that park because they were just glad to go to an amusement park. But they had rides you could ride on. You couldn't go in the swimming pool. They didn't allow blacks to go into the swimming pool. So that was out. But you could ride on the different things. While there, my mother decided she ought to have a picture of me. So I looked at the pictures they had outside on the wall showing what the pictures would be like and I fell in love with the picture of the boy on the donkey. So, I said, "I'd like to have a picture." So we go in to get the picture made and I go to get on the donkey and my mother says, "No!" She says, "You don't get on a donkey." So she had me to sit. My mother had a picture taken of me in Shellpot Park. And as I look at it lately, I see I was burned. I was all upset because I couldn't get on the donkey. Well anyway black people used to go to Shellpot Park that one week out of a year. In those days they evidently didn't have respect of themselves enough to tell 'em,

"We wouldn't dare to come to your park if it can't be regularly." But that was an early time in the history of the United States.

EDITH ELIZABETH FAULKNER DICKERSON

My name is Edith Elizabeth Faulkner Dickerson. I was born in Woodall, Delaware, December 8, 1921. My mother delivered me. She was in the house by herself and she delivered me and cut the umbilical cord. She wiped me off and wrapped me in a blanket. Took a little rest then decided to take care of me.

It looked like wilderness to me. It was Covered Bridge where my father drove for Senator Ball. Well, he drove for Senator Ball and that's the best I know of him. Then he settled in Washington. My mother lived with my brothers and they helped to raise us. We moved to Twelfth and Orange in the beginning, right around old Howard High School and old Shiloh Church and the Clover Dairy was right in front of us, number 21 West Twelfth Street. Well, my mother actually wanted to move so she could be near people and get out and go to work, because I was like the tenth child. She liked to take in washing, ironing and she wanted to work. She needed to get away from the country life. Well we lived near Zimmerman Drug Store and my mother started working for them right across the street., right in the area. Then we moved to 1121 Tatnall. She would come to the window, when we were home, a certain window, and look across at us while she was working. It was a pharmacy and that's what I can remember. She saved money. I have her bank book now. And when it was filled, she would take that and put it in the bank. We had bank books at school that we would save. She always gave use money to save. It was just a part of me. I knew there was tomorrow. I remember

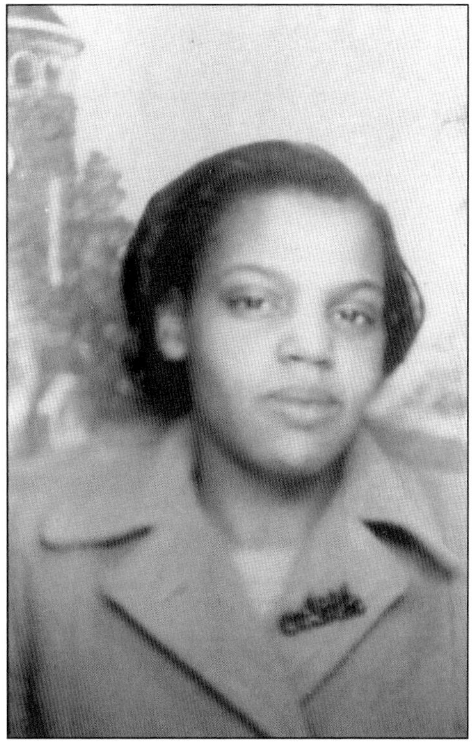

TEENAGER ELIZABETH FAULKNER DICKERSON.

going to Sunday school. She would put us in a cab and take us to Walnut Street to church—Seventh or Eighth and Walnut after we left Shiloh as children.

I went to #5 elementary school from kindergarten to I guess the fourth or fifth grade. And then they made us transfer because we were living at Sixth and Jefferson. So we had to go on the "Hill" to school. So that was #21. And that was two of us going. out there. Another was going someplace else. And then we moved to 427 East Fifth· That transferred me to #29 to finish the sixth grade. Then from there I went to Howard High School. It was strange that day going to all the classes. It was the first time, being the younger child, always had a sister or something over me. It was hard to get to the classroom until I made friends with someone and we could go together.

I've always sung all the way through school—from elementary, from

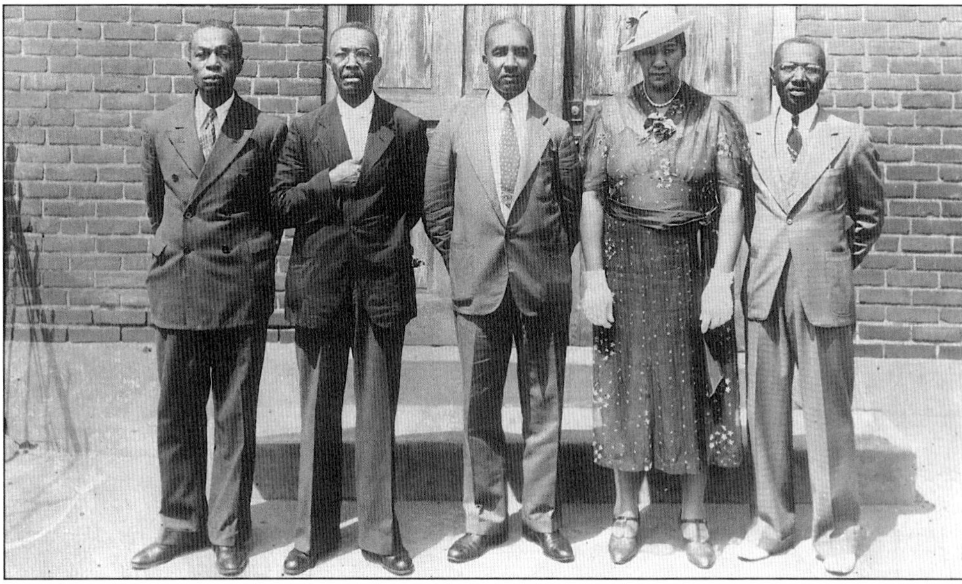

CORA PRITCHETT'S FATHER AND OTHER MEMBERS OF THE 1939 DELAWARE STATE BAPTIST CONVENTION. *From left to right are William Pritchett (corresponding secretary), Reverend Price (Eighth Street Baptist Church secretary), Rev. Arthur James (Shiloh Baptist Church), Mrs. Gordy (president of missions), and Harvey King.*

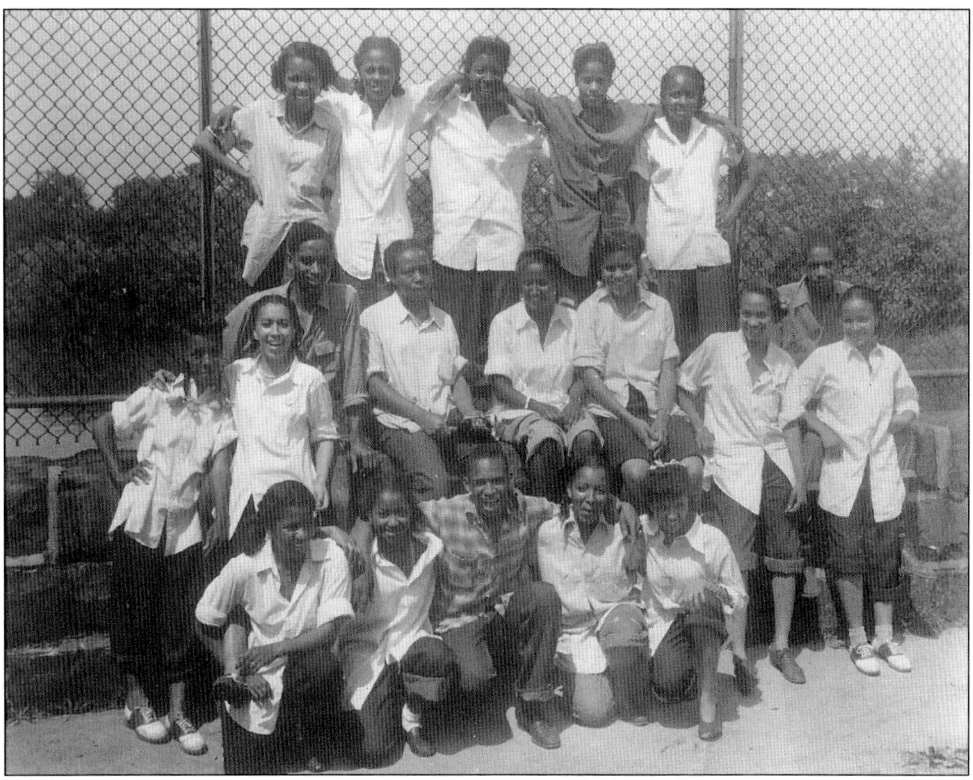

"TRAMP DAY" AT HOWARD HIGH SCHOOL, C. 1945. *Cora Pritchett is on the left in the top row.*

kindergarten. We would go to town to sing. I was an alto. And I remember, Mr. Hitchener was telling someone that he wouldn't be afraid, with the volume of my voice, to put me into an auditorium and I could carry it. We always would say we were the best because we really had a good glee club. I think I was in my seventh year—in the 1930s.

Cora Pritchett Toliver

I was born at 1123 Walnut Street on February 24, 1929. My parents were William Pritchett and Cora Williamson Pritchett. My parents were basically from Pittsylvania County in Virginia. My mother was actually born in North Carolina, but she moved to Danville, Virginia, at about six months, and she didn't know anything about North Carolina. I had two brothers and one sister. My sister died in 1940 when she was 13 and I was 11. And then I had two brothers who are five and seven years older than I am.

One of the girls I played with—we started kindergarten and graduated from high school together. That was Clydas Colder. Her family lived in a three-story house. It was about four families who lived on three floors. Her parents lived on the third floor. One daughter lived on the second floor with her family. Well, an aunt lived on the first floor with her family. And lots of families did that. They lived in a house together. I would go around there and they would come to my house. You know we enjoyed playing together because there wasn't too much to do. We couldn't even go to the playgrounds in the neighborhood because they were segregated at that time. I think the nearest playground we could go to was Decatur. And I couldn't go that far by myself. My brother went. It was near Eighth and Locust, somewhere I think we called it the "Hoodle"—down in the "Hoodle." I think anything below Bennett Street was called the "Hoodle." Around Seventh and Eighth Street near Christina Park. I don't think it [Christina Park] was there at the time. But I remember when it was built. It was in 1938 and they had the tercentennial. It was a big to do with that.

I grew up, until I was 13, in Shiloh Church. At that time it was at Twelfth and Orange. I remember Sunday school particularly. We enjoyed that with picnics in the summertime. Our superintendent was Mr. G. Oscar Carrington and our church treasurer was Ms. Caroline Betsy Williams. At that time there was only one high school. Very few large churches so you sort of knew everybody. When new people came to town and went to the churches, you met them that way. May be I shouldn't mention it but there was a lot of fighting at that time, because they eventually separated and formed Central Church. I was only 13 and I didn't want to go but I had to go where my parents went. My father was active in the Baptist church. He was a deacon in Central Church. They didn't make him a deacon at Shiloh but at Central he was a deacon. And even before that when we were at Shiloh he was a corresponding secretary in the Delaware State Baptist Convention. He was always active in the church even before he came here. My parents came here when they got married in 1917, and they joined Shiloh Church when Reverend Moore was pastor. Mom would go around with him like to weddings and things, sort of like a secretary. And so they stayed there from 1917 to 1943. And then they left and went to Central Church. The founding minister was Reverend Arthur James. And after him was Reverend Albert Rowe, I believe, I'm not sure. I guess he was pastor emeritus. And the Reverend Rowe came and then Reverend Holt.

My father was a plasterer by trade. He didn't practice because you really couldn't get a job in the trades if you were black. But he went to St Paul's College and he was a plasterer and he was good. He could do private jobs when he was on vacation and things like that. The Pritchett house in Buttonwood, he did that. Right after they finished it, it burned down.

Well, actually at that time you had to be dressed properly in our school [Howard High] and we just wanted a "Tramp Day." We just wanted to wear jeans to school. So we weren't allowed to do it, but we did it anyway. We didn't get put out or anything like that. We did it for the fun of it and someone took a picture. We were seniors then, so we defied authority and did that. When we graduated we wanted caps and gowns, and Mr. Johnson wouldn't let us do it. It would have been cheaper because you had to buy the dress and boys that didn't have a dark blue suit had to buy one. I wore ... I guess many other people did too. Some of them made them. I bought a wedding gown and had the sleeves cut off. I have a picture of it. Because my brothers girlfriend cut the sleeves off. They were sort of puffed sleeves.

ROBERT J. FLEMING JR.

I was born on November 4, 1926 in Wilmington, Delaware. I lived originally in the 200 block of North Union Street. Then we moved in town to East Ninth Street and then we moved back on the West Side when I was six years old. My mother's name was Mary Lewis Fleming. And she was born in Greenville, South Carolina, but she came to Wilmington, Delaware, I think in the early 1920s. My father, Robert J. Fleming Sr., became a police officer in 1927. He was the second black person to become a policeman. My mother worked mainly as a domestic. She was a cook for many of the well-known families around town at the time—mainly in the Westover Hills area. She was also very much interested in civic work. She was a member of the Carver Garden Flower Club. She was very much interested in solicitations for the NAACP. In fact, I used to always kid my mother a lot. "When people see you coming they're going to turn and run the other way afraid your going to ask for some money." And we would have a good chuckle about that. But she was a tireless individual and I think I learned quite a bit from her. She never raised her voice that I can remember, but when she said something you knew that she meant it. And I took my cue from that.

My father, as I said, was the second black policeman on the force. He never really talked too much about his work. He might come home with a little anecdote now and then. He might complain about some of his superiors. I remember the superintendent at that time was Andrew Kavanaugh. Mr. Kavanaugh had three or four sons. In fact, I know one of the sons very well. As I said, there were only three black policeman at the time I was growing up. He had a lot of white policeman who were friends with him. I remember one person who lived on the "Hill." He was Italian. I can't think of his name right off, but he was Italian. He was coming to my house quite a bit. My father liked to drink beer. He loved beer. And they would sit in the kitchen, just drink beer and I guess they would swipe tales between the two of them. But as I say, he never really talked about his work too much, at least that I can remember, except for a few amusing things he would say. Like the time he told me they had a riot or disturbance over Third Street Bridge. When they sent him out there someone said to him, "Why would they send only one cop?" He said, "There's only one riot, so we need only one cop!" So that was the little joke that he used to have with that. But otherwise, he was kind of strict with me. He would tell me things which I thought at the time, well, you know, "What does he know?". But I found out later that he did know something, because that's the way young people are.

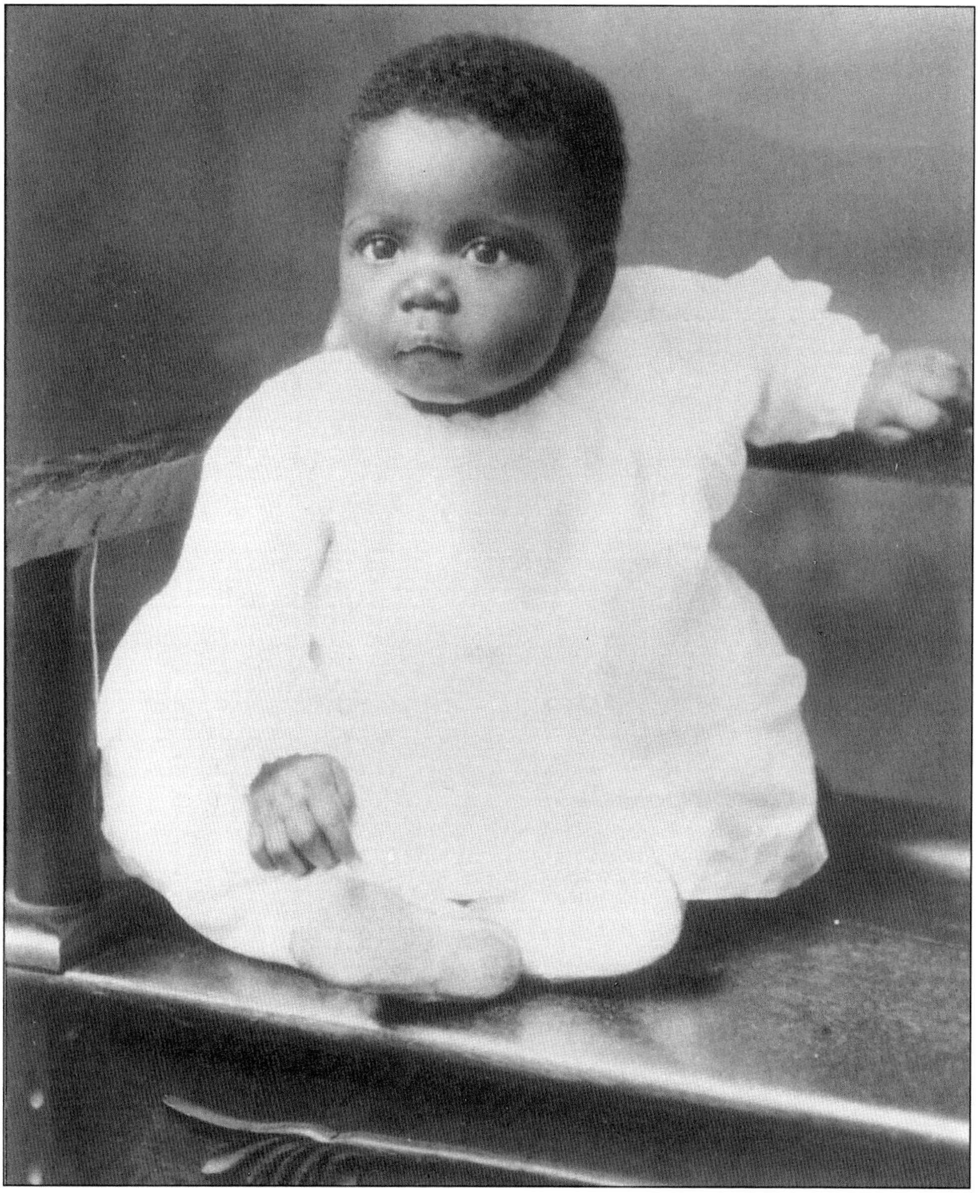

ROBERT J. FLEMING AS AN INFANT IN 1926.

Getting back to growing up on the West Side. It was a good relationship we had with the Italians out there. We were very close to them, because we were in between, you probably heard of Browntown area, and also what they call Forty Acres. Forty Acres was were the Irish lived. That was around Delaware and DuPont Streets. Most people at that time worked for the Rhodes Company they had built it on Bancroft Parkway. They had built homes for them to stay in and most of the Irish migrated to that part because the Polish people lived in South Wilmington, what they call Browntown and Hedgeville. And woe be to you if you, not so much being black or Italian, but if you were in their territory—you didn't

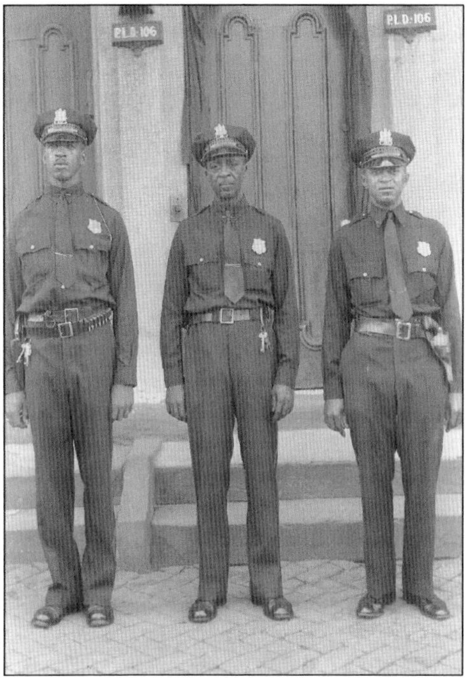

***The First African Americans to Serve in Wilmington's Police Department.** From left to right are Ralph Harris, Lockwood Purnell, and Robert Fleming Sr., Robert Fleming's father.*

live there. You saw hard times. So not only the blacks there saw hard times, but the Italians there too, because we were right in between the two. And if we ventured too far to the north we hit Forty Acres and, too far south we ran into Browntown. So I think that created a bond between the blacks and the Italians during that time. Because I see some of the guys I grew up with, with the Italians, and we reminisce about the old times. But I remember going, one time, yeah. We got caught down at Delaware and DuPont and that's when they used to have the B&O Railroad was down there. And about four or five Irish young guys approached us and demanded what we were doing down there. Well, there were three of us and about four or five of them and I remember the guy moved to Curtis Daniels. You probably know Jean Daniels and that was Curtis. She married Curtis later on. So we looked at each other and we said, "Well, the only thing we can do is we will hit one of these guys real hard and run." So I remember I hit one guy and Curtis hit another guy and the third guy ... We said, if you're going to get whipped, we may as well get the first lick in. I remember doing that and we ran so fast that the guys never did catch us because we ran back to DuPont Street and we crossed over Pennsylvania Avenue (which they didn't cross over Pennsylvania Avenue). I wasn't much of a fighter and I knew we would get a whipping. So we're going to get the first lick and I struck one guy and Curtis hit the other guy and the third guy probably ran ahead of us, as it was. Those little things, that you know, that happened as we were growing up. But we had a good time on the West Side. My nickname at the time was "Copper" because my father was a policeman, and when someone calls me "Copper" today, I say, "Oh, that's somebody that I grew up with a long time ago." You know we still do because everybody on the West Side had a nickname. I can think of maybe one or two people who didn't have a nickname. So it was a good time coming up and I think I stayed on the "Hill" until I met my wife and moved out here. That was in the early '60s so I stayed on. We moved out here in 1932 and I remember my father and mother paid $3,000 for the house from Jay Montgomery. I remember that insurance company. And they paid it off, I guess in the prescribed amount of time. The house was my mother's pride and joy.

There were always a lot of children at that time, and we always walked to school. We never rode the bus or anything. Anyway all the black kids would start congregating. They would start picking up as they walked along and by the time they got to Howland Street, which were the last black families on that street, there might be 25 or 30 children walking along Ninth Street going to Howard High

School. Everybody knew everybody else and the neighbors were very protective of the children. We thought they were being nosey but they weren't being nosey, they were being protective. And I say we had a very tight group of youngsters on the "Hill" and I still see most of them today. A lot of them are still living. They don't live on the West Side any more, but they're around town occasionally. We'd get together and we'd talk about the old times on the "Hill." It was a lot of fun. We had a lot of fun together and although we were being segregated, we really didn't let it bother us that much. We were raised with the Italians and we got along fine. They would always say, "How come you all go to a different school?". And I said, "Well, this is just the way it is." But we'd come home from school. We would go out on the playgrounds and play together. During the summer we would play all summer long and when school came, we'd always play when I came home from school. But we had a very close association of not only the black children but the blacks and the whites at that time on the West Side. I do go past my neighborhood occasionally and I just feel a little sadness because I don't know anybody on that block—maybe one person. That's all. But I still keep in touch with my former neighbors. I think one thing about growing up together, we remained close.

BARBARA WASHAM

I was born in Wilmington, Delaware, and most of my life I've lived on Walnut Street the 1300 block. My mother and father were Robert and Mariam Washam. My mother's maiden name was Mariam Jefferson. My mother did domestic work and my father worked for a drugstore. Well he did work for Eckerd's Drugstore at the end. That's where he retired from but he also worked for Sun Shipyard and that's about the only ones that I remember. He was a custodian for Eckerd's and at the shipyard he was a custodian there too.

The Walnut Street Y was built in 1939 and I remember going there when I was not even a teenager. When I was about 11 years old that's when I started going to the Walnut Street Y and learned so many things like the same things they were doing when I use to teach there like the ballet, swimming, and the gymnastics. And then after I got to the age where I could choose what I wanted to do in terms of a career, I decided to go away and came back with a degree in physical education. I was hired by the Walnut Street YW. At that time it was the Y&YW.

Well I think the primary thing that really kept me going to the Y every day was the

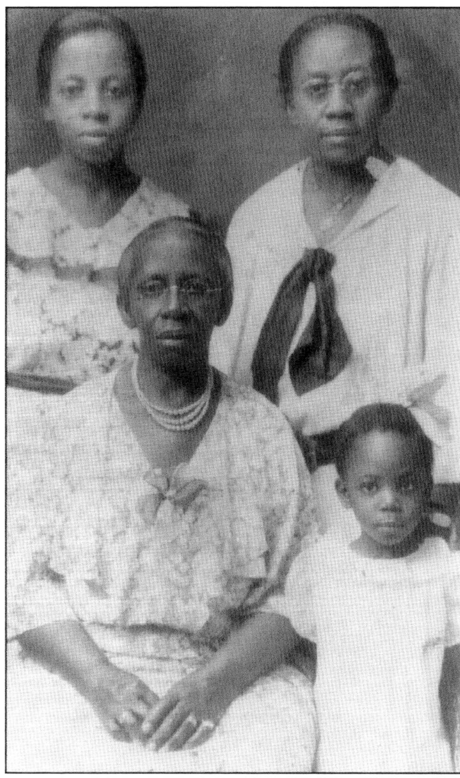

FOUR GENERATIONS OF WOMEN. *From left to right, are as follows: (front row) Annie P. Richards (Irene's mother) and Barbara Washam; (back row) Marion T. Washam (Barbara's mother) and Irene A. Ball (Marion's mother).*

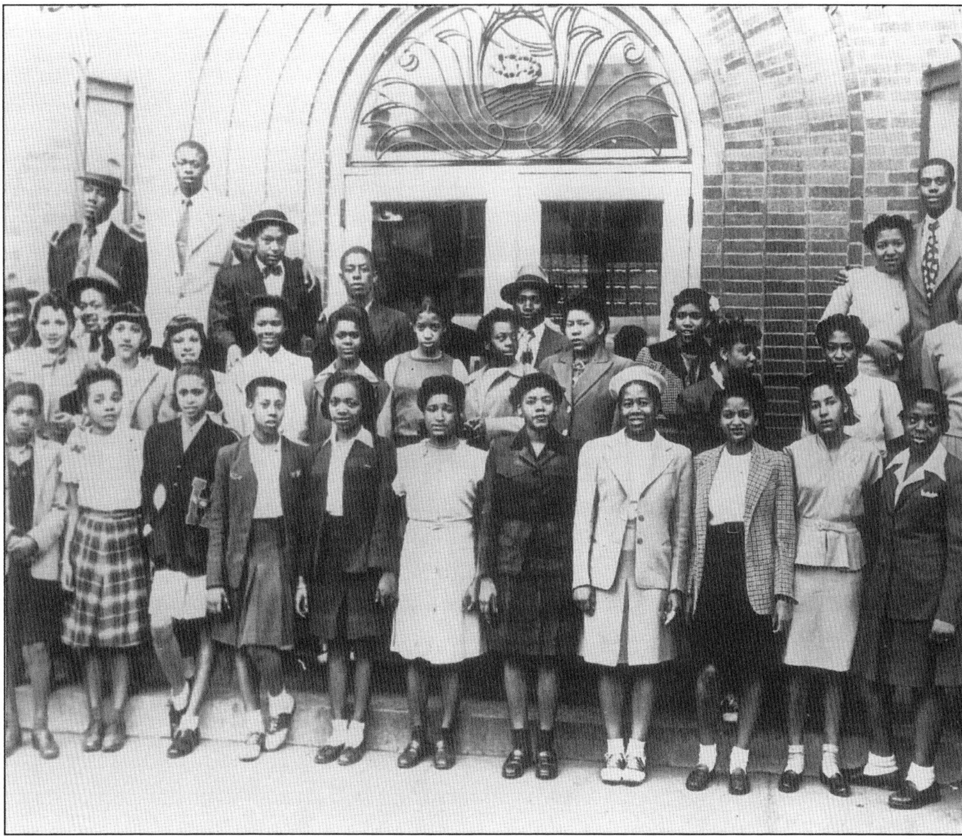

***Barbara Washam and Others from the Walnut Street YWCA and YMCA.** Barbara is in the second row, fourth from right, in front of the young man in the hat.*

swimming and the ballet. We did have recitals and we did a lot of other things in terms of bowling—we did bowling. That was something that was different for the community since it was so segregated. It was so wonderful when the Y did open and we were able to just get all of those activities and we took advantage of them. We had basketball teams too. So we did do the team sports. And there was a girl's basketball team and we went on trips and played against other YWCAs and it was a great thing for the community—the Walnut Street Y and YW and I keep saying YW because a lot of people think it was just the YM but it was the YW and it was the one I worked for when I got out of college. We had some people who were on staff there. There was the teenage director or the physical education director and I just can't remember all their names because they did change off and on. They were very supportive. They lived in the area so that made a difference too. You always came in contact with them at the Y or somewhere else so that made a difference.

Well, let me say that the people who had the most impact on my life were my mother and father. They were my role models. They were the ones who encouraged us and supported us and showed us what the great things in life were and how. And that's why I'm where I am today. We knew that we had to go to school and get an education and move on from there and continue to move on. Keep focused and have an idea about what you want and go on and pursue it. She [mother] liked to participate with us in activities, also. Like bowling we were bowling together and things like that. It's probably not unusual now but at that time it was a great thing to have parents and children doing activities together. And so that's one of the things I remember.

Well, the swimming started at the Kruse pool like I said because of segregation. We had no indoor pools so all of the swimming was done in the summers. We had swimming meets and everything like that down there at Kruse pool because we could not participate in state swimming programs. I guess I was about 11. And from there the YM and YW had an indoor pool so we were able to swim all year round. So we got involved in synchronized swimming. All I remember is that we started the synchronized swimming and I just can't remember too much about it. We also had diving classes and things like that.

Well I liked to shoot marbles. So that was one of the things I liked to do. So that was what I was doing. The rest of the people I don't know. I did the hopscotch and the jump rope and the other classic games Chinese Checkers and dominos.

The #5 School was just like a block away from my house so I can remember going to kindergarten and having very nice teachers. And just like I said the difference now is that most of these teachers were living right around the neighborhood so it was like one big family.

I was on the cheering squad at Howard. I was like a mascot. I do know that. I would do most of the cartwheels and things like that. I was on the basketball team and I sang in the choir. I remember Mr. Andrews, one of the greatest choir directors. I think most of the teachers were very interested in the children and the parents were very supportive of whatever the teachers were doing. We had musicals. We always had musicals. I remember participating in *Carmen* and *El Travatore*. Those are the things that were impressive to me because everybody got to participate. You were either a singer or in the dance section. So there were lots of things you did. There were proms and you decorated. That was that kind of thing to look forward to also .

I remember people who came to work for the YWCA they had to live in rooms rather than apartments because there were no apartments that allowed blacks to live in them. Then when the time came when it was suppose to be available to anyone people were still not able to get apartments because as soon as they saw your face they knew that they weren't going to rent to you anyway. You couldn't eat downtown at Woolworth's or any of those places.

My life wasn't that bad because we had the Y. It was something.

Floyd W. Van Riper

I was born April 30, 1938. Reflecting on my years that led up to becoming an Eagle Scout or even a boy scout, I would say that it was instrumental that I joined the YMCA because they structured me, when I was young in how to swim. We started out like a minnow. Then we'd go from a minnow and then you'd progress to become a shark. That helped me out—the YMCA. At that time they used to call it the Y on Walnut Street—Tenth and Walnut. Later through the years I joined Troop 80, which was under the umbrella of the American Legion. At that time we were located on East Eleventh Street but that building is since gone. But we used to meet upstairs on the second floor. We had our different programs there. But I do give the Y a lot of credit because they helped me in the basic things like swimming and when I used to go to day camp. So that was a little structure. When I went into scouting, I started going through the ranks, I call it the ranks. First you were a

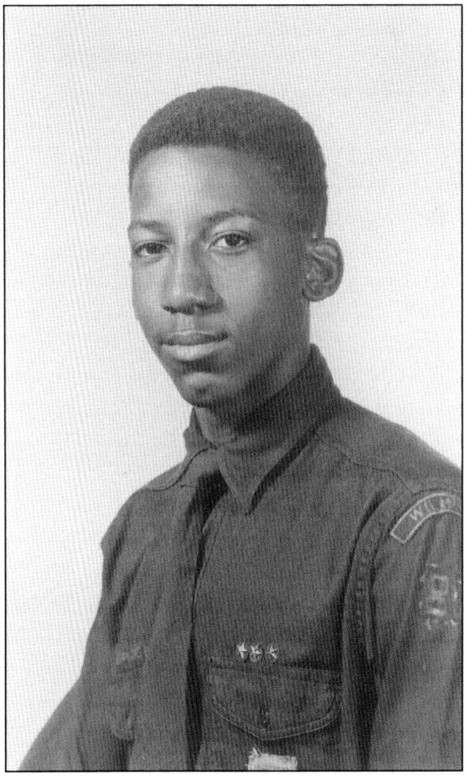

Floyd Van Riper, the First African-American Eagle Scout in Delaware.

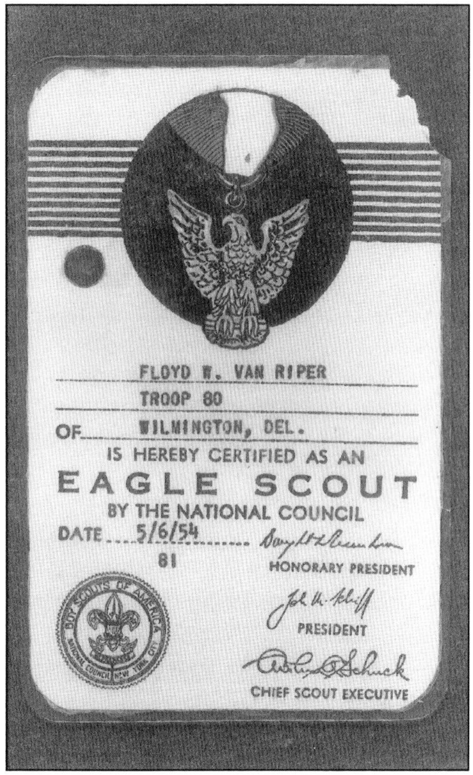

Floyd Van Riper's Eagle Scout Membership Card.

tenderfoot and then you learned how to tie a square knot and some basic things in scouting. Then my other rank was Second Class and I became a Second Class Scout. I went to camp. At that time we were segregated. You know, it was the black scouts and the white scouts. And our camp was Camp Horseshoe. I attended Camp Horseshoe and by being active in camping that helped me to get my experience so that I could go on to becoming a First Class Scout and then next Star Light and the eventually I became an Eagle Scout. I give a lot of credit to the YMCA because in achieving Eagle Rank, you had to know how to swim, you had to camp out. You had cooking merit badges—different merit badges that structured around some basic things. I think I had 20+ merit badges. That's the gist of it. I came up through the ranks but I had a lot of help. I had a lot of family members that were very supportive and I had other people in the community. They knew what I was trying to achieve. They were very supportive because I had to go to counselors. You had certain requirements for each badge. You had to make a presentation. But most of the merit badges I got at camp. Through the years when things opened up, we could go to Camp Rodney. Camp Rodney was located on the Chesapeake. Ned Brown, he's from Belvedere, was a good scout also. And we were the first scouts to get the All Rodney. That was the highest award they gave to a scout. So Ned Brown and myself were the first ones to get that All Rodney. Scouting was good to me it structured my life and it helped me to eventually go into photography. Because that's when I started photography when, I was a Boy Scout. I used to look at Ed Anderson.

Ed Anderson was one of the premier photographers in Wilmington, Delaware. And when I was a kid I used to go there and peep in his window, you, know, and its gave me inspiration. Because I didn't really have any role models other than people like Ed Anderson. I never talked to him personally, but you know, I would just go up and look in his window. I got a little inspiration from that and eventually I got a camera and I moved along those lines. After coming out of the military, I went to photography school

Well my troop leader was Charles Brown. He was very instrumental in my going up the ladder to becoming an Eagle. He was very supportive. And Mr. Fletcher Brown, also. I think he was on the board. He was very supportive. Scouting was very popular at one time. When we were in scouting it was the thing to do. You had a lot of activities.

I'll tell you that day will stay with me for the rest of my life because I was awarded the Eagle Scout at Longwood Gardens. And you know the place itself is just, just overwhelming. I believe when I received my Eagle, I was the only person of color. I believe it was about six or seven other scouts that received their Eagle. But you know, you walk across the stage. It was something to remember. As soon as I received my Eagle, I remember some of the other scouts came over and congratulated me. Gave me hugs and all. And I gave them inspiration, I guess to stay in scouting. It was something I wanted to do. I'm glad I did it.

Pastor Aretha Morton

My name is Aretha Morton. Maiden name of course Adams. I was born January 19, 1938. Well, during those days the insurance people would come to your house to collect the money. My grandfather had a favorite chair that he sat in the all the time. The insurance man would come in and he'd say, "Well, Pop, how are you today?" And my grandfather would say, "Frustrate, Frustrate," which meant, of course, "first rate," which I learned later. And my grandmother didn't appreciate that so I guess maybe after three or four visits he came in and again spoke to my grandfather and he said, "Well Pop, how are you?" And my grandmother said, "I need to say something to you." And he said, "Yes what it is?" And she said, "My husband is not your father. And I would appreciate it if you would stop calling him 'Pop.' " So, of course, he apologized and the next time he came into the home, he said, "Good evening, Mr. Jackson, how are you?" And from that time on, he addressed him as Mr. Jackson and of course my grandmother as Mrs. Jackson.

Well, my grandfather, in his days in Wilmington, was a retired farmer, but I'll tell you what he did do. He would go back downstate, well at least two, three times a week and he would get eggs and he would bring them back to Wilmington and he would sell them from his car.

And my grandmother, was of course vice-principal of the Millside School and she loved teaching. She loved children. My grandfather used to say he and I got along fine during the course of the day. I would always get home from school before she got home, and we had an opportunity to sit down, laugh and talk and he was—he was a little guy, but the minute my grandmother hit the door, that was the end of my grandfather and my conversation. But she enjoyed teaching. A lot of times, she would bring children here to the house. She said, "Never call a child dumb." They might be slow learners, just need a little bit more than everybody else. And they would come right here at this dining room table and sit there until they got it. She made sure that they got it. She never wanted a child to just be passed on to the next grade, she would take her time and make sure that they got it. Frank and Ethel C. Jackson. The "C" stood for Clark for my grandmother, that was her name.

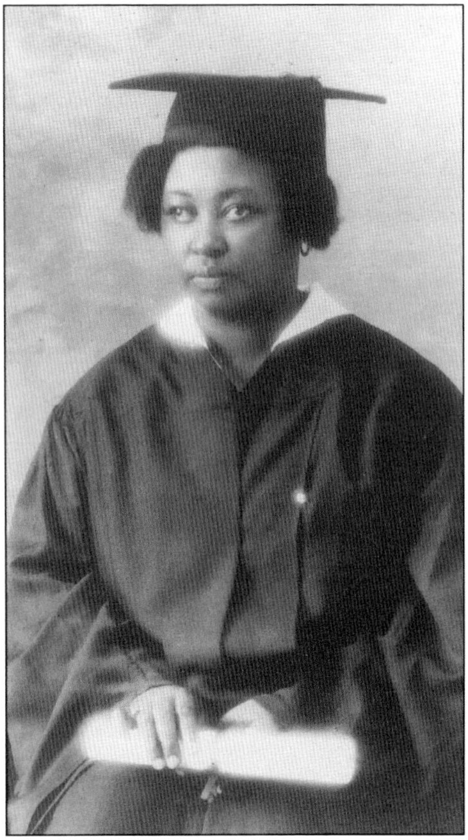

Aretha Morton's Grandmother, Ethel Clark Jackson.

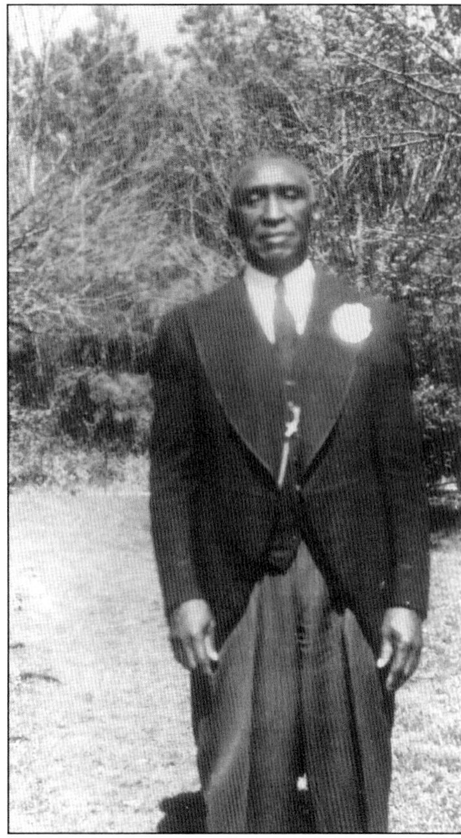

Aretha Morton's Grandfather, Frank Jackson.

There were times that I would leave my mother and father, and they always knew where I was, and I had my own bedroom. My bedroom was in the back here and you know, I would just come stay for days and weeks at a time and my mother followed me right up the street.

My grandmother, she was one who was a stickler for paying bills on time. I could show you the book where she paid the mortgage for this house, $21.20 right down the line until she got it paid to buy this house. So she loved to know that she was paying her bills on time, Braunstein's and Arthur's she had credit, and that's where my clothes came from that I was wearing as a little girl. I was wearing clothes from Benheim's and Arthur's. My feet, you know, they always wanted you to take care of your feet. Your feet and your hair had to be right. Anyway, there was a restaurant at Eleventh and Wilson, and the man had a little girl and all of my hand-me-down clothes went to her. So one day as we got older, I was walking down the street, Market Street, and she was walking with some friends and I spoke to her. And she didn't speak to me, and that hurt my feelings. I'm saying to myself, I'm black at that time, no such thing as African American, I'm black at that time and she was white okay, and all of my clothes were going to her. I couldn't understand why, so I walked up behind her and I passed her and I said, "You didn't speak to me," and she said, "Oh hi," like that, and I said, "Have you forgotten?" "Well," I said, "Well, okay ... don't worry, you don't have to speak to me." And I'm sitting here now, 62 years old and I guess she's around the same age, I guess, I don't know, but I hadn't seen her from that day.

Well, one thing I talk about this all the time because it's a passion. We were blessed to have our own businesses. I think about the only thing or the only times that we went to Market Street or near French and all of those areas was to go to Wilmington Dry. We got our stockings at Wilmington Dry. Then on the East Side there was a place down on Bennett Street where James and Jessie are now. There was a store there, I think, I forgot what his name was, but we had two of those stores, where if we didn't want to go to Dry Goods, we could either go to Sands which was on Eleventh Street or we could go down at Bennett Street and Tenth to get stockings. Now, they were, along with Dave's (Dave's was on Eleventh and Lombard), the only three white stores in the area, other than Swinger. Swinger was up near Tenth and Wilson. Now, during that time was the time we used to put the stamps in the books to get the food, okay? They had books and we would collect stamps. We put the stamps in the books and the books would get thicker and thicker and we'd trade the stamps in for more food. Okay? Shields at the Eleventh and Popular, she had a grocery store in the later years, okay, and then we had the Wright Stores. They were a grocery store, Swinger was a grocery store. The other two places were like Dry Goods. But now your other businesses were professions, okay? And they were African American—the doctors, Dr. Goens, Dr. Brown, Dr. Anderson, we had all of that, on the East Side we had our own doctors. We weren't in the grocery business, we had professions. We had our own dentists, Dr. Sykes, I can't think, Dr. Peaco. All on the East Side. If we needed our shoes repaired, we had our own shoe shops. Dr. Loper was here at the corner of Tenth and Poplar. We had our own pharmacists, our own pharmacist, Dr. Smith. We had another one at Ninth and French. We had our own print shop, Skip Butler, at Tenth and Lombard, We had our own, during those days. We didn't have paneling, we had wallpaper. So we had our own wallpaper store, which was Mr. Hazzard down here at Tenth and Lombard. Okay? Most of our African-American women went to Miss Dora Lee for cosmetology. So those women that graduated (and of course my mother was one of those women that opened their shops), they did not settle for doing it in the home. Some of them did it in their homes but they would take perhaps the first room and make their own business. My mother was one of the first that had her own shop. When Miss Dora Lee graduated, she, my mom, and Bella Lee and a few other ladies whose names I can't recall right now, but they owned their own shops. They had their

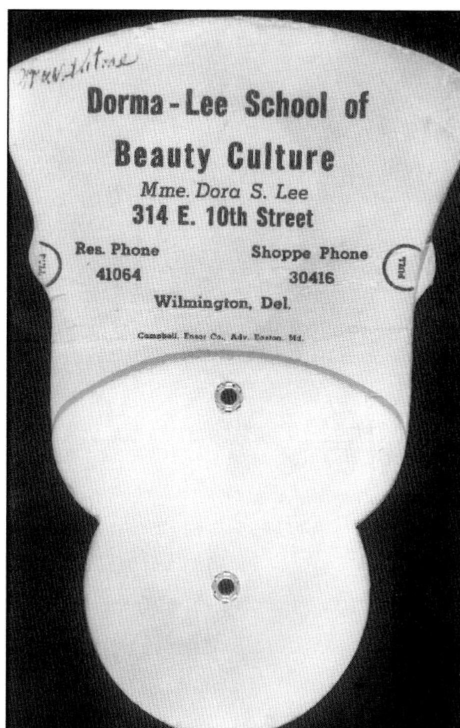

An Advertisement from Ms. Dora Lee's School of Beauty Culture.

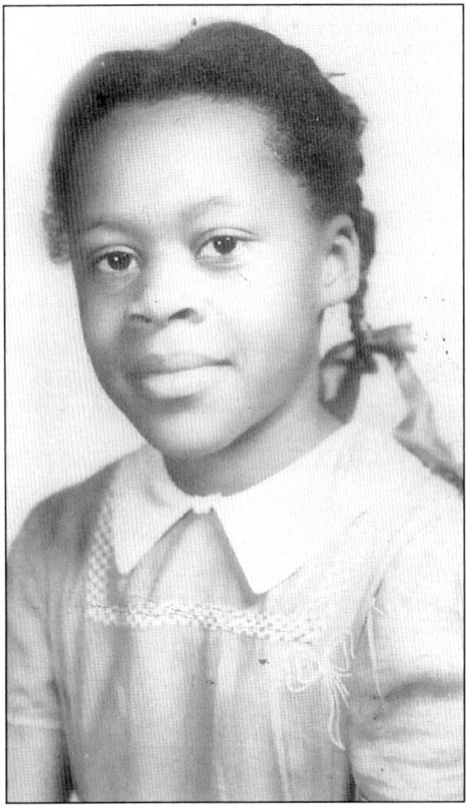

ARETHA MORTON, AGE EIGHT.

own business, there was no such thing as working for anybody else. Everybody had a mind to have their own profession and their own business. That's the way it was. And then up the street here, we didn't have to go anywhere to get our clothes dry cleaned. Right up the street, I can't think of his name, anyway, where Tom's barbershop is now, that was a dry cleaners. We had our own dry cleaners, Olin Thomas. Okay, and it was, it was just, I mean, as young people back in that time, we had no other mind other than to be something professional because the white folks were having grocery stores. But we were in professions. And Howard High School, that's all they turned out was professionals. The parents worked in private families. I don't know, what they call it now, but we called it working in private families. And some of our parents raised the children of the folks that they worked for, you see, so that's what made everything exciting. Then from time to time, they were allowed to go to the house where they worked and we'd played with the kids and stuff and it was an exciting time. But as I look around the city, I think that's what gets me the most is when I know where we once were. When I do funerals from time to time and I look at the older set, those that are older than myself, the men are still dressing the same way. They still have same pride. They still have the same manner. There's a guy who lives around the corner. I've never known his real name, and we call him "Eggy." Eggy still tips his hat when he sees a lady coming toward him. That's something we were used to. Men walked on the outside, to the right of women, on the curb side for protection. They tipped their hats when they saw ladies coming, you know. And it's just today to see things the way they are, and I'd never thought, I really and truly never thought that I'd live to see things the way they are. I'm glad I was born when I was born. That's why a lot of times when I go somewhere to preach they always want my biography and stuff and they won't read it. I know it's a lot, but two things I always want them to read. I always want them to say that I was born in January of 1938 and I'm 62 years old. I always want them to say that, if they don't say anything else, because I'm glad I was born when I was born. To have been raised the way that I was ... because it's still in me and it's never going to leave.

CANON LLOYD STUART CASSON

I'm Lloyd Stuart Casson. Born February 17, 1935, in Dover, Delaware. I was a twin. I was five minutes younger than my twin brother, Floyd, who from the time that I can earliest remember was always just a little bigger, a little taller, and a little tougher than I was. In fact we were two boys of six siblings. I had three other

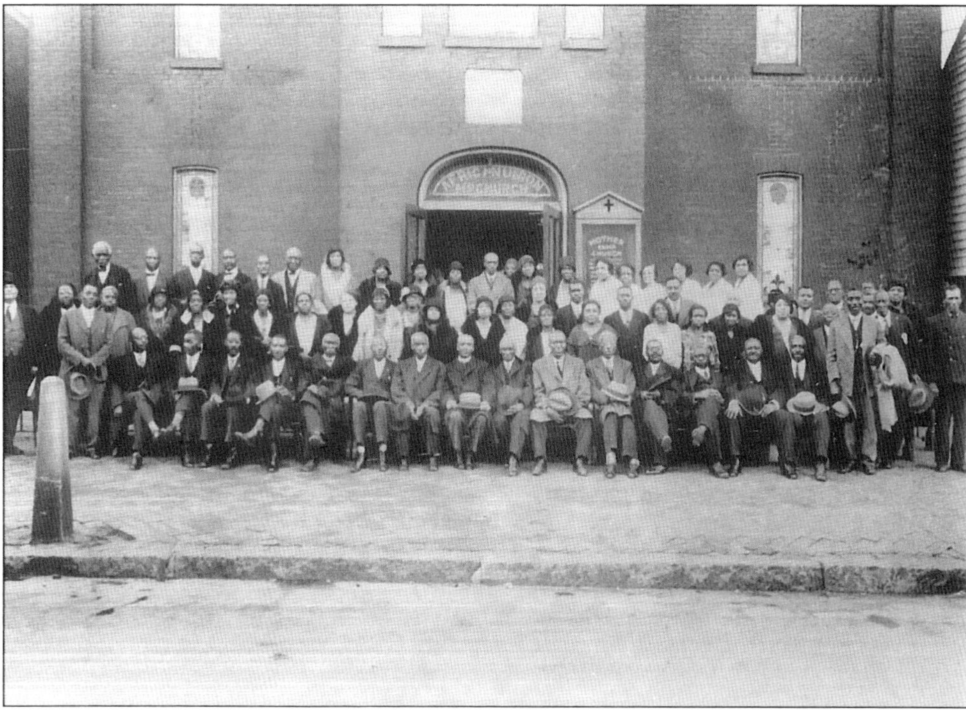

The Mother AUMPC Church. Lloyd Casson attended this church as a child.

brothers and a sister. My brother Floyd, who as I say was five minutes older than I, died in 1989, and I also had another brother, older brother, who died just a few years ago in 1997. My brother and I were born in Dover, but by the time we were two years old, we had actually left our home. My parents divorced. I think we were about two, two and a half years old or something like that, and we became wards of the state of Delaware. We didn't really know what any of that meant because the people that we lived with were people who knew our parents, and so we didn't really know anything except that we were "on the state." Very interesting. We lived first in Newark, Delaware, for a brief period of time. I think I've got this right, and then we lived ... no, no. First we came to Wilmington and we lived really with an aunt of Bill Young Jr. on French Street. As a matter of fact, he still recalls how when we came to live with her for a brief period of time, she called him to say, "I've got these cute little boys I want you to come and meet." Well of course many years later Bill Young was a teacher of ours and a very dear friend and mentor and at that time when we were just a couple of kids he would not have expected that I guess. In any case, we left there after a short period of time and went to Newark, and the people in Newark were really totally insane. I can still remember their insanity. They were very strange people, and rather abusive to say the very least. So our stay there wasn't very long, and we came to Wilmington to live with Aunt Mary and Uncle Eddie, Mary Hodges and James Hodges. Her maiden name was Redding, and of course ... she claimed to have been related to Lawyer Redding. Whether that's in fact true, I've never been able to figure out. In any case, Floyd and I were about four when we came to Wilmington. We were twins. We were always together. What I always remember is how we held hands, and

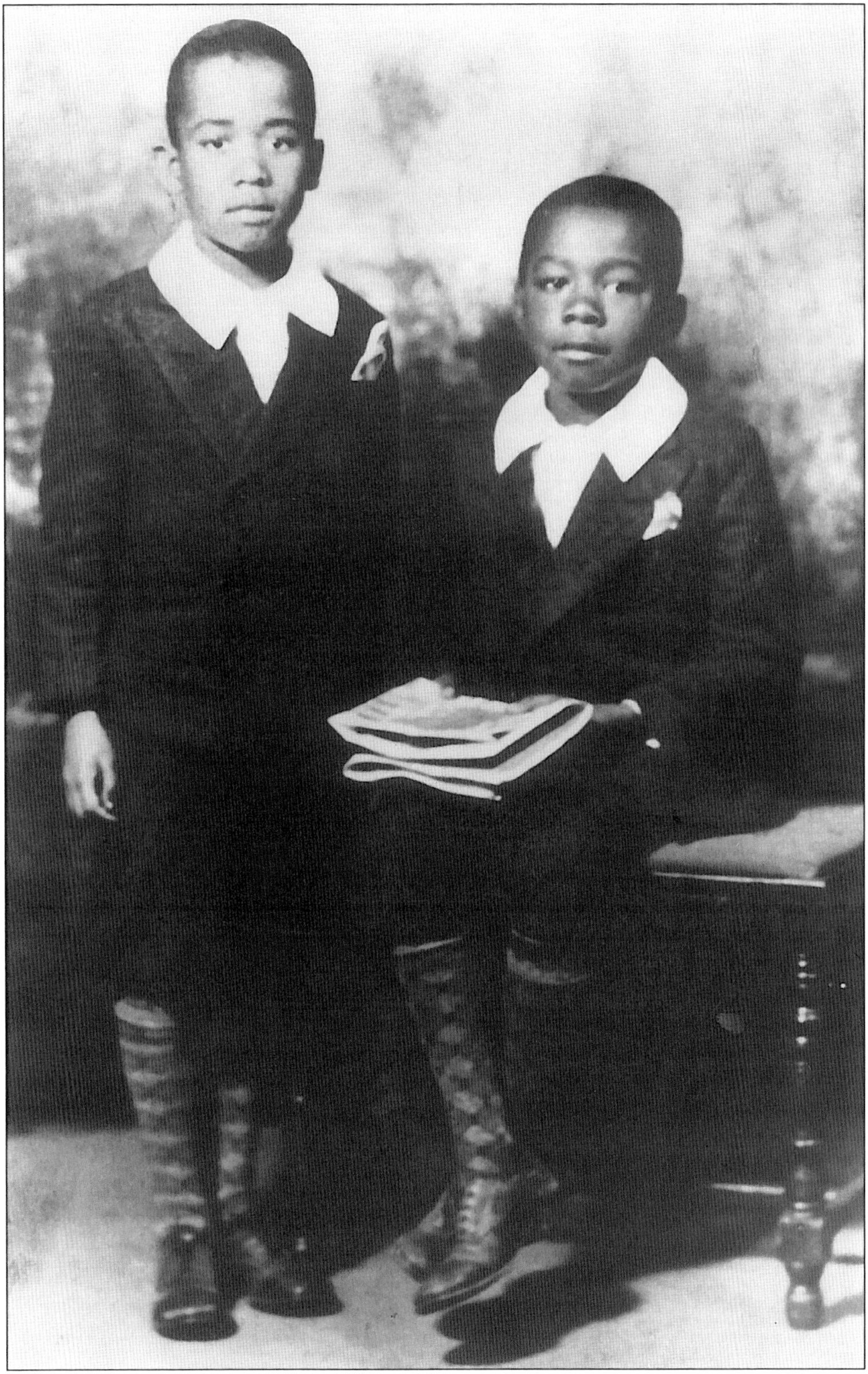

Lloyd S. Casson (standing) and His Twin Brother, Floyd.

because he was just a little taller, he was always told, "Now you take care of your little brother," and he really enjoyed doing that. But I used to get ticked off about that because I felt that I could just handle my own self, "thank you," but when we got to the corner to go from 1225 French Street to kindergarten around the corner to the #5 School you know we always held hands until as we got older. We both had our own friends and we kind of walked together. One of the things I really, really remember and enjoyed about growing up is walking to school. I mean we went to #5 and you know what? I can remember every single teacher to this day starting with kindergarten all the way through ... every home room teacher in our school until the day I graduated. There ... there may be an occasional teacher I don't quite remember, but it says a lot about the impact that these people had on our lives.

The war was on, by the way during this time, and so we were always mindful of the war. I should have mentioned this. When we were still at #5, I can remember learning war songs like "Praise the Lord and Pass the Ammunition," "When the Lights Come on Again all Over the World," you know, and the war was just a part of life, and as a matter of fact we had these little milk bottles. We got free milk, I think it was free every day. And there were these bottles the caps of which were paper disks which covered the opening. And the paper disk had a small tab which you took your fingernail in order to pull the tab off and drink the milk. Well these tabs became dog tags. Let me tell you what I mean by that. The teachers would take these pens. You know in those days we had the inkwells and the pens you stick in, and so you write very finely. Well the teachers wrote our names, ages, addresses on these little tops shellacked them and ran a string through them, and we put them on our necks. They were dog tags in case of bombing, and we could be identified. I thought of that years later when I was soldier, and was issued my set of metal dog tags. I remembered that when I was in something like the second grade, I was actually wearing a dog tag.

As I say, I remember the teachers. The main reason that I remember all of our teachers is not only did they really get to know each of us, they knew us well, and they knew our parents by and large, so you couldn't pull any wool over anybody's eyes. Many of them went to church, the same church. When we first came to Wilmington, we went to Mother AUMP church which was up on French Street. Ed Bell, the funeral director, was the high muckety muck, and his father, I believe it was Reverend Bell, was a ... was the minister when we went there. And you know it was a famous church. By that I mean a very old one. They were the church that sponsored August Quarterly. So we were always a part of August Quarterly, but even though that's the church we were going to as real young kids so ... vacation Bible School was held primarily at Ezion Church at Ninth and French or Mt. Carmel at Tenth and Lombard those were ... or Bethel at Sixth and Walnut. Those are the three places maybe because they were the largest buildings. They were all huge buildings, and most of the Bible School teachers were teachers in the Wilmington Public School System, and so we'd just always know them. They were always there. They were our mentors and guides, along with our families and extended families all the way through twelfth grade. You know, that situation probably will never repeat itself again. We should never have broken that up, because we will never be able to pull that back, I don't think at least not in our time. Another thing that I remember is how we were nurtured by the Y. The Walnut Street Y was just an incredible nurturing influence for us from the time that the Y was built. I remember to this day Floyd and I standing there holding each other's hands. And I believe it was raining when the cornerstone ... when the Y was opened or the cornerstone was being made. Something like that. It was an important day. I believe 1939. We would have been four years old or something like that, and the people standing around for this building to celebrate this building. Maybe it was being opened then, or maybe it was the cornerstone, I don't remember that, but what I do remember is that for as long as I can remember, I was a member of the Walnut Street Y. Floyd and I were members of the Walnut Street Y, and people like George Taylor, who was the Boys Work Secretary, who really loved us, cared for us, and would take us on trips. We would go walking into the Brandywine and he would ... he would take us places and point out things. I remember a Jewish volunteer ... an Italian volunteer named Mario Grieco. G R I E C O. I remember him because he was a volunteer at the Y who was the advisor of the Junior High Y Dragons, which was a Y club that we all belonged to. We had these green jackets, and it was really great. One of the things that I remember about that is that I was the secretary, and Mr. Grieco taught me how to take minutes. And you know something to this day, one of the greatest skills I have is taking minutes. I mean I'm serious. I even love to take minutes, and it all happened because of what I learned at the Walnut Street Y. You know it's where we learned to swim. We learned to box. We learned to fight and defend ourselves by not depending on our temperaments and so on. Not only Mr. Taylor, but Mr. Redmond, Mr. Jensen . ... this is Yvonne's father-in-law, a wonderful human being. An absolutely sweet guy. Mr. Forester Lee, Paul Haughton, by the way whose wife at one point one of the social workers that Floyd and I had you know with our connection with the state board of welfare.

Well going back, I was about to tell you about when we were going to #29 school we used to always stop at Dr. Smith's [pharmacy] down on Tenth and Poplar Street, and one day coming home from school, we stopped by Dr. Smith's, and Floyd stole a pack of Choke Charlie's. Choke Charlie's are cheese crackers with peanut butter, and they choke you. I mean they were ... you really had to have something to drink in order to eat them otherwise they really choked you. Anyway we stole these Choke Charlie's and we were eating them on the way home. Now understand that we lived between Ninth and Wilson. Excuse me between Poplar and Wilson on Ninth. Dr. Smith's store was at Tenth and Poplar. So right around the corner. So we ... by the time we got home we were still chewing Choke Charlie's, and we got in the house, and Aunt Mary said, "You boys stop and buy anything?" And we could hardly talk because our mouths were full, and she says, "Just want you to know that Dr. Smith called and he thinks you stole some crackers. Did you all steal anything?". And we could hardly speak because our mouths were full of Choke Charlie's and we said, "No we didn't steal anything." So anyway we got a beating of course, and we had to go back and pay Dr. Smith, and so we ... that was a part of living in a village where the grownups knew who you were. Knew that if you did anything wrong they could discipline you or otherwise punish you, send you home, and that the parents weren't going to go fussing and fighting the way they do now. They were going to affirm their action and take similar action. That was the story of our life.

Chapter 2
New Castle

Gladys Green Clark

I was born in New Castle, Delaware, on January 9, 1919. Well, my mother worked in Wayne, Pennsylvania, but I lived with an older aunt, who is my mother's sister. And my mother's sister also reared many of her brother's and sister because her mother died when they were young. So she reared my mother and some of the other brothers and sisters, and then she also reared me. And she was an excellent, excellent person. She taught me many good things and kept a good reign on me. And I am glad for the things she taught me and how she raised me.

And I went to school at Booker T. Washington in New Castle from the first to eight grade. I started there in 1923, and I started first grade in 1924. And I went from the first grade to the eighth grade. It was a two-room school and two teachers that taught all eighth grades. We had a little room, first through the fourth grade, and a big room was from the fifth to eighth grade. And each teacher taught all four grades.

The name of my first teacher, who was also the first teacher to teach at Booker T. Washington School, was Mrs. Bertha Battle—Mrs. Bertha Howard Battle. And she came from the Washington, D.C. area, and she taught the first through the fourth grade. Mr. Albion Unthank was the principal and he taught grades five through eight at Booker T. Washington School. And Mr. Unthank taught there until his sudden death. He was there for many years and so was Mrs. Battle.

My aunt's name was Isabella, I S A B E L L A, and her last name was Guy, G_U_Y. And she always taught us, first of all, to be honest. And she said if you ever have to borrow—she didn't believe in borrowing at all. She would do without things before she would borrow. But she said if you did ever borrow, always pay back. And if you couldn't get there to pay at the time you had agreed to pay, go to the person and let them know that I don't have it now, but I will have it at such and

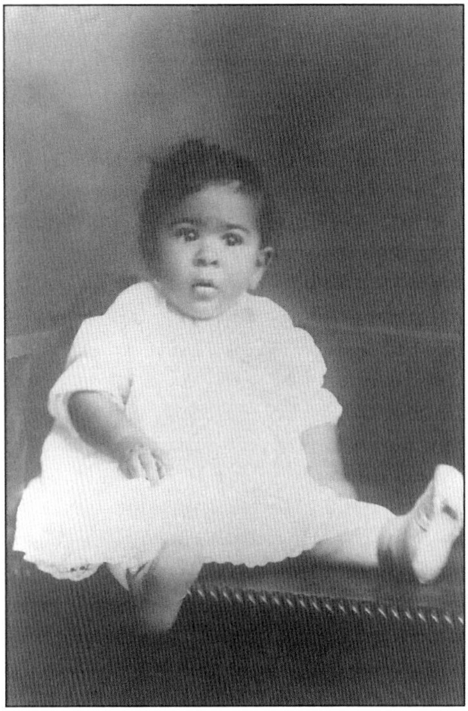

Gladys Green Clark as an Infant.

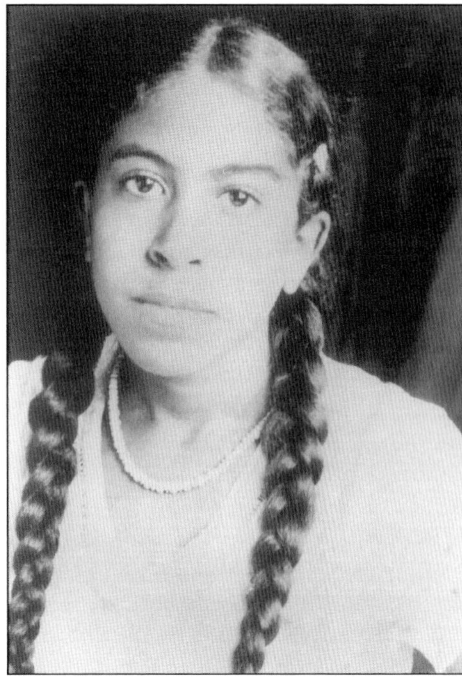

Gladys Green Clark as a Student at the Booker T. Washington School.

such date and keep your promises. And she did domestic work.

Well, as a child, the neighborhood I lived in has always been a mixed neighborhood. We had Irish, Italians, and of course were we called "colored" at that time. And we all played together, and we didn't have any problems at that time, racially, because as I said, the neighborhood we lived in has always been mixed.

In fact, New Castle has always been—most neighborhoods have been pretty well mixed. I think they are less mixed now then they were then because as the colored people have sold their homes and whites have improved them so that the prices of them have become so high, I don't think there are very many colored that have been able to buy back into the neighborhood. So we have less mixture now than during the time when I was growing up. I remember many streets in New Castle like on Cherry Street there was a colored family. On Second Street there was a colored family and almost—they were pretty well mixed. But now it's less of a mixture I would say.

There were many places that you could not go. In fact, as I said, none of those eating places could you sit in. But there weren't too many places. Ice cream parlors you could not go there and sit. Of course the schools, you could not go to the schools. There was not much—-and the theater. That was another thing. We had a theater in New Castle and you could not go there. The theater was at Fifth and Delaware Streets, which is now across from where the post office is now. And that was segregated. In fact, I don't think you could go there at all. I never tried to go, but I don't think you could go and sit upstairs. So it was segregated as far as any kind of social activities, very segregated.

Now we had a very famous tea room where the courthouse is. It was called the Courthouse Tea Room. At that time, it was always owned by the state, but I guess, it was rented out to this couple who ran the tea room. And it was known all over the country, the New Castle Tea Room. At that time people traveled on the New Castle ferry, the New Castle Pennsylvania ferry, and there were loads of people that would come through with their chauffeur driven vehicles at that time. And they were always driven mostly by colored chauffeurs. And this tea room was so famous that everybody went there. But what would happen when the people would go there? They would say, "We have a chauffeur with us," and she would say to them, "Well, they can't eat in the dining room." So what they did, they had a chopping block in the kitchen, and they would fix them a meal in the kitchen. And they would eat in the kitchen. But that tea room was known all over the country, New Castle Old Courthouse Tea Room.

And I can also remember when we had no sewers in New Castle. Everybody had outdoor toilets, even the rich people. They had the big toilets with the very big wells. It was so scary because when you looked down there all you could see was this darkness in there. And there was this one time there was a lady that worked for J.T. Eliason at the corner of Fifth and South Streets. And she went into this toilet in this backyard, and the floor gave away from under her. And the only way she was safe, she braced her elbows on the framework of the toilet. And she was screaming and the men that worked across the street heard her screaming and went there and they got her out. Otherwise, she would have drowned there. And that was always frightening. Our toilets were not deep. The poor people, they had little toilets that were not deep at all. But those other toilets, they were so deep I was fearful of going in them because they were so deep and so scary looking down in those.

But about Mr. Wright, when they sewered New Castle, that was around 1928 or 1929, they brought a contractor here from either Alabama or Georgia, the very deep Southern state. And they brought all of their men with them because I imagine they worked very cheaply. And they brought all of their equipment. And they ran the sewer through all of New Castle. And I can remember the men that came. Of course there was nothing to do here, so up in this area where Mr. Wright had the garden, they had a lot of little "chalets" up there where people lived. Sometimes the men lived by themselves and they used to gamble there. And a lot of these men that came with the company from the South, they would hang up there and gamble. And one day someone said a man had been shot. That's one thing my aunt always taught me, you never run to any tragedy because you know, you might get shot. And my friend Pearl Day (Henry), we were together; we were inseparable. And she said, "Oh, there's been a shooting over by Mr. Wright's house. Come on let's go." I jumped off the front step to go, and

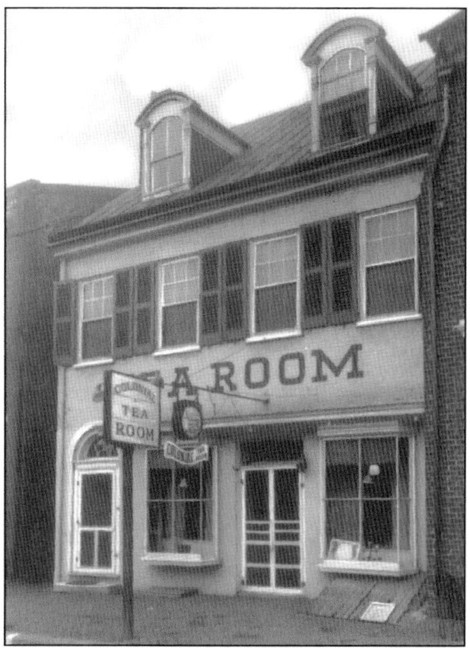

Pictured here is the Colonial Tea Room. The Courthouse Tea Room was located across the street.

my aunt heard it and said, "Come back." I had to come back. And I could not go.

Well, when Pearl came back, she was a nervous wreck. She was crying and screaming. And she said when she got there the men were all gathered around, and she wanted to see what it was and she got her arms and jumped on two men's shoulders and looked down. And when she looked down this man's face had been shot. And she said blood was coming out of his ears, his mouth, and his eyes. And she could not sleep for days. I'm so glad my aunt did not let me go. She did not let me go there. But Pearl was so upset she was a nervous wreck. But there was a shooting over a gambling game up in the same area right near the bridge, but that was something.

And when they finished sewering New Castle, the contractor moved on, but there were two or three men that stayed. And one of them married one of the ladies in New Castle and stayed here. But most of them moved on with the contractor to other parts of the country, I guess.

Althea Unthank Harmon

I was born September 4, 1928 in New Castle, Delaware, and it happened to have been the morning that school opened and my father was late for school. He taught there at Booker T. Washington School and when he arrived Pearl and Edward Henry told me he smiled at everybody and said, "I have a new baby daughter." Okay, a little bit about my father. He was born in Philadelphia, Pennsylvania, in 1896 and his mother and father moved to Allentown, Pennsylvania, and shortly thereafter my grandmother passed away. My grandfather did remarry and the wife tried to raise the children but it didn't work. So the children as teenagers at time for college, went to North Carolina. They were sent to college or helped with their college work by my father's sister, my Aunt Alice, who helped send them to college after graduating from Livingstone College. My father started his career as a teacher and I believe, the first place was somewhere in North Carolina. Then eventually he got into Pennsylvania but then later on, after a few years of teaching, he was asked by the board of education here in Delaware around the lower part of the state, if he would accept a job in a community where the people were, they were called Moors. They were not white and they did not want to be black. So my father accepted that job and arrived there and stayed in a room with a family until he could bring his wife and new baby down. They often invited him to things that pertained to the community and he would attend. But when he brought his wife down, they would invite him and not invite my mother. So one day he was approached by someone as to why he would not come to their affairs any more, and he said, "You invite me but you don't invite my wife." And they bluntly told him that, "We love you. We think you are great, but your wife is too black." And you would have to know my mother to know how she handled that situation. She got them all straight! She told them where they came from. So that was an incident in his life and then he moved on to the lower part of the state of Delaware, down around Milford and Georgetown, somewhere in there. And then from there he came to New Castle. And he was everything, I must say everything to the people of New Castle. They were very, very fond of my father because he was so much to them. He was their accountant, their tax preparer. He cut hair. He cut hair because he had boys that he would have to take into Wilmington and have their hair cut plus his own. So he learned how to cut hair to save on that. They would go into Wilmington because they were not welcomed at the white barbershops there. So you had to travel. He learned this new trade to earn extra money on the side. On

Saturdays, he cut their hair. Well, he was just their advisor. He was just everything, I say everything to them. They really loved him and at his funeral, they all just fell apart. But for years after he passed away, whenever I went back to New Castle or met someone, they would say, "Althea, you don't know how much we miss your father!", that went on for about 30 years. Of course the young people there today don't remember him. He did a fantastic job as a teacher, because in those days black teachers not only taught you the Three R's but they taught you about your own history, which a lot of young people today in school don't get. They have this black history studies but it's not the same as coming from someone who has had that experience and can tell you from life's experience how it was. So we got that kind of thing. I must say my mother and father always said to us drilled in us that we were just as good as anyone else. And that stood with us through the years. "Don't be afraid to reach out and try to better yourself." "And you don't need to stand back because of color." So we never got in trouble. Except I remember one incident. It was me who, I didn't have a fight but almost had a fight with a white girl that lived up the street from us. Her father was a policeman and this happened early in the day. He waited until it was time for him to go to work and put that uniform on to come down to our house to sort of talk about the incident between the children. You have to know my mother. She was fiery. Her father was an American Indian, full blooded. She had a temper and she could get you straight in a minute. She straightened him out. But nothing ever came of it because she reminded him that he waited until that time to come as if the uniform would frighten her away. But she stood up to him. So that was the other incident I had in New Castle with a member of the other race. We all got along pretty good together, but I'd like to tell you a little bit about my home life there. Okay?

The times I remember most and talk about most is the dinner hour. We had

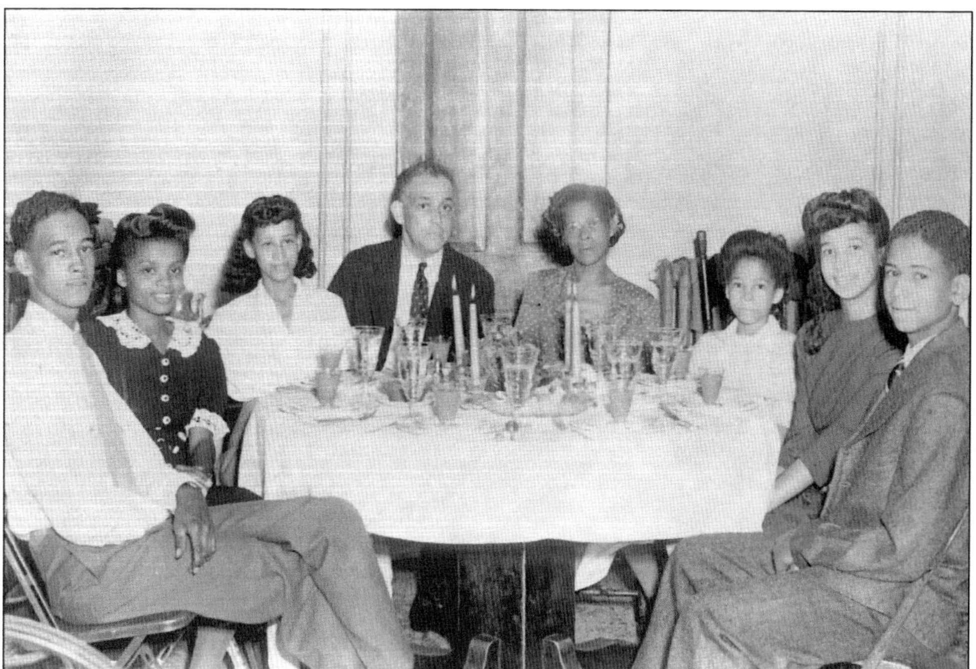

Althea Unthank Harmon's Family at Dinner. *Althea is seated second from the right.*

dinner in the dining room every night. And we set the table like we were the Vanderbilt's, with no money. But we would light candles on most nights, not every night. We would have all the best that we had. Then we would sit around this table until late in the evening. In fact, we didn't have dinner until 7. I guess that's in me today, I have late a dinner. But we would sit there after dinner and we would just talk and laugh and have fun. When we learned new things in school, words and that type of thing, we would try that on our dad. Find out if he knew all of this. This was new knowledge for us. "Do you know that we learned this new word today." So it was fun. And then the other time is Christmas. Christmas is memorable. In those days people didn't lock their doors at night. We slept all night. Nobody bothered you. This wasn't just our family. So the house was open Christmas eve. As we grew and left and came back, everybody came home at Christmas. And it was just talk, talk, talk, talk, all night long. And then we would have the people of the neighborhood. People that my father taught would come in. They would talk to him and reminisce with him.

And one other thing that pops in my mind is they never, with all the children they had, they never turned anyone away who needed help. One Sunday morning, this happened. I'll just say he was white, it doesn't really matter. This old man came by, well, he was old to me at the time. But I wouldn't think so today. Looking back on it, he was around in his 40s or 50s. He knocked on the door and of course you'd say "Come in." So he opened the door and he saw that my mother and father had all these kids around the table eating. And he says, "Oh, that's alright." So my father says, "Well, what's the matter? What do you want?" He said, "I was going to ask you, if you'd give me something to eat." So of course they invited him in and they feed him. He told them, he said, "I'm not a bum. I'm trying to make my way some where in the South, to my sister." He had gotten out of the hospital and he had TB and he felt if he could get in the country, the country air would do him well. He was trying to make his way wherever and so they fed him. He had breakfast and mother even packed him a lunch. It must have been Christmas time, that we got this big package—this big box. And it was from this man who had found his way, made his way, because he was hitchhiking to wherever his sister lived. He was now helping her with the farm. And he sent all this food, you know, vegetables and stuff. And that was something to remember.

Elizabeth Bungy Baylor

I was born August 3, 1908. Everybody knew each other and sort of looked out for each other. John and Anne Bungy were my parents. I had 13 brothers and sisters, 6 brothers and 7 sisters.

Well, my father was a farmer and he owned a lot of real estate. He lived in a place called Walnut Hill and then moved into New Castle. Yeah, he bought real estate, quite a bit of property there—a little place called Dobbinsville. I guess you call it an extension of Delaware Street. He owned quite a few houses out there and he owned some on East Fourth Street. We had a beautiful garden and he used to sell these vegetables.

My mother was gentle and kind. She did a lot of knitting and quilting. The ladies had these parties and they'd go out quilting. They'd go to each other's house.

Well winter we didn't have a furnace of course, we had what we call a big potbelly stove, a big round stove that heated the downstairs. Then at night when we would go to bed, my mother would heat a brick and wrap it in newspaper and put it in bed to keep us warm.

CHAPTER 3
BUTTONWOOD

DOLORES TWYMAN MCCRAY

I was born in Newark, Delaware, November 25, 1934, on Wilson Street. When I was three years old, we moved from Newark, to Buttonwood. When we first moved to Buttonwood, we lived in the house that the Pinketts live in now. That was owned by my Aunt Cathy Street. And she in turn sold it to the Pinketts. So after that we moved down the road, where Gene Petty lives now. I remember my grandfather, Reverend Twyman. He used to come up every weekend and bring us grapefruit—a basket of grapefruit and a basket of oranges. Then we had Grandpa Harris, that I used to call Grandpa Ha Ha. I don't know why, but I used to call him that. And I remember I used to go up there all the time to his house and always go upstairs to his room because he kept peppermint lozenges. To this day I still love them. I used to ask him. "Can I have some?' He used to say, "Go upstairs and get some." I remember we called it the "big house" because it was so big that it had three floors. Then you could go up two ways. You could go up through the kitchen and through the front door. It had two ways upstairs. Then they had two kitchens. They had the shed kitchen and the regular kitchen. Then they had the barn, and grape arbor and the well. And they had two gardens.

I remember when they used to have hog killing time. When they had hog killing time, they would meet and go down to the pig pen. That's where they would kill hogs. And my great aunt had a great big old-fashioned iron pot. That they used to heat the water in. Then I had to help clean the chittlins and make the scrapple. And when they used to get the meat all done, they would put it in the smokehouse on the side of the house. Outside the house they had a smoke house. I remember that. At hog killing time, before they killed the pigs and all that for two weeks, they feed the pigs nothing but corn and water. That's what they called cleaning out the system. They feed them nothing but corn and water before they killed them. They

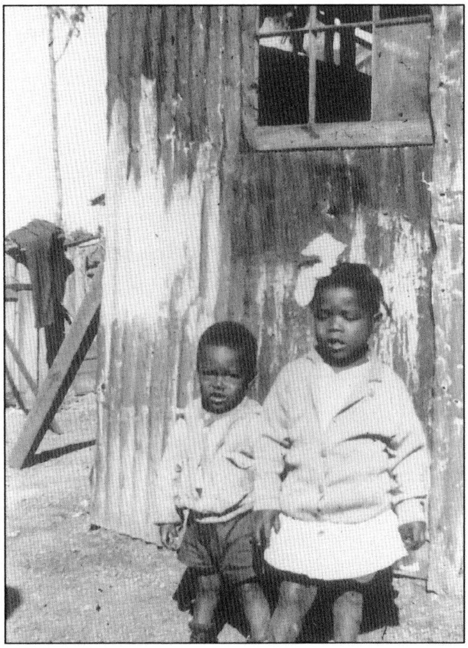

DELORES AND HER BROTHER THOMAS NEXT TO THE SHED AT THE "BIG HOUSE."

hung them up on them big ... they made these racks and things, like an "x." They had a long board going across there. They would kill them and then they hang them up and make the blood drain out of them. I cleaned up many a chittlin. We had to dip them and wash them chittlins out, wash the stuff out of them. Wash them out get them clean. Put them in a great big pail they had and then they would go over them. And they made sausage, scrapple, souse. They made everything. Well, I didn't generally realize that we were poor until I got old enough to know how to spell poor and know what it meant. You know, you get the definition of poor. But we used to eat good. My mother made bread. Like even after we got finished dinner and all of that, she's sometime in the evening, she would make some bread and we would have pear preserves and hot bread. You know biscuits and all that. And she used to make a whole cake on top of the stove. Hey, we ate good, you know.

My mother, she was one of them people, we had everything because we canned. She canned anything they grew. If it was edible, she canned it. She made her own ketchup. She made mayonnaise. We worked when we was growing up. She made everything. And we had to make butter. They had the old-fashioned churn, we made butter. I never saw so much butter in my life. I was trying to make it so fast, because I wanted to get out of there. She made string beans, potatoes. I mean everything, that you could can, she canned.

I've never gone without a meal, Although we cooked on that wooden stove, and all that. Then we had to bank the stoves off at night. And then we had each of us had a chore. We had to make sure before evening them lamps were filled and the globes were washed and we had chores to do. Kerosene. That's what they used. Kerosene, we had to fill them lamps up. And then we had the night buckets that we had to take out and take down to the outhouse and empty it and clean it and put disinfectant in it and let it set there. And then whoever's week it was to bring it, you had to have it in by a certain time. And if you had to go to the bathroom at night, they had a lantern, you'd go down there to the outhouse and somebody would go with you and you'd light the lantern.

My mother could sew. She made most of our clothes. I've had clothes made of things like bags. You know when they get the great big bags of flour or whatever, the feed and all came, they would bleach them up and all of that. They'd make us dresses and make dresses and stuff out of them. And, mother, as I say, my mother could sew anything. She could see a dress in the store and she wouldn't even have to get a pattern. She'd go home and from her mind, she'd cut a pattern from newspaper. And she would cut that dress out and make it. She could really sew.

Oh, that was fun. That was great fun.

See most of the time I stayed with my aunt. They lived across from the school. I was always—I was running over there when the bell was ringing. Everybody was in school. I lived next door and was always late. Always late. But it was nice going there. And you know I went to Buttonwood School when Mr. Coleburne and Mr. Woolford were the teachers. And Mr. Coleburne played such an awesome graduation march. Ah, it was so pretty. I don't know that name of it or anything but I looked forward to marching out—when I graduated him playing that march! And the year I graduated, he resigned. I was so disappointed because I wanted to come right on that march. I wanted to graduate on that march. I didn't make it. He resigned. But that was another thing. Mr. Coleburne—my aunt cooked lunch for him every day. He came over to our house, over to the big house, and he had lunch every day. She fixed lunch for him every day. He used to come over and eat his lunch with Mr. Woolford. Mr. Woolford was nice. Mr. Woolford was a good teacher, but we gave him a hard time. I remember, he used to get so upset with us. We would go in the bathroom with chewing gum. He'd make us spit it out. Mr. Woolford was a nice teacher but we was a mess. It wasn't him, it was us. And I remember Mr. Coleburne ... when they opened up a kitchen on back of the school. I remember every now and then he would make us apple brown betty. It was so good. I remember that apple brown betty.

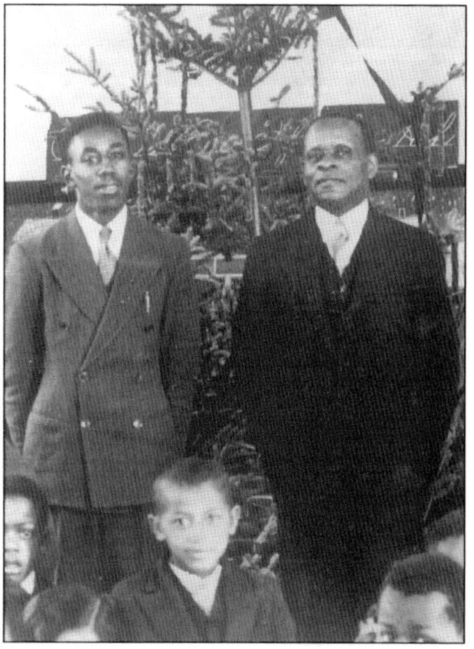

Sylvester Woolford and James Coleburne, Teachers at the Buttonwood School.

I don't remember having any white friends for years. I was way up there when I had white friends. But most of our friends were just people in the community. And then when we graduated from Buttonwood, we went to Howard. It was just all blacks, you know. I didn't have any white friends. All the white people when I started Howard, you know, I babysitted for. But I remember when we couldn't get in the Rialto Theater. I remember when we couldn't go to the theaters and all that growing up. And the only reason I got there was because I took care of the children. The two white girls, I had to take them to the movies on Saturday. And that's how I got into the Rialto Theater. I sat with them. 'Cause see they were small children and I had to take care of them. By me being with them, they'd let me in there to watch them two girls. And that how I got into the Rialto. That was in ... I went to Howard in the forties. It was close to the fifties, '49 or '50. Cause I was in there in '49 and I got that job after school watching them children on Saturdays. They lived on Robinson Lane in a big farm house way back in Robinson Lane on Maryland Avenue. I don't remember taking them out. I didn't have to take them anywhere. I remember their mother used to bring us up to the theater and give us money and that's the reason why I got there to see the little cartoons and the stories and all ... and that was back in the fifties.

Leona Black Pinkett

My mother's name was Elizabeth Black and my father's name was Thomas Smith... Well, to tell you the truth, I don't remember too much about my parents. About my mother, because she died. My grandmother and grandfather raised me. My grandparents had died, and then my aunt and uncle raised me. Well, that was great, living with aunt and uncle. Wonderful, because they did everything they could for me, and I got everything I wanted, just about. We lived down to Hocum's Lane. They had bought a piece of ground, so long, I almost forgot from Mr. Bungy, from Newcastle. And they had a house built down there. And, well, when they had the house built, it was nice, and we moved there. And it was wonderful. The house was, it was bungalow-like type house. I think it was six rooms. Bath, another bath. Six rooms. To tell you the truth, I didn't stay with that aunt. I stayed with Aunt Levah. She lived right next door.

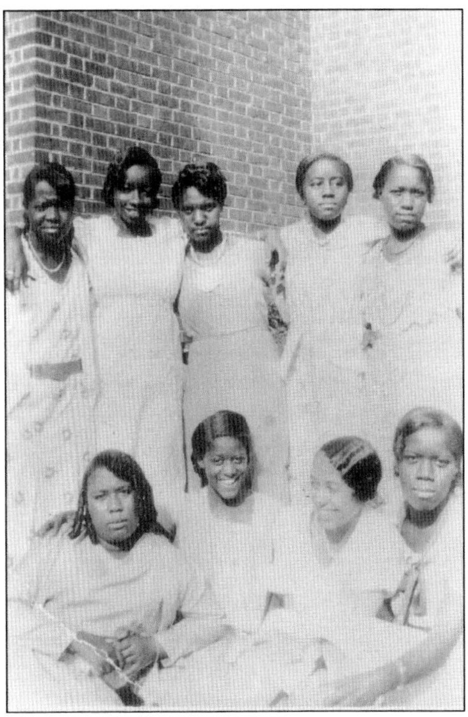

Leona Black Pinkett and Friends at Howard High School.

I went to school in Buttonwood. Mr. Coleburn was my teacher. Oh, he was a nice teacher. I remember that, and he, it was ... I think it was a two-room school, no, one-room school. It was the Dupont Building School and he used, we used to sing a piece that Mr. Coleburn wrote for Dupont. And, he was a very good teacher, he taught eighth grade, which was the school ... and, of course, he taught all classes.

Reverend Fullman I remember him. Oh, he was a nice minister, and he was sort of a relative like. He was sort of, you know, family like. He was, he had a brother, we used to call him Uncle Mike all the time. Mike. Use to call him Uncle Mike. He was a minister that liked people. When I used to go places like to the parks and places he would go with us. And he would take us on rides and like that, that sort of thing. He liked to do things. Yeah, we did. We used to pack lunches. Oh, fried chicken, one thing. We had fried chicken. Somebody would have a watermelon or—we'd share with each other, you know. We would share with each other the lunches. What somebody wouldn't have, the other one would have. And we shared with each other.

Well, on the girls team, we used to catch for our girls, and we did everything on the court. I used to play on the girl's team and way back then yeah. And we had a nice girls team. I played. Mostly I played third base and I pitched. And he used to catch for us. But no girls didn't get back there to catch. But, we did everything else. But they wouldn't get out there to pitch, so, I had to do that. We had a good time. We used to play. Oh ... we played, we played all ... No, we played white and black. We played as far as Glasgow. Played teams there. We made all the rounds. No, we didn't have any uniforms. I don't remember there being ones. We didn't play in uniforms. I guess we'd just to play in pants. We didn't have uniforms. I started to play basketball—but I didn't finish because of transportation.

Teal Taylor Petty

I had 17 brothers and sisters, 5 of them are deceased. My mother's name was Embiola Wolf Taylor and my father's name Elliot Nathaniel Taylor. My father was a Maul from Lewis, Delaware. They were one of the prominent families in Lewistown, as they called it. My father was a minister and on the side he was a custodian. My father pastored five or six churches. He pastored Elizabeth AME Church in Newport. He pastored Ringgold Chapel in Middletown. He pastored in Pennsylvania. My fathered started out as the assistant pastor at Bethel AME Church. He was assistant pastor to Reverend Noisette. I was real small then. After he finished his internship he was able to go out on his own and they sent him to Elizabeth AME Church. That's the church we went to growing up. Elizabeth AME Church was on Boxwood Road in Newport. They have since torn it down and have replaced it with another church down on Clyde Street in Belvedere. We sang on the choir and we had pagents. We just did the usual things you did in church. Wherever he went we went with him. My brothers helped him build different things in the church and it was sad because they tore it down when the highway came through.

I lived on 60 Buttonwood Avenue. We went to school at Buttonwood Elementary School. It was right up the street. And we had a good time. We were poor. Of course ministers in those days didn't get paid much money. They hardly got paid anything but we had a good time. We had a lot of fun walking to school. We played and if we wanted to play because we were the largest family in the community, most of the kids came to play with us. Or we would go and play with them. My mother

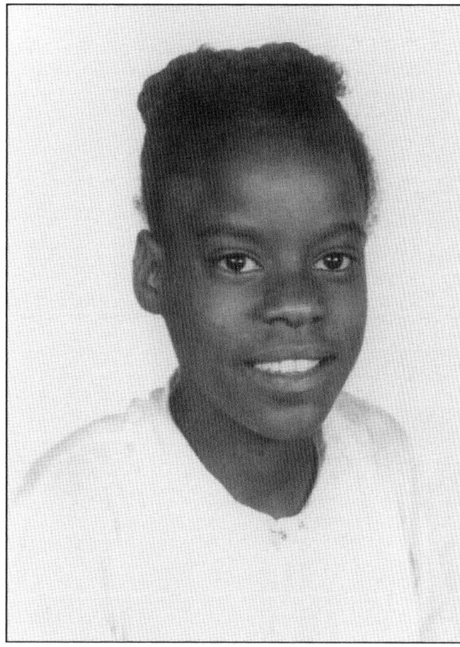

Teel Taylor Petty.

always needed to know where we were. If she called us and we couldn't answer her we were too far away. And if we didn't answer when she called and she called a second time or third time you were in trouble because you knew we were out of the distance of her voice. That's the way all the parents kept control of the children. When they called and you didn't answer, you were in trouble.

In the summertime was the fun time because you could run around with no shoes on. You could just play all day. We just had a good time. I remember going to George's Market. He had little brown bags and you could fill this brown bag. If you had a nickel you could buy penny candy and we would always buy Mary Jane's because you got more Mary Janes for a penny. Or you would buy malted balls. You could buy 10 malted balls for a penny. And we would come back with this little brown bag full of penny candy. That was one of the good things.

We had our own little grocery store. We had a gas station. We had our own little

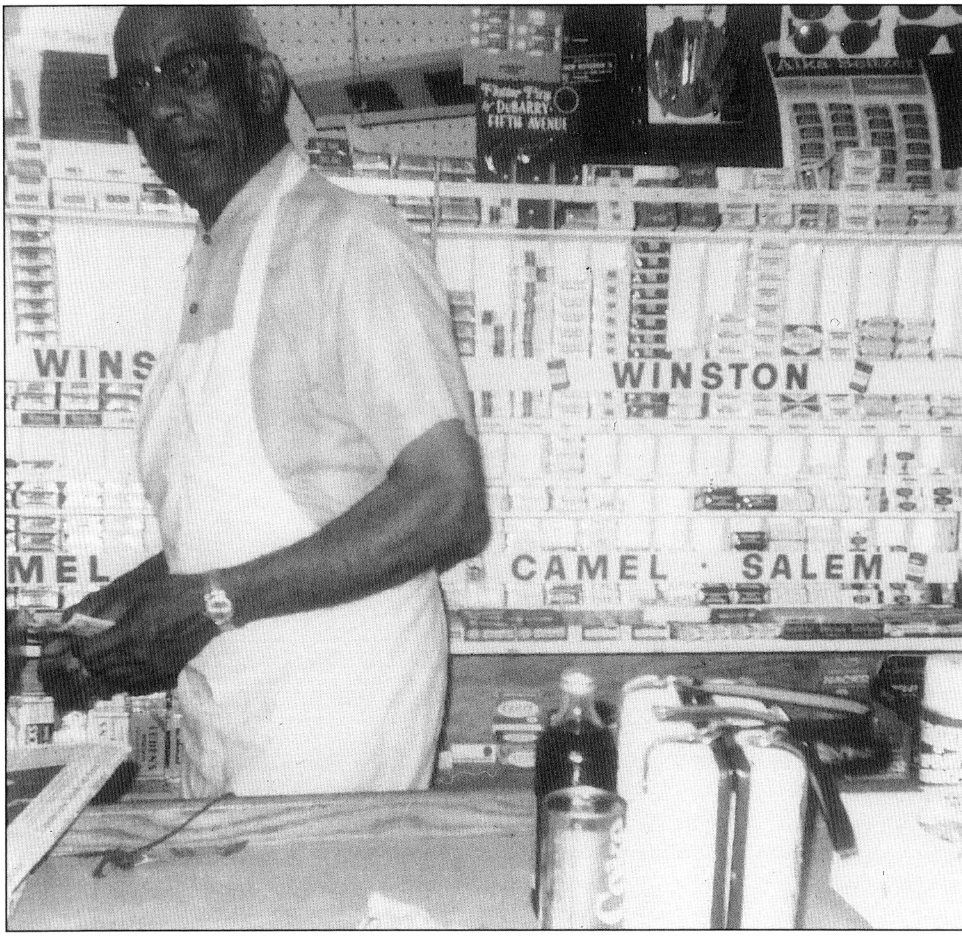

George Pennington in His Store, George's Market.

school. We were really in our own little world. We were kind of protected. We always lived around white people but we didn't associate with them. We had our thing. They had their thing. And that's the way we lived. This went on until the late fifties.

What we did in the summertime, every summer, we had to make quilts. I am going to tell you from a girl's perspective. My mother would make quilts. And every summer we had to sit and make quilts. That was a must. Every summer you had to can food. So she would bring in big baskets of apples and peaches and pears and we would have to sit there and peel these peaches and pears. She would cook them and can them for winter. That was my job in the summertime. The boys job during the summertime would be feeding the pigs, which would be year round.

But then when wintertime came everyone had their own pigs and they would have to slaughter the hogs. This was the meat for the wintertime. They would pack it (the reason black people have high blood pressure). They would pack this meat in salt and then they would cover it with pig fat. And it was in a big barrel. And it stayed there all winter. And when you dug it out, you had to wash it off and then you had to eat it. Hog killing time everybody would get together and help one another kill the hogs. You would go to Reverend Taylor's house. You would go to Mr. Anderson's house. Mr Anderson was one of the prominent people but he lived right next door to us and all the men would get together and they would do this while the kids stood and watched. When they cleaned the hog, they would take the lid of a tin can and they would give the kids the lid to the can. We would scrape the hair. We thought that was fun. We would stand and scrape the hair off the hog and then he would turn pink. That was our job.

Another activity they had in the springtime was that everybody changed their toilet. You had to change the toilet spot because in winter to summer it was time to moved their spot. So you had to move the spot. One year my brothers were out moving the toilet spot. My brother must have been about ten and he got too close and fell down in the hole. So you can imagine what happened then. Well, they got him out and I hope he didn't swallow any. He's alright now. But those were some of the things we would do.

We had several prominent people in Buttonwood. Mr. Anderson lived next to us. Mr Anderson had a car and it had a running board on it. Mr. Anderson would slow down when he got close to his house. And we would run and jump on the running board. He would stop so we could jump on his running board. Then we would run and open his gate and he would ride us in to his yard. Mr. Anderson has a daughter name Izetta. We all went to school together. And Izetta was our playmate. Whenever we saw Mr. Anderson coming not only did we get a ride, if you got to the gate first and opened the gate for him to go on in. You got the nickel. So everybody would race to try to be the first one to open the gate. And if you were not the first one to open the gate then you would run down the street and get on the running board. And he would give us a little ride. That was our thrill.

Mr. Anderson had everything. He had a beautiful home. He had the pump inside of his house, where our pump was outside. They had linoleum on his kitchen floor. Mr. Anderson had a rug. Oh, we thought Mr. Anderson was it! Mrs. Anderson would bake cake and she would give us cake and things like that.

Going to the Buttonwood School Mr. Woolford was my teacher. He was very nice but he was strict. Mr. Woolford was a stickler for etiquette. He not only taught you what you needed to know but he made sure you had those manners you were suppose to have. We learned a lot. We really learned what we needed to know because you had to stand up and recite. You couldn't read. There was no such thing as having a part and going to read it. You had to know it in your mind. If you were in a play you had to know your part. I think those things have helped us along the way. It was quite different ... he use to say to us, "Well you're gonna go over there with those white folk and you better have manners because they really know what to do." He was just telling us that. We go to William Penn and it was really an experience. I felt the kids were rude. They were sassy. They were just different from what we were. When Mr. Woolford said something to us, we had to get out of our seats and stand up and answer him. If he called us we were suppose to say "Yes, sir!" If a grown up talked to us, we had to say , "Yes sir. No sir." And when we went there, they said, "Yeah! What?" It was just an entirely different world. I went to William Penn in 1954. The first year they started integration, and closed Buttonwood School. We went there. Not only that it was huge! From the size that we came from to go to the big huge school. There were a lot of kids and you had to do all of this moving.

I was a majorette when I went there. I just figured I could be a majorette. I wanted to be a majorette. If it wasn't for the teacher that was there at that time,

I would not have been one. We had to share uniforms and the girls did not want to wear a uniform that I wore. So what happened was I got to keep my uniform. That was the way I was allowed to be a majorette there. I was the only black majorette there until I graduated. I think they had one black cheerleader the same time I was there. I don't know what her experience was, but that was my experience. You had some girls that were very nice but the majority of them were not.

I remember the Earle Theater in New Castle did not allow blacks into their theater. But at Christmas time they would open their doors and invite the children from the Buttonwood School and the Booker T. Washington School to come and spend the day. You could get into the movie but you had to go up into the balcony. Other than that we had everything that we really needed right here in our own section. It's something to say for black communities because we had a nice time. We really didn't miss out on anything. It was just the idea that it was separate and if you wanted to go there you should be allowed. I think I've had a good life.

Eugene Charles Petty

I was born on April 21, 1927. My father was Edward William Petty and my mother was Hester M. Petty. There were seven of us. My father worked for the bridge force. He helped build bridges. When he left the bridge force he worked for the B&O Railroad.

Well, one Sunday afternoon, I came from church and it was about 10 of us cousins together. We were playing cops and robbers. And the other guys were deputies and the other guys were crooks. So what we're doing is to put one of our cousins up on top of the pig pen. We had pig pens in our backyards. And we had put a rope around his neck and we were going to push him off. And being kids, doing crazy things, you know, like boys do. We were going to push him off. I was the sheriff who said "Push him off!" And my mother comes out screaming "Stop! What are you doing!!!!" That scared us to death. And we never forgot. None of us ever forgot that day to this day. I haven't forgotten it—that we almost pushed him off there. And we would have hung him because he was about 6 feet off the ground. Just think about ... goodness! ... that we didn't push him off. My mother stopped us from doing it. So, sometimes you have to think what kids will do ... playing and doing funny things. Sometimes not necessarily meaning to hurt anybody. It was something that could have changed our lives ... and it did. It certainly changed my life.

I went to Buttonwood School and I graduated from the Buttonwood School in 1941. When the war broke out I was an air raid warden. Because they were afraid the Germans were going to come and we had something down in the Delaware Bay—submarines. I was about 14 or 15 but they had no men because most of the men had been drafted into the service. I made sure that everybody cut their lights. In those days you had half a light blacked out so the lights wouldn't shine in case of an air raid. When that siren went off you had to make sure that everybody put those lights down and kept them out. You had a little flashlight. You carried the flashlight during the air raid. You wore a cape and hat. That was about it. At the age of 17 I enlisted because they still needed men.

Bernard Pinkett

My parents were very good providers. My mother always, if we ever did something wrong, she would not beat us. She would always say, "I'm going to tell your father

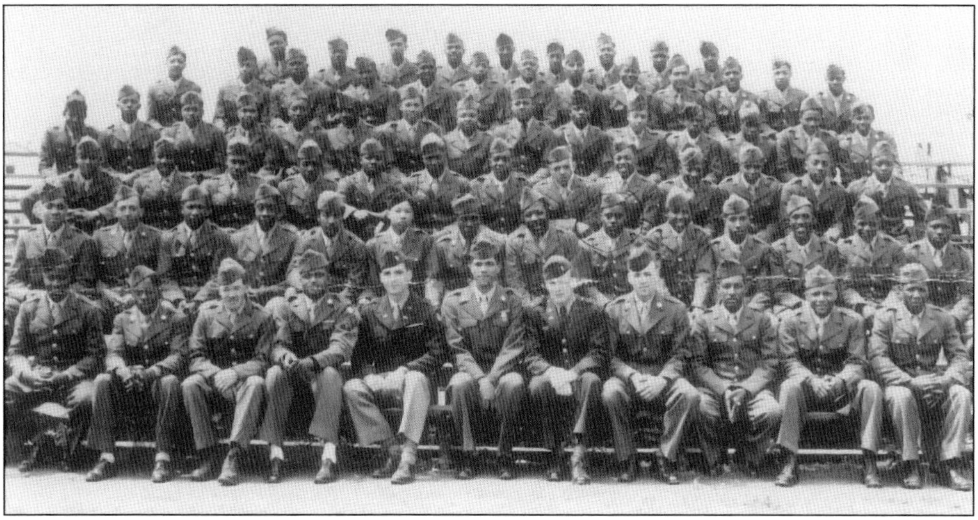

Eugene Charles Petty's U.S. Army Outfit.

on you." That statement really made us do the right thing. My father, he had a number of jobs. I remember his working at Amalgamated Iron when he was quite young. And he was a mechanic. He used to work on cars. But he did almost anything to make an honest dollar. In addition to that he always had a garden and he was up before daybreak. The sun was starting to come up, he'd get out in the garden and after that back to work or the chores around the house. He was always busy. Always busy. In a little truck farm we grew tomatoes, peppers, corn, beans, lima beans, string beans, lettuce, cucumbers, sweet potatoes. We really had quite a few things. We had chickens, pigs, ducks, turkeys.

Well, Buttonwood was sort of an archaic little community with dirt roads. We had a three-room school, one church, a baseball diamond, and George Pennington's store, which was an all-purpose store that sold kerosene, gasoline, and all types of fresh produce, can goods, sugar, flour, whatever you needed he had. And if you needed something that he didn't have, he would make sure that he had it the next time you came to the store. But it was an all-purpose store. And what I remember about Buttonwood is the fact that people got along so well before Collins Park, our neighbors. You very seldom had family feuds or fights. Oh, you had some little things that happened in school, but nothing that lasted more than that incident, and I always appreciate growing up in the area because it taught me how

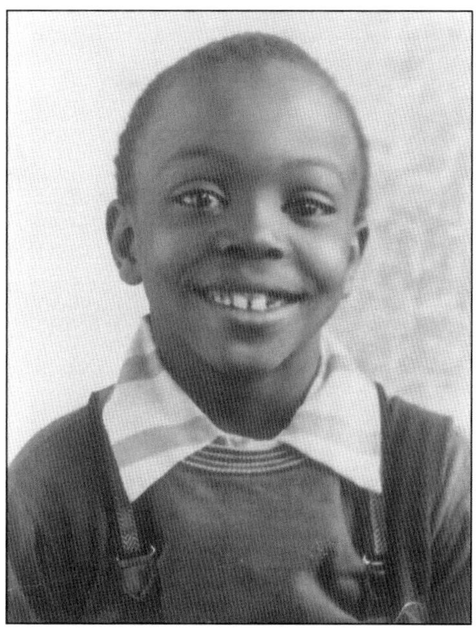

Bernard Pinkett, Age Eight.

to respect others—respect myself and respect others.

Ah, Collins Park is about 50 years old, maybe 45 years old. And until then, we did not have white playmates. After the building of Collins Park we did play sometimes with a few of the neighbors from Collins Park.

Yes, I've always been athletic and loved to play baseball, football and track. But I was the mascot at 10 years of age for the second team [Buttonwood Tigers] but the team dissolved and formed another team around 1946. It lasted four years, I believe, but I enjoyed being around the other fellows. I really loved to play baseball, and liked the traveling. We used to go to Dover and Wilmington, and South Bridge, and Odessa. Most of the games we played were on Saturday. And at all the big games on Saturday, they had food and sodas and watermelon usually. But the comradery is the thing that I really remember and a few other things. I remember the Harris boys, Cyrus Truman, the Mitchells, Shirley Mitchell, Ralph Tiller, Rosco Simmons, and the father, William Simmons. My father played second base and Dick Faulkner used to pitch left-handed and right-handed. A fellow named Dick Pitch, he used to pitch left-handed and right-handed. He always had a good game. Some players came from Wilmington and New Castle to play with the Buttonwood Tigers but quite a few came from the community.

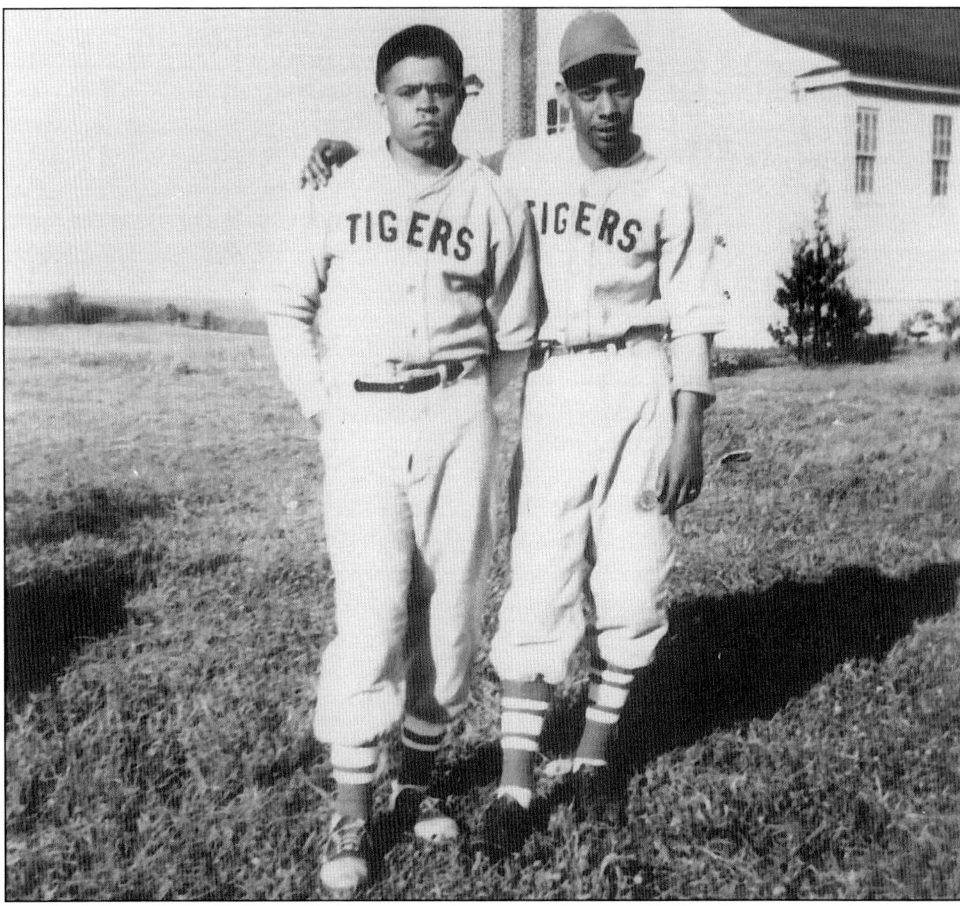

Ralph Tiller and Another Member of the Buttonwood Tigers.

CHAPTER 4

BELVEDERE, NEWPORT, AND MARSHALLTON

VIRGINIA COOK MARKS

I was born on January 17, 1917, in Newport, Delaware. And when we were living in Newport, we had winter from Thanksgiving on up until Easter almost. Snow would get so deep. And kids would have to walk from Newport up here to school. And my brother, he died with frosted feet. He caught frosted feet walking up and down the road. And Ralph kept—he did everything he could possibly do. He went in the service—and there was nothing they could do for him. And it wasn't that they bothered him all the time. But every now and then they would itch. And I'd seen him in church—he'd ease his shoe off and just rub his foot. Oh, it used to hurt him so bad sometimes. He would try anything. Someone told him to take horse manure and heat it. And put your feet in that, and then that would cure it. We were out sledding. And we came in. Ralph had come in because his feet had got cold. And he had this horse manure in this big bucket, sitting on the coal stove. And honey, that was right in there. It would cut your eyes open. And so he got that warm enough and then he set it down there and put his feet in it and wiggled his toes. It felt all right for a while, but that didn't cure it. Someone told him to take turnip skins, boil them and put your feet in it. Whatever anyone told him, that's what he would do. But it all came from walking to school. Because a lot of times, they would walk from Newport up here to the school. They only had two rooms. So Ms. Molly would get the biggest boy to get the fire started. But if you had to sit around and wait, you're cold, you've walked all the way from there. Sometimes the snow was up to your waist. There was no such thing as a snow day. We're going to have to go to school. And kids just got out and walked. Many a time, even a horse and buggy hadn't even been up and down the road to make a path. So, therefore if you were walking, you just waded through that snow up to your waist or however, until you got up the road. And you know we were good and cold when we got up there. And then to get up there into the school, and then no fire. So you wait until the fire is made, and then you'd get warm and then you've got that same journey back down the road. But we lived through it. We just looked forward to it every day. And we were happy. We could go out and sled in it after we got home. If my father was working from three to eleven—was his main shift. And he would be gone when we came home from school. So we had from then until eleven o'clock to do our chores. Either go up the road and sled or do whatever we had to do and sled and get back home before my father got home from work. That's how we used to work it. Sometimes we would come all the way out to the Cedars, which is all the way up Newport Pike, and then you go down past where the little train is up here, anyhow, it's a big hill. And that's where everybody would go sledding.

Oh, August Quarterly was a big thing. Even when we were little, people used to come up in horse and wagon, and they would take their horse down to Michael's stable, down at Second and between Market and King. That was the place where you would keep horses, because that's where farmers used to keep their horses when they came in. And they would just leave their wagons on the street. And walk their horses down to the stable, because they couldn't stay there all day. But the people would start coming in Saturday. Virginia, Maryland, wherever they came from. And they all would come getting ready for Big Quarterly—that's what they call it—Big Quarterly. And it was something to watch. This was their one time in the year where they could meet their relatives and celebrate religiously as they did. It was a religious thing. But the parade in these gowns—I'll never forget—green, red, blue, pink whatever. They saved for the Quarterly. In the poem, Paul Lawrence Dunbar, when he says, "Gals all dressed in silks and satins. Men all dressed up in Prince Alberts." He said, "I ain't seen such fancy dresses since last Quarterly meeting day." And that's what he meant. Everybody saved their best. They had a special thing for Big Quarterly. And they would walk all the way from Tenth Street, all the way to Second Street on French and just walk back and forth and meet their different friends or relatives or whatever. And stop and talk and those that didn't have relatives that were staying or lived down on the East Side or wherever they lived close by, and this is where they met. I loved to go. They would sing. They had quartets singing. And one thing, you didn't see white people. It was our day and this was our day. There wasn't such things as balloons and all the rigmarole that they have now. They've taken the religious part away from it. People would be singing and praying, and everyone could preach then, I guess. They had a preacher on every corner. But this was what it was all about. And the food was given, you didn't buy anything. People brought watermelons, and they cooked up all this food that they brought. Some of them would have it in the back of these wagons, but they didn't have the wagons on French Street. They'd be down on the East Side and they'd be carrying food up there. As fast as they got rid of one pan full, they'd have another. Go back and get some more out of the wagon and bring it up there. And this is what they ate. You'd go by, and they'd ask if you wanted something to eat. And there it was. Watermelons were so good. But we just would walk to see and giggle and grin and laugh and make fun when we were little. After we got bigger, we stopped. But it was a sight to see. People coming in, and all this modeling, They think they were just looking good. And they would just walk and walk from one end of French Street to the other, up and down, up and down, meet, sing and whatnot. And of course the Mother church was there, then that would be where they had the big service. But all those Quarterly people getting ready for July. Even as I got older, people started selling. And oh, you couldn't get enough fish off King Street because people were getting ready for Big Quarterly, and they'd have—everybody had a table of fish, chicken and whatnot. Of course, they were selling in later years. Everything was sold. Everybody wanted a table so they could make some money. But it wasn't about making money, it was about meeting your relatives. Some of them hadn't seen each other for three or four years. It was something. They should have had videos then and they could have taken down all this and now you could sit and see just what was what.

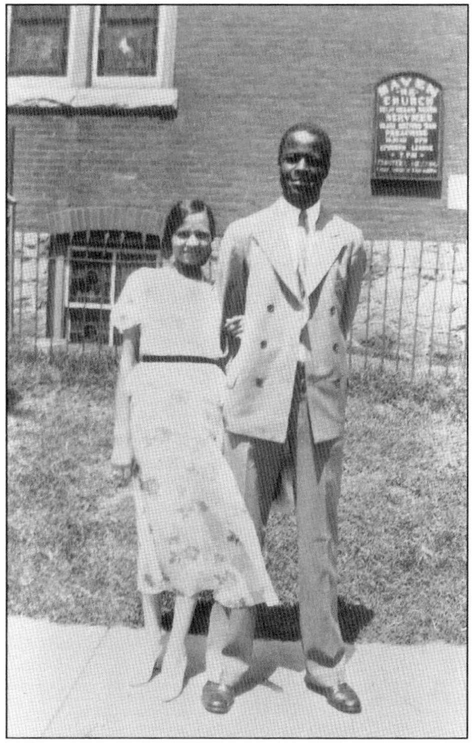

Richard Fleming's Brother William and Girlfriend in Front of Haven Church.

Richard Fleming

My birth date is March 14, 1912. I was born in Marshallton, Delaware. That was on Lancaster Pike and Route 141. It's called, that area, is called Marshallton, Delaware. I was, when I was small, as much as I can remember back to 1916, when we were living on the farm, I had four brothers, I mean, five in all, all boys and my father's name was Daniel L. Fleming. My mother's name was Luberta Fleming and most all the Flemings lived on the Hoffecker farm. We lived there up to the time that my father had an accident and caught pneumonia. He passed away in 1918.

He caught pneumonia during the time when the Hoffeckers used to send the cattle or stock to the Delaware State Fair, which is held in this area, in the Prices Corner area. He was leading one of the cattle down the road to the fair and this particular animal started running, my father jumped across a ditch which he didn't know was there and caught pneumonia and he died.

My brother's names were Kenneth, he was the youngest. I was next. Richard. Then Walt, he was two years older than I. Then there was Eddie. We used to call him Daniel Edward Fleming and that was my father's name and then William Fleming. We used to call him Boob. He was the oldest. And, on our farm, I guess I was about six years of age when I moved off the farm. And I think the day that my father had the fall and took sick, my mother had a pair of opera glasses and she could, someone had told her that there had been an accident, that he had fallen and I think I was with her, and she could use the opera glasses, looking across the field near the cemetery and that's where he fell when he broke his leg, that's where he was, and caught pneumonia. And we had to move off the farm because of that. The Hoffecker's wanted someone to take care of the farm. They were doing it because we had no father. So all the Flemings, including grandfather's family, moved off the farm.

I used to say, when I get a bicycle, I'm going to ride all over the place. My brother had a bicycle, he rode to Atlantic City on the bicycle with friends of his so when I learned how, after I learned how to ride a bicycle, I said I was going to perhaps try to do the same thing. I think I heard, I must have heard that Lindbergh was going to come to Wilmington. So I got on my bicycle and I rode some distance from here, since that farm was something like, I'd say about 3 or 4 miles and I saw him fly over the farm where I used to live. And he landed on the Dupont Air Field and he went on Route 41, came around, came in Pennsylvania Avenue, I forget the route number now. I could read the writing on the side of his plane, "The Spirit of St. Louis." And it was one of the most exciting things that I could think of during that time.

I recall one time, I still have a picture of when they had a push mobile derby and the first time I entered the push mobile derby I won third prize.

Reverend Clarence "Clyde" Herbert Knotts

I was born on January 30, 1932. My mother's name was Irene D. Knotts and my father was Edward L.B. Knotts. I was born at home, delivered by Dr. Clyde Clark Neath. I was named after the doctor. My middle name was Herbert. I was a complete breach birth and almost killed my mother and almost killed myself and I had problems with my legs and my mom had to massage them constantly in order for them to straighten out, and my left leg has never gotten right to this day.

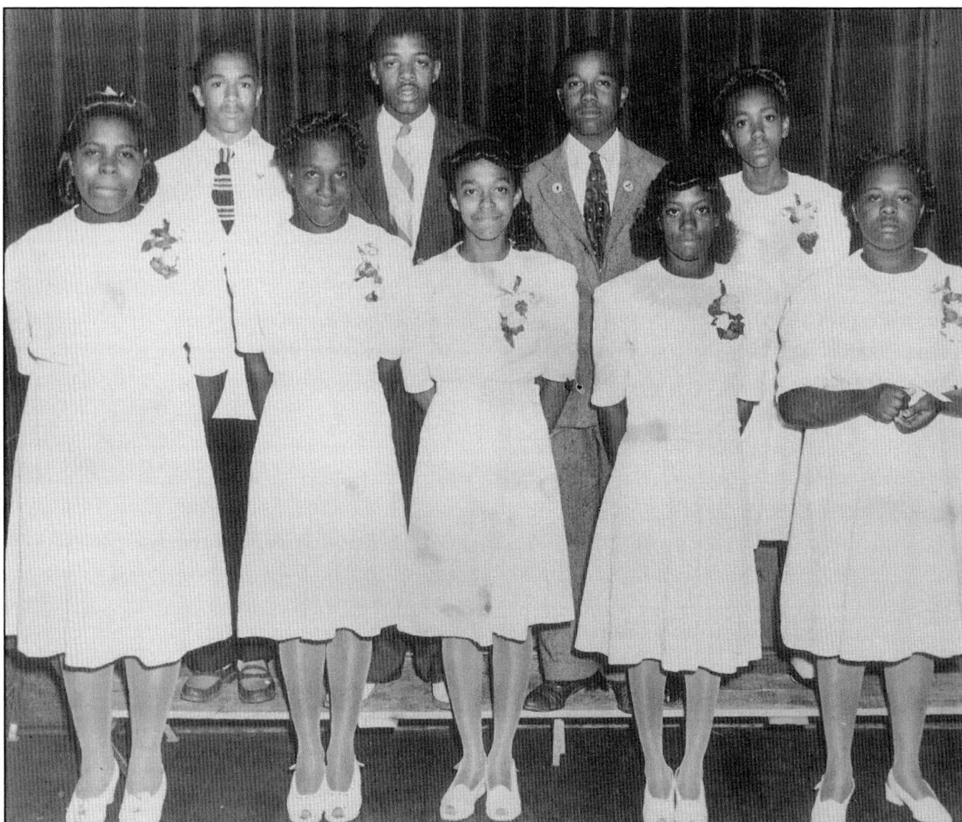

Clyde Knotts (back row, first from left) and Members of His Class at the Absalom Jones School.

We were six girls and four boys and some of them died in infancy, but we always had our lawn parties, lawn ball games, everything we did ourselves as a family. I didn't need anybody else because we had so many kids.

We lived at 214 Kiamensi Road in Belvedere, right beside the school and daddy was the janitor of the school at the time, when I was born. And he was also a butcher, butcher for 50 something years. Mom was a homemaker and she did day's work in some homes and things, but everybody had to work. That's the one thing, you worked and you added a little bit of money to help support the family. It wasn't much, but just enough to help you know.

I went to Absalom Jones School in the first grade, but it was at Simpsons Church, at that time and was getting overcrowded so some of us, Evans Smith, Jean Winfield, and I think Alan was there with us and Harry Anderson. We had to go to the basement of Simpsons Church where Ms. Johnson was our teacher at that time. She had taught everybody in the family except my oldest sister Bea. But I enjoyed it, because we made butter and stuff, a lot of interesting things, so it's not just learning. She was a beautiful teacher. I guess that's one reason I wanted to be a teacher too. And then after that when I got out of the first grade I went to the school up on Kiamensi Road. I think it was a four-room school then and I was in the second grade and Mrs. Alexander, Mrs. Armstrong then, was my teacher. But the thing that really changed my life was Miss Rhodes, who later became Mrs. Matthews, who was a beautiful woman and a beautiful singer. She had me join the junior high school choir in the third grade and I sang "Somebody's Knocking at Your Door," the lead part, for that solo for the junior high school choir. But I stayed with her for the third, fourth, and fifth grades and she passed away. But I knew, from that point, the third grade, that I wanted to be a music teacher. I never had any other thing about being anything else but a music teacher. My mom and dad wanted me to be a doctor. I told them I wanted to be a music teacher. My mom said, "Be another Roland Hayes," because I sang fairly well. I said, "Nope, I want to teach" and that's what I did. I went to teach.

Mr. Saul Miller had a horseshoe pitching place down in his yard and we tried getting in the hole to pitch horseshoes. And I was a very good horseshoe pitcher when I was in high school. And I was up there and I wanted to pitch horseshoes, but they would never let me pitch horseshoes. They said, "No you go on to college, and when you finish you can come back and come back in the hole." After graduation, I got into the hole and I beat everybody around there. But I mean, it has just stuck with me Because these men thought enough of me not to let me ruin my life by being in the hole and doing things that perhaps I shouldn't do. Although I wanted to pitch real bad, but they would not let me do it. They said, " No, you got a good mind, you go on to college, and when you finish college, you come back and you can get in the hole." And I did that and I beat them all. It made a real impression on me that they would think enough of a young man and encourage him to get an education, so I did. And that was great, and I was able to go back after I graduated from college. Another compliment they gave is me was, "College didn't change you like it changed other people. You're just the same guy, we loved you and you grew up as a kid." That just touched me too.

In the wintertime, we were going over to the hill, to go sledding, cause that was a favorite place to sled. And the white boys came over and wanted to chase us off the hill, and we said we weren't going. They said, "Send out your best, and we'll send out our best." So we sent Joe Webster who was also a good boxer and Webster beat him. It was a very sad thing to see, because he really beat him very badly, and his nose was broken and blood was flying everywhere, and that was very disappointing. It was very disappointing to me. I didn't think that should be. I was upset because of what had happened, but it didn't have to be and from that point on, though, we didn't ever have any trouble getting the hill when it snowed. When we come, they'd be over there on the hill sledding. But when we all came up there, they left. But that, it was very disappointing to see that happen. I still remember that to this day. It was very sad.

We didn't have problems with the Italians in our community with the Cuccios and the Marianos. It was just sad because the snow was all red from the young man's blood and everything. It just didn't make sense to me to have to do that too. We could all stand on the hill together. I didn't understand that. I was too young to understand I guess about being prejudice and stuff.

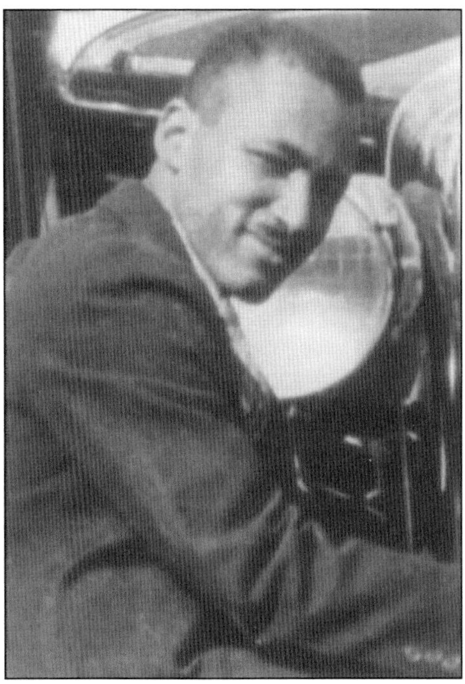

JEAN QUINN LEWIS'S FATHER, LUTHER J. PORTER.

JEAN QUINN LEWIS

I was born November 26, 1928, in St. Michael's, Maryland, to Rev. Alfred and Esther Quinn. My father died when I was very young, at 14 months old, and I moved to Wilmington with my mother and grandfather. My grandfather was pastor of Haven Methodist Church at that time. And Roma, my sister Roma was four years older than I, lived there with me until mother married Luther J. Porter. We moved immediately since they were married, into Belvedere. And daddy was a teacher at Howard High School and he carried us by car to the schools in the city because he was going in there everyday. We both went to #29 Elementary School on Twelfth Street in Wilmington and he would pick us up at my Aunt Helen Holland's after school and take us home to Belvedere and that's all I could say.

My mother taught school. In 1948 when the University of Delaware opened up to black folks, she was one of the first to apply, but she had been to school in other places, in Hampton and other schools. She had home economics training at Pratt Institute in New York and she signed up for elementary education. She was in one of the first graduating classes at the University of Delaware when black folks graduated.

I was never afraid, never worried about locking the doors in Belvedere and I had friends there in the neighborhood and I was usually going to school or working or reading or something and I was quite content. And we were never afraid in Belvedere, and I had many friends. Lois Bailey was one, and her whole family. They were so good to me, they lived next door to me, and we played all kinds of games that children play, in and out of the chicken houses. We raised chickens. Daddy subsidized his teaching income raising chickens and sold the chickens and the eggs. And I remember collecting the eggs and we had to clean them and bag them by the dozens. And he sold them to the teachers at Howard High School once a week. And he had a big garden in the yard. We grew all the vegetables there, cause mother canned them in the summer and I had to sit out in the garden and pick the corn, and it was awful when it was hot. But I didn't complain. I had to do it.

We raised chickens. We had an incubator. Not an incubator. 'Cause we called it a brudder, because the eggs had already been hatched. We would buy them from someone and buy a hundred chickens at a time. And the brudder, they called it, was in the kitchen. Of course the kitchen smelled but we had to change the paper everyday. It was a horrendous job, but it was something we had to do and we did it. We raised them until they were substantial enough in size, you know to go right into the next chicken house. It was three levels, and then you had the hen house which was not in the same place, where the hens would lay the eggs. When daddy wasn't there, Roma and I had to sell the chickens and had to wash them and pluck them if the people wanted them. We couldn't let a sale go by, and people came by and bought it. So we raised those bitty's in the kitchen. And, several times a week, we'd lift them up. It would take two or three of us to do it and roll up the debris. And put fresh paper down, lots of newspaper. So we had breakfast, dinner, and lunch with the bitty's right in the kitchen, a hundred of them. And of course, many of them would die.

He [my father] was, he was very honest. Very honest man. Very upright, very fair. And he was very kind to us, to Roma and me. He was a great reader and studier, and he made us save. Every Sunday morning we got our allowance and it wasn't very much, just a few cents. Some mornings we had to say the Golden Rule, "Do unto others as you would have them do unto you." And we recited that, and then we got our allowance.

Even when I was a little girl, didn't know what I was doing, I had to make a budget every August. Everybody in the family had to make a budget of what you needed money for during the year. I had no idea of what I was doing, but we had to do it every August. Of course as I got older, I understood it better.

He wasn't as strict as people would think he would be. And he told me he used to like to do carpentry work and building closets and things. I used to sit right under him and watch him work. He worked hard on that garden, and during the war years, he worked in the summer at Dravos down there, you know, in the shipyards. And he pooled with the men in Belvedere. He was very happy, jumped in with the men in Belvedere. And he was just a third class, cause he didn't know that type of work, but he learned. Third class machinist, in the summertime, during the war years. They were among his good years because he was with his friends in Belvedere, and he liked them very much.

Well, as a child, we just saw him going to all these, you know, at that time, the civil rights people. The proponents of civil rights, would come to either Howard High School or Walnut Y usually on a Sunday afternoon. And of course I had to, even as a child, I had to make them all. And I wouldn't pay that much attention because I was young, but I had to be there. I just had to sit there in the back until they were ready to go home, because at that time they didn't leave me home alone. And he went to all of them, Walter White, Daisy Lampkin, Thurgood Marshall, you name it. And at different times, they did come to Wilmington, not often, but at one time. Of course it was a big deal for Wilmington, those who were interested in that sort of thing. And we were always there. We had to hear them. And the Crisis. He studied the Crisis, he was in touch with this. So once he became a national representative to the NAACP, he was in touch with

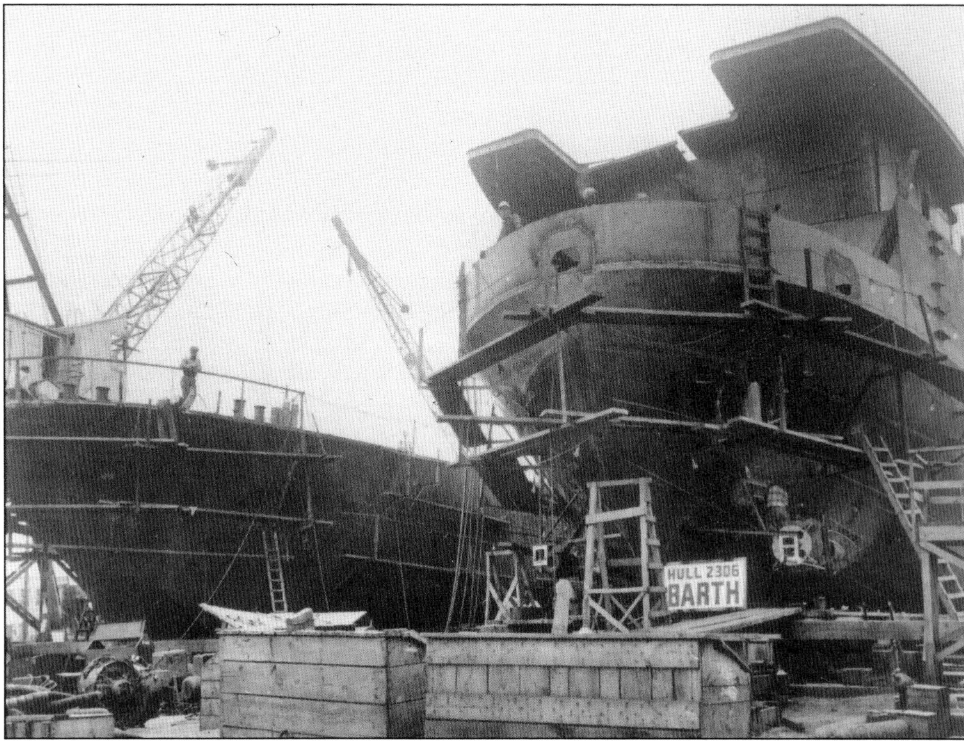

DRAVOS SHIPYARD. Luther J. Porter worked here to supplement his teaching salary.

them. And Lit Mitchell, he was very fond of, very proud of Lit Mitchell. They had many conversations together. And, that was his whole thrust. Then we were called "Negroes." How Negroes could get their place in society, to be accepted as first-class citizens. That was the main thrust.

He loved the NAACP and he was devastated when they began to have financial problems, because he believed in keeping their books straight here. I think the 25 years that he was treasurer, he never lost a penny nor did the other lady who proceeded him named Gertrude Henry. She was in the early years, she was treasurer and then she gave it up, and every penny was accounted for. And he loved the NAACP. All that he could think of was getting to the national in the summer. He was very proud that he was a representative, one of the representatives from Region I for many years. He had such faith that some day men would be accepted for what they were and not whether they were black or white.

DORIS LYDIA CAMPER CROMMARTE

My date of birth is June 26, 1937. My name is Doris Lydia Camper Crommarte. I think most of all what I do remember is the day of the May Day I went home to get dressed, and I lived down in Newport which is about what? 4 or 5 miles away from the school, and something happened. My ride that was supposed to bring me back to the school couldn't bring me. I just didn't have anyone to bring me, and I was getting very nervous because I knew all the audience was waiting, and the program was suppose to have been going on, and I'm home in my gown and no way to get there. And our milk man ... we used to have a milk man that used to deliver bottled milk to the door, and he'd come by in his little truck. His name was Curly. And Curly came by to deliver the milk, and he said we could not miss our May Day. So he moved the milk crates all aside, prepared a nice seat for me on top of the milk crates and way we went. And I arrived just in time to be able walk up the aisle to my throne. I think that was the most thrilling and memorable part of that May Day for me. Let's see. I was in the ninth grade at that time, so I was about 14.

Representatives from all the high schools in the state are gathered for one week for a music camp. I believe that was 1954, yes, and of course Patty Harris and I were representatives. As far as I can remember there were only 6 ... 6 black Americans there compared to ... oh I believe there was like 104 something like that of the white children there. There were only 6 black Americans, and then about 3 of them dropped out. So there were only about 3 of us I think by the time it was all over, well by the time we had the concert at the end of the week. You know ... of course we felt very honored just being chosen to go. But by being raised in an all-white community, we used to live down in Newport before we moved up to Cedar Heights, and of course there were only just a handful of black children that lived down there in Newport and we were raised down there until we went to high school. So there was no problem as far as me mingling. To me it was just wonderful. I had no problems at all mingling, and I was especially surprised and feeling very proud when the leader chose me to sing the solo part to one of the songs that we were going to sing. Out of all of the children, as he had us to sing, he decided he wanted me to sing the solo. So I felt very honored. Well, one thing I do remember. We had recreational time when we weren't practicing. So a group of us decided to walk to town. We were within

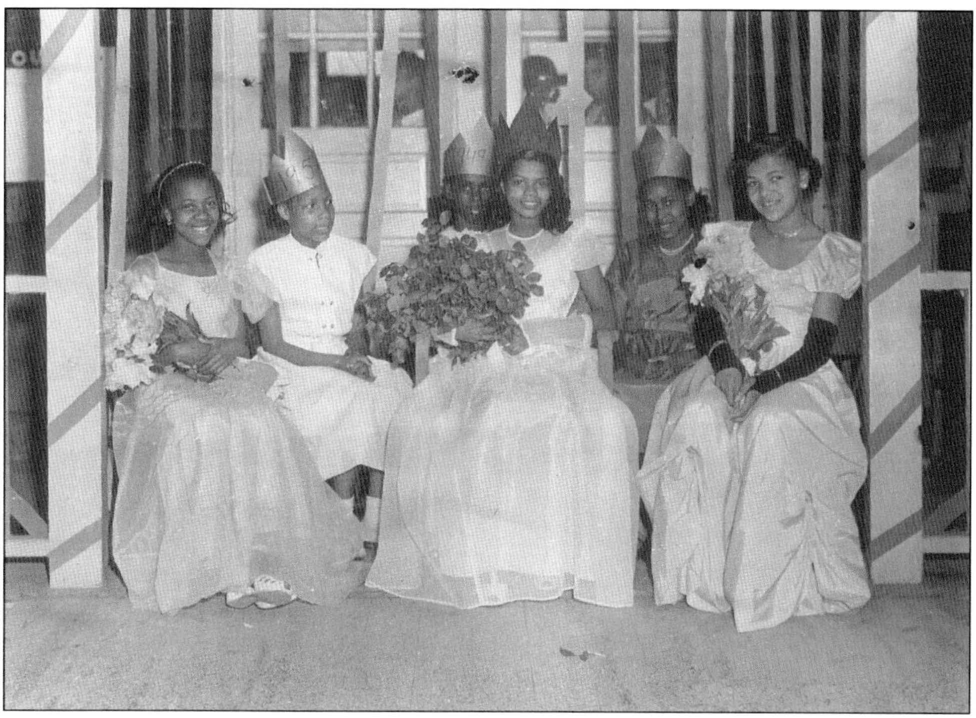

Doris Lydia Camper Crommarte (Center) and Her May Day Court at the Absalom Jones School.

walking distance, to go to the movies. There were our white friends along with us. When we got there to pay for our tickets, the lady was ushering me to go around the side. I didn't quite understand what she meant. What it was, the black people were supposed to go around the side and up the steps up to a balcony. Black people had to sit up in the balcony, and the white people could go inside the regular door. It shocked me because I had never experienced anything like that. And of course, all my little white friends hey ... they said "Hey we'll all go." And they went ... we all went together. And we all went up to the balcony. Of course we all had a good time because we had made you know a lot of very good friends down there. But I never forgot the experience because it was my first experience really of that type of separation that I could ever remember. To me it was like being down in the deep South. And I guess at Dover at that time that's the way it was, and I did not know that. Well you know I never remembered that [in Wilmington] because we always went to the Hopkins Theater. And of course that was a black theater only. So I just don't remember experiencing being ushered to a balcony upstairs ever before. Now if my parents had maybe so, I don't know. But by just going to the black theater, that's all I knew. So by this being a mixed theater, I had ... this was the first experience being separated where. They were going to separate our friends from us. And we had to go up, and they had to go down, but they chose to go up with us you know. I believe ... let's see when we ... when we went to the vocal music camp I was about 16.

Loretta Bruton

My mother was a schoolteacher. She started teaching in Newport and then she ended up at Absalom Jones School. I guess this is even before I was born. I went there, and then we lived on Fifth Street in Wilmington. I would go to school right there sometimes. It depended upon I guess how they felt—down the street to #21 School. And then at other times, I would come out, she was to bring me out to Absalom Jones. Oh, I remember playing with the other children. Mainly, we just had a good time. But school itself. I look back now and I can see it was teachers, good, good, good teachers. And I also remember, when I went to college, how many people, I mean, how further advanced I was because of their teaching. The things that we had in high school, Howard High School. But that was true.

Well, my mother was very decorative ... and loved little touches like that. I remember the house at Christmas. She would decorate it. She would put a lot of herself in it. And Daddy he would have to do the outside. My grandmother and grandfather were there. And they had their friends from Philadelphia. Billy Anty, the baseball player (he played for the Wilmington Renaissance) and his wife. And then there were other relatives like John, my father's brother, and his wife and his daughter.

We had peach trees. We had apple trees. We had pear trees and we had lots of grapes. We had lots of jelly. I can remember the peach pies. They had lots of apples pies and I liked apples pies.

Yes, they made my clothes. She and my grandmother made my clothes. And to tell you the truth, a lot of the clothes that I had came from my grandmother who worked for a family and at their daughter's. She had children and I got all their clothes. So, I was well dressed. I can remember those dresses. Ah, they were beautiful ... But I remember the blue. You talked about this lady that wrote this book about blue eyes [Toni Morrison]. They had blue eyes and every dress I had would be a reflection of their blue eyes. That's something but that's true. Every dress, and I mean there were several dresses and the girls were

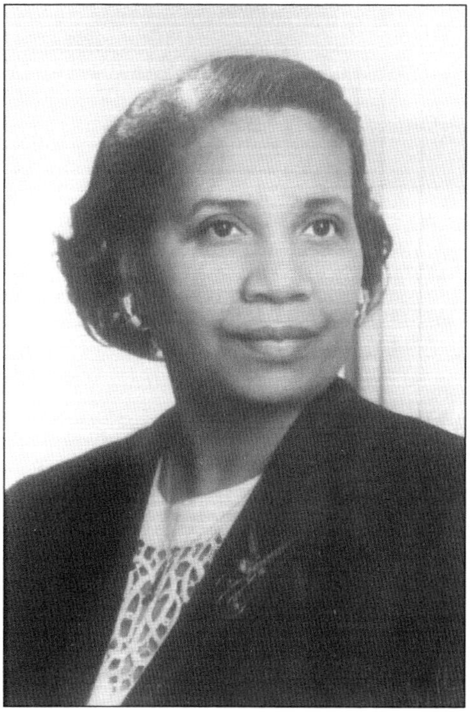

Loretta's Mother, Anita Johnson.

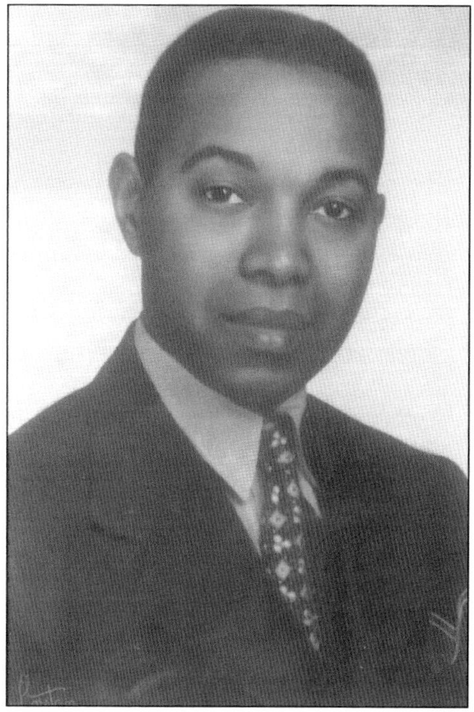

Loretta's Father, William Johnson.

different sizes. And the girls were dressed alike, so I got that dress that they wore, that she wore and I got the sister's dress.

About my father [Judy Johnson played for the Negro Leagues, the Pittsburgh Crawfords] ... I could remember going to Pittsburgh and he played there. We would go there and stay for the summer. I can remember that. I had to go on the train by myself. I can't remember too much about it, except there were hills. We'd have to go up and down the hills. And I remember the woman that we lived with had a store. We'd have to go over to that store every day. And of course there was candy. But that was before I was eight years old. There were other children there but they wouldn't play with me. Well, they would play with me, but there was a boy that didn't like me and so it made it very hard for me. But we went through that, too. I can remember going to the games, but I don't remember anything about them. I just remember being there.

A lot of players came to our house in Delaware. In fact the whole team came one time. They were coming up from the South, so they came by. I remember that. They were everywhere.

Yes, Daddy was gone quite a lot. It was horrible you know. Well, my mother adjusted though. She was well adjusted in a lot of ways. Because she just expected it. If he was gone, he was gone. But here life was full. She kept me busy. Believe me. She kept me busy. He was really gone a lot and until he quit and when he quit, everything went down. He quit in '34 or '35. He worked for several years until he retired. He was half way in business with John, his brother for a long time. They had a store, you know. And then they opened up another store up the street, on Dupont Street. And then he opened a store in Millside, and that went well. That was good. I had to work in the store. That was another job I had. I didn't get paid, so you had to eat what you wanted. Then

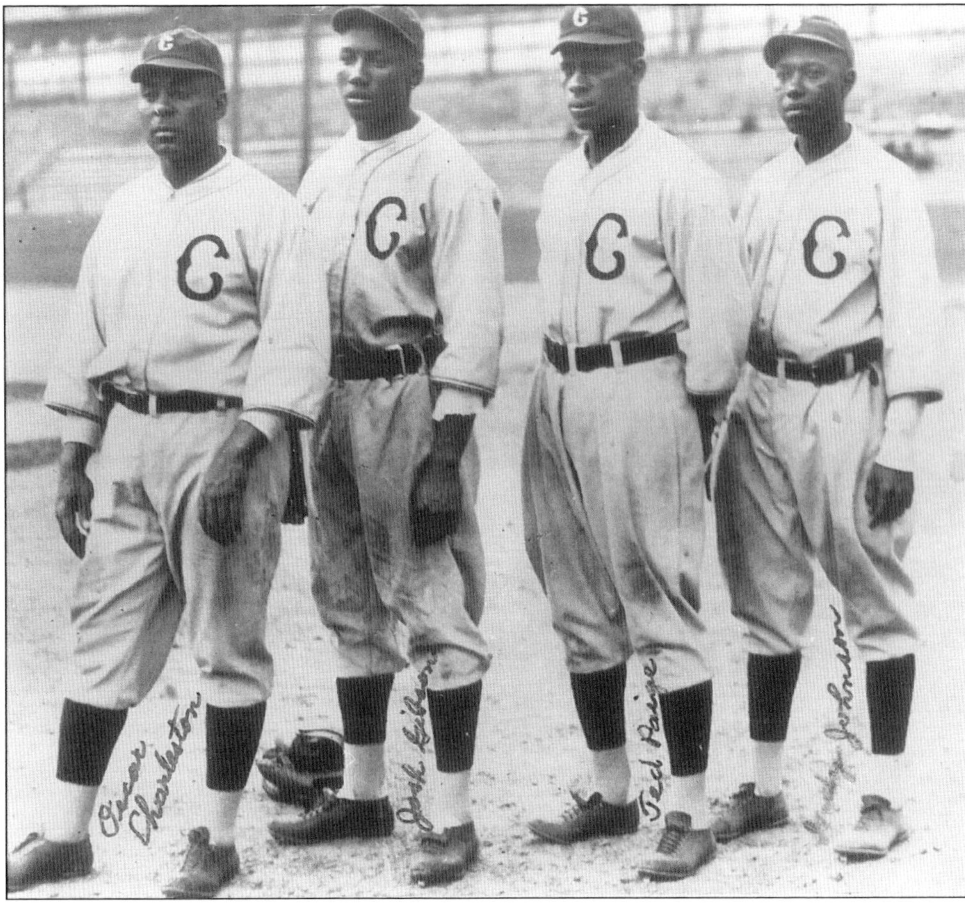

William "Judy" Johnson (Right). *He was a third basemen in the Negro Leagues from 1923 to 1937. Later, he was inducted into the Baseball Hall of Fame.*

he was driving a school bus from Absalom Jones School. I think that's mainly what he did. [About race and baseball] Not outwardly. I think a lot of his was right inside. It was right inside. It stayed there. He, I don't think he could afford to let it go. I don't know if he talked about it. He kept it in there, and if it came out it was with another player. I don't even think it came out with my mother pretty much. The resentment was there ,though. You could feel it. And you knew it was there. And you were brought up with it too. So that still it was getting better. I guess it was supposed to get better.

They had lots of different parties. They had lots of friends from Philadelphia. And they would come down and spend the day. Or they might come and spend a couple of days and it would be fun. But they used to love to play baseball. A lot of baseball in the yard and they enjoyed it. And she'd cook and cook and cook.

Chapter 5
Claymont

Jane Watson Mitchell

My mother's name was Sara Louisa Woodburn. My father's name was Charles Elmer Watson. My father worked in the steel mill in Coatesville. He worked in the steel mill. My grandfather worked in the steel mill. Everybody worked in the steel mill. Luchens Steel Mill in Coatesville, Pennsylvania. So everybody worked there. When Worth's Company Steel Mill (I don't remember when it was built) opened they all decided to migrate to Claymont, Delaware, to work in the steel mill. That was grandfather and his three boys. They all went to work in the steel mill. So I remember seeing my grandfather because he lived in a shanty, they called it, just below Hickman Road in Claymont, Delaware, and we lived in a house. These houses along Hickman Row were all owned by the Worth Steel Company and they had very nice houses there for their workers. And even though we were black "colored" as they called it in those days, the colored families had the nicest houses. They were all three stories. The first floor had a cellar to it and a kitchen. The second floor had a living room, the bathroom and one bedroom. And the third floor had two bedrooms upstairs. So we lived in these houses and the houses were just lovely. And they still are. We were children and we talked about who had the best looking house on Hickman Row. And we had contests about the best looking houses.

Now, what I remember most about my mother and father is that they seemed to be very close to each other. And what I remember so much about them is that they used to have house parties and all the neighbors, the grown neighbors would come to each others houses and have these parties. We weren't allowed to go, but you know, these houses were three-story houses and we would creep downstairs from our bedroom and sit on the stairs. There was a banister there and we'd watch them dance around the floor. I could see my mother now. She was ... she just seemed like the most beautiful person in the world! And she was making little turns and her foot would go up in the air. They looked so nice together. As soon as they looked up there and saw us looking at them, they chased us all back to bed. But I do remember that.

I remember in Claymont that when I got to be five years old, we all went to State Line School and Miss Deason was our teacher. There were six grades in that school—from the first to the six grade in that school. I began going to school when I was five years old. When we were living in Claymont, you didn't have to be six to go to school. You just went to school because everybody was going. Also we had school during the week and then on Sunday there was church service. And the church service was Baptist. So all the songs that I hear now and the hymns are familiar to me from the Baptist church. "What a Friend We have in Jesus," "I Walk Through the Garden Alone." And the entertainment we had most of the time was made up of men who did this singing. I remember how they were really singing these songs. And the one that I remember more than anything was "These bones, those bones, those dry bones. One bone was hitched to the other bone."

And all of us went to school. I remember when we finished sixth grade we had to go to Wilmington to go to school, because there were no schools. We were living under segregation and there were no schools there. So we had to go to Wilmington to go to school. I could remember a couple of things about my father and mother. I remember my father was the first one in the group to own an automobile. He had, I guess a 19 ... I don't remember the date now. Ford, one of the first

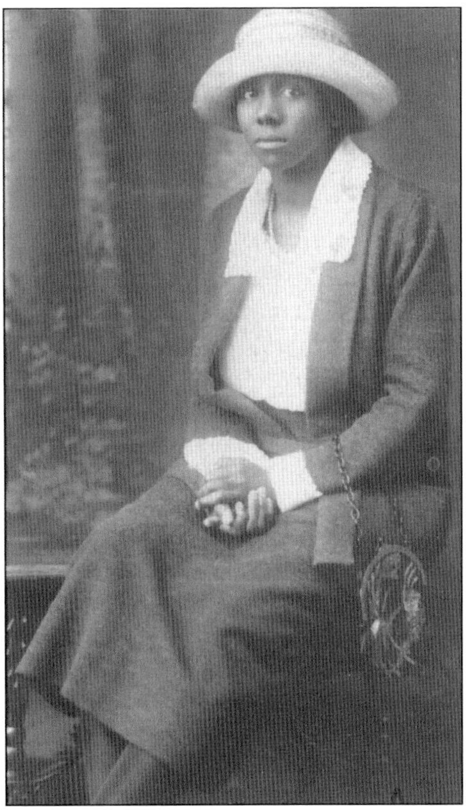

Jane Watson Mitchell's Mother, Sarah Louisa Woodburn Watson.

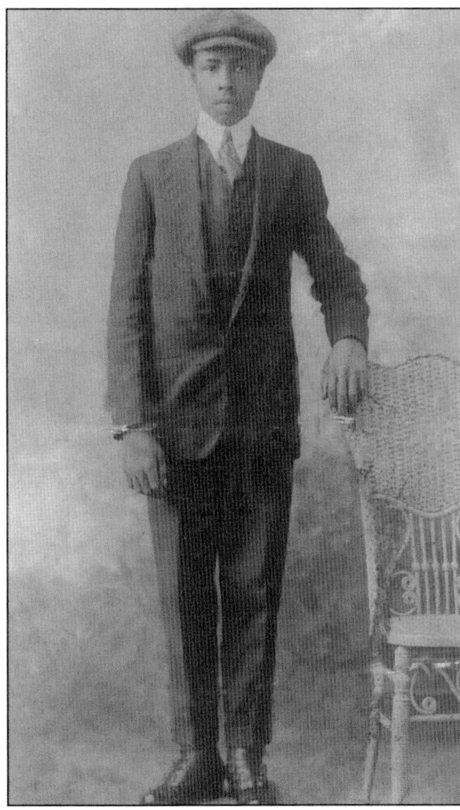

Charles Elmer Watson, Jane Watson Mitchell's Father.

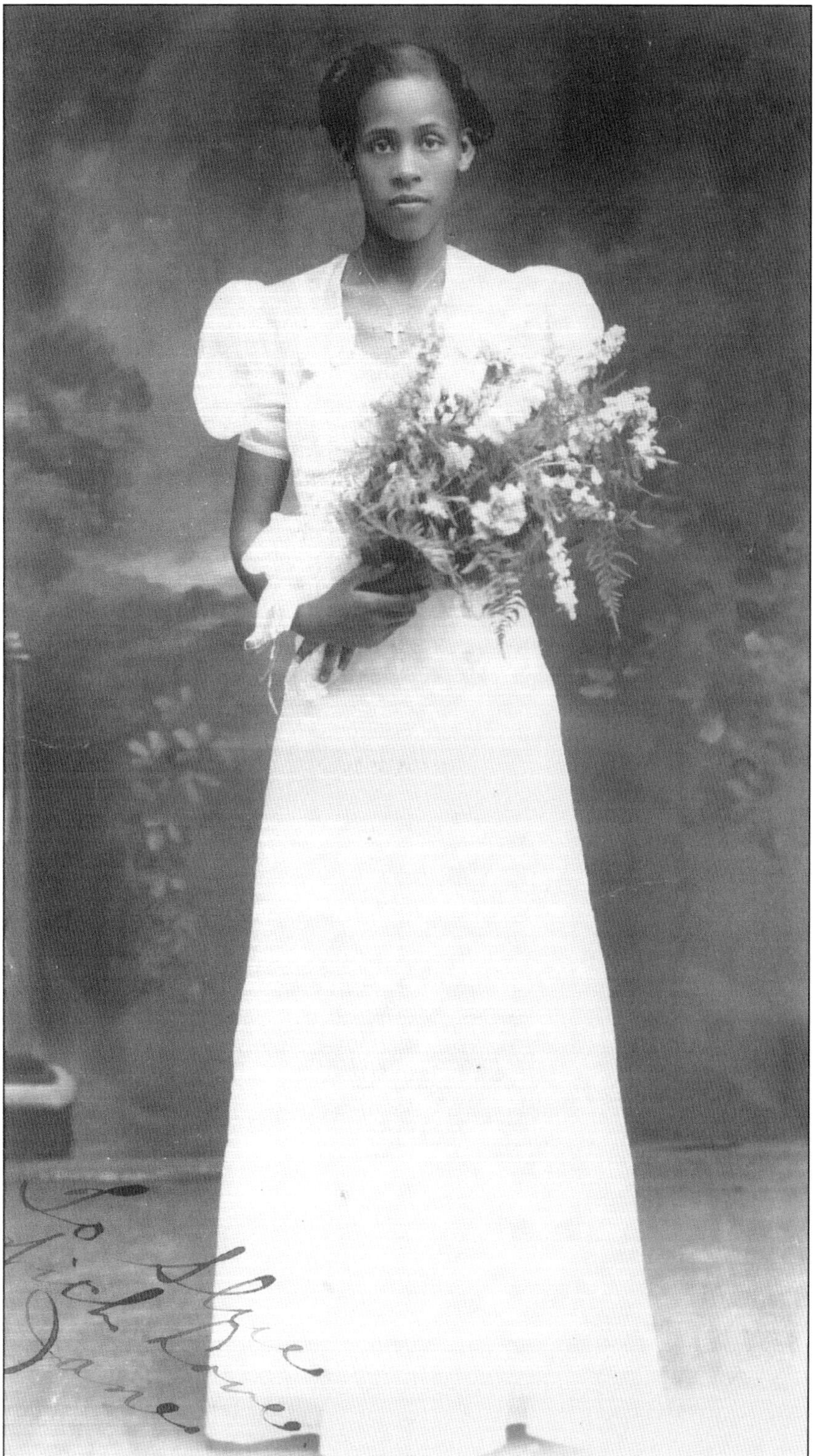

JANE MITCHELL DRESSED FOR HER PROM AT HOWARD HIGH SCHOOL.

Fords to come out. I can see it now. Everybody was so proud of him. He comes riding around, off Hickman Road, in his car, and everybody was so pleased. It was a Model T. I can remember that, of the car. And we used to have a thing, a contest about who had the best looking house. And there was Mrs. Richardson down at one end of the group of houses. And her house was the prettiest of all.

My father worked at the steel mill and I think they handled molten steel. I didn't know too much about it, but later on I remember that it was a very, very, tough job. And he and my two oldest brothers began to work there too when they got old enough. But I remember how hard he worked. But Mr. Worth had a great big house. I think that house still stands right there in Claymont. He used to have fireworks for us every Fourth of July. And we would go there and sit on the lawn and look at the fireworks. I remember that as we would leave our houses to go to the commissary which was owned by Worth Steel. We would go there to buy all of our groceries. I guess that was taken out of the salary. I don't remember how they handled that, but we'd buy all our groceries from Worth Steel. We used to walk across a trestle to get to the commissary. And we used to have more fun going too, because underneath it was water, you know. We'd have more fun going across from one part of the trestle to go to the store. It was really nice. There was another store in there called Scarpitti in Kinemart at Hickman Row. We used to walk there to the store sometimes.

Everybody knew each other. Most everybody there came from the South. The people migrated from the South and this was all around in the early twenties. My father moved there when I was two years old and then the rest of the children began to grow. My sister Elaine was the next child after that. My father, he had the rest of his children and we ended up being nine in our family. And I was the fourth child down.

Also, in Hickman Row, across from where our houses were, there was a street and then there was a pond across from that with trees—a little park over there. And then a big hill that led up to the Crossland Farm. We used to sled in the wintertime down the hill. You know we had to be careful about the pond at the bottom.. And I remember, it's so vivid in my memory because this is the Crossland Farm that we looked up there one night and there was a great cross burning. It seemed as if it was a meeting place of the Ku Klux Klan. Now that is one thing that stays in my memory. I will never forget, that cross burning up on that hill. And we were all frightened to death. We all ran home, you know, and got in our houses and shut the doors because we were so frightened by this display of the Ku Klux Klan. I don't remember what happened about it. But they were across from us and you could see that thing burning.

Retha Johnson Kelly

I was born January 30, 1924. My parents were Lola and Robert Johnson. And I had two brothers Robert and Augustus Johnson. I was born in Philadelphia and then I was brought to Hickman Row, three days after birth. And I have been there up until the time I was grown. My father worked at the steel mill. My mother was a housekeeper. You know she worked at home. She used to bake a lot of pies. And when times were hard in our community, people had to supplement their income, you know. Mother used to get up at 3 o'clock in the morning, and she would bake pies. She was noted for her sweet potato pies. She would bake individual pies, and my brother Augustus would take them out to the Congoleum and to the steel mill to sell them. Robert worked at the Dupont Hotel up until his illness and his death.

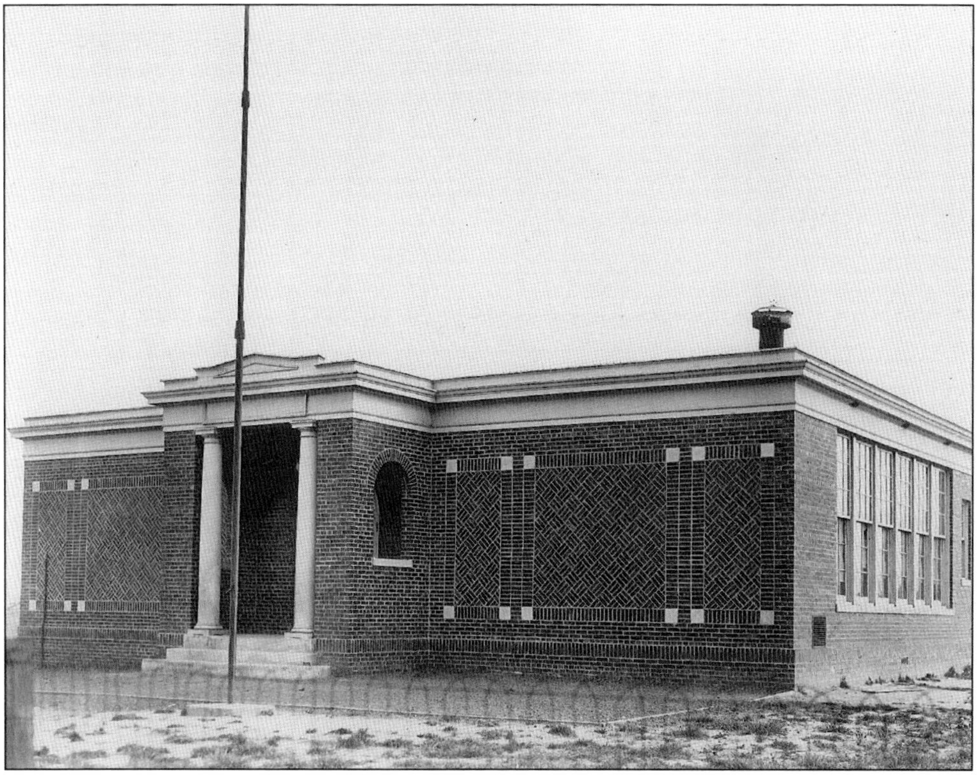

***State Line School in Claymont.** Retha Johnson Kelly attended school here. (Courtesy of the Hagley Museum and Library.)*

It started out as a very small church. There was a two room building up on a hill in back of the houses. We had row houses. And there was this two room building up there. Mrs Rowe, who was one of the founders of the church who worked for one of the presidents ... I think he was at the mill. She asked him, "Could we use one of those rooms for a church?" And he said, "Yes." We were already using one room for the school. There were six grades in this one school with one teacher, Pauline Gyson. And oh boy she was really something. Because at that time schools were not integrated, and we went there. They started the church in Mrs. Rowe's house—Mr. and Mrs Philip Rowe. The church was started in their home. My mother of course was one of them and they had service there, you know. They organized the church there. The first minister, Reverend Butcher from Woodland, Pennsylvania, I believe it was. He was a friend of the Rowes and they asked him to come down. And he became the first pastor of that church. And then they got a few members when they moved into that second room up there. That's where we stayed until we built a new church. And they built a church for us right across the street from the houses—a beautiful little church. And the church grew. We stayed there on Hickman Row until the Worths sold the mill. And the people that bought it did not want it below. So they sold the building and everybody was heartbroken. We had services at the Y in Wilmington for a long while before we built the church at Twenty-sixth Street. And then we moved up a little higher to the top of Twenty-sixth Street where we are now.

That was the name of the school, State Line. Every May Day we had a big affair with the Maypole. We wrapped the Maypole and we would all dress up you know. And everybody had pets—I had two little rabbits. We would take our pets up there you know. Mr. Stahl was the superintendent of the school at that time. He's dead too, He would always take pictures of us. He had a movie camera and he would take pictures of us at this May Day and all of the special affairs. They weren't called camcorders at that time.

People would have rent parties. They would have rent parties and there was a big oh a big tree right across the street as you come down the hill. On the left side was a great big tree, and they and a platform built there. And a couple of the tenants John Arthur Robinson was the one. They got a jukebox and put it on that stage. And that was a place for us children to dance and play. Of course our parents could sit on the porch and they could watch anything that's going on. So you could go out there and you could have a good time. And they would sell dinners and all kinds of desserts. It was a nice clean place to live and the people were nice. There was no feudin' and fightin' among the people you know. You didn't have to lock your doors.

Way up in the back of the houses that's were they had pig pens. They had these pigs and they would slaughter the pigs. There was a certain day when it was real cold. The men would stay off from work and the children had to go to school. We didn't want to go. We wanted to see what was going on you know. But we had to go slow. There was a store down at the bottom of the hill coming into Hickman Road that was owned by Italians. And when they were going to kill the pigs, they would always come up and catch the blood because they like to make blood pudding. When we'd come from school, change clothes, and run right up to see all these pigs hanging up. They'd been gutted and cleaned. In great big black kettles women were stirring up this fat to make lard. They'd be stirring these black kettles to make the lard from fat. That's when they made what you call it—cracklins. They made cracklins and they would give us a chunk. Hey, those were the good ol days. You got me goin' back, girl, I'm tellin' you! They were the good old days! Yup, but things change and people do so, too.

Chapter 6

Christiana and Hockessin

Bernice Jackson Anderson Hilton

I was born July 23, 1928, in Christiana, Delaware. My father was Reverend Milton W. Jackson He started pastoring at Christiana, Mt. Pleasant United Methodist Church. He later transferred to the UAME Conference and he served in Ironhill, Delaware, Kennett Square, Pennsylvania, Avondale, Newark, and various other churches in the UAME Conference. My mother was Helen Elizabeth Hall Jackson and she was a housewife.

I had seven brothers and six sisters. Of course, we weren't all there at the same time because there was a two-year age difference in all of us. But there were about eight of us at home at all times. And we had to go to church every Sunday. Well, I especially loved Children's Day because we would always get a new white dress and patent shoes and we had to say our recitations.

Well, there was a family of Browns—three brothers. And hence the road where we lived was called Brown's Lane. One of the daughters, Mrs. Alethea Galton, was my Sunday school teacher. It was a nice quiet little town. Where I lived it was an all-black community. We loved each other and everyone looked out for everyone else. When we went down to the main corners, which were mostly white people, we were treated with respect. We never had any trouble because back there then I guess we stayed in our places. They thought we should, so we never had any trouble with the white community.

I went to a little one-room school, Christiana 111 C—the "C" stood for colored. Our first teacher was Mrs. Thelma Brown. She taught there for one year and then she moved somewhere else. And then there was a lady named Dorothy Lewis and she came from Lewis, Delaware. She married a man named Bobbie Saunders. So she was Mrs. Dorothy Saunders and she was there until we graduated in the sixth grade and went on to Howard. Oh, I forgot. I did have another teacher a Miss Spence. Her father was Reverend O.H. Spence and she taught for one year and

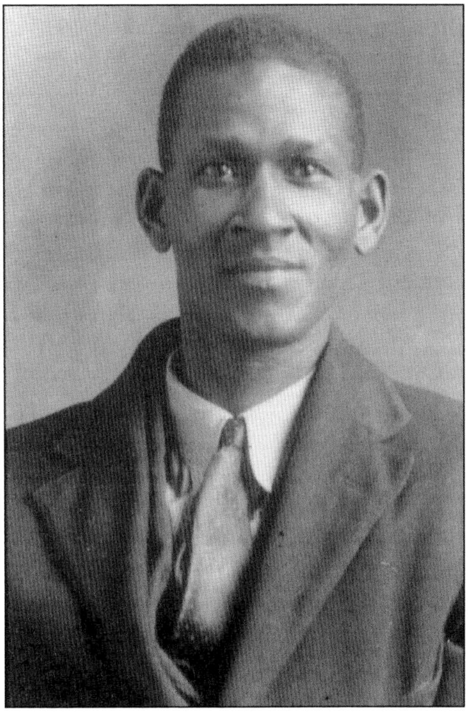

Rev. Milton W. Jackson, Bernice Jackson Anderson Hilton's Father.

retired because we worried her to death, I guess.

Well, I remember one time we had a big rain, and they were putting a basement under the Mt. Pleasant Church. It rained a lot. We were going by and we looked in there and saw all of this water. So we decided to go swimming under the church. So we took all of our clothes off and went swimming without any clothes on under the church. A man named Harry Blake came by and saw us in there and called out, "I'm going to tell your mother." Well, by the time my mother got to the corner I had my clothes on and ran around the corner. She didn't catch me until I got back home.

We had horses and when my father would go out, we would steal the horses and ride bareback. We had a horse named Dexter who was very mean. He was white ... a beautiful white horse. If you ever got on Dexter's back, you just had to hang on for dear life because he would run, run, run, run, until he got tired and then he would come home and stop abruptly and throw you off his back.

There was always something to do because my father had a little truck farm. So we had to bug potatoes, and help drop potatoes and pick beans and work the garden. Then he would go to the market and sell the things. And every now and then he would let one of us accompany him to the market, which was always fun. At first it used to be on King Street in Wilmington. Then they moved the farmers out to Madison Street in Wilmington and that's where the farmers were when he retired from going to the market. We had chickens and pigs, one cow, two or three horses. We never had any sheep, but we did have lots of pigs, a cow, horses, and chickens. We would get fresh eggs every day. My mother would milk the cow, and we would churn the butter. When they killed the pigs we would always have good meat all winter long.

Samuel Bernard Peterson

I was born on the fourteenth of February 1909. My parents were Dorsey E. Peterson—that "E" stood for Edward—and my mother's name was Martha C. Peterson—Martha Carter Peterson. She was born in Kennett Square, Pennsylvania My father was born in Wilmington, Delaware. I was born on Limestone Road in Hockessin, Delaware, by mid-wife. And we lived in a little two-story house. We had chickens and pigs and everything that we needed for living. So we didn't have to worry about anything happening as far as not having food or anything like that was concerned, because we had plenty of that. But we lived about 2 miles outside of the little burg of Hockessin. So anytime we wanted anything we had to go to Hockessin and get it. And of course, after I got big enough, I was the one that would go to Hockessin and get what we needed for dinner or whatever it might be. We called dinner, "supper" at that time. So, we lived on Limestone Road and I guess it was about a quarter of a mile from the corner where Limestone and Valley Road met. We rode down to Valley Road and then out Valley Road to Hockessin. But the farmer whose house we lived in, allowed us to cut across his field and that I guess cut out around a mile. And we cut across that field and hit Valley Road. And that's the way we went all the time. But our school was Hockessin Colored School—Hockessin Colored School #107. And we went there all the time. But we had to walk 2 miles from where we lived. I don't care what the weather was, snow or anything like that—we had to go to school. And you'd get sick, your mother would tell you, "Well, I'm going to give you this." I don't know what it was, but she's give us some kind of medicine and send us to school. So we didn't miss many days. We had to go to school. And of course, we went to school until eighth grade. After eighth grade we had to go to Howard High School. But then when we started going in to Howard High School we had quite a time going from home out to the railroad track. And the train would come along, the milk train would come along. We would get on it, ride on to Sixteenth and DuPont and from Sixteenth and Dupont to Howard High School. We had to walk there. We didn't mind walking. We didn't have any other way, so I guess that's the reason why. I remember one time my brother and I were walking a long time and had to hurry to catch the train. A man came along with a wagon. He had this wagon coming along and said, "You tired of walking?" We said, "Yes, sir!" And we started running and he'd kick the horse and made the horse run. And he said "Run a while!" We missed all that, but we had fun doing it though. I'm glad I lived in Hockessin because there were lots of boys that lived in that little burg of Hockessin, didn't make it for some reason. I think they were too slick. And

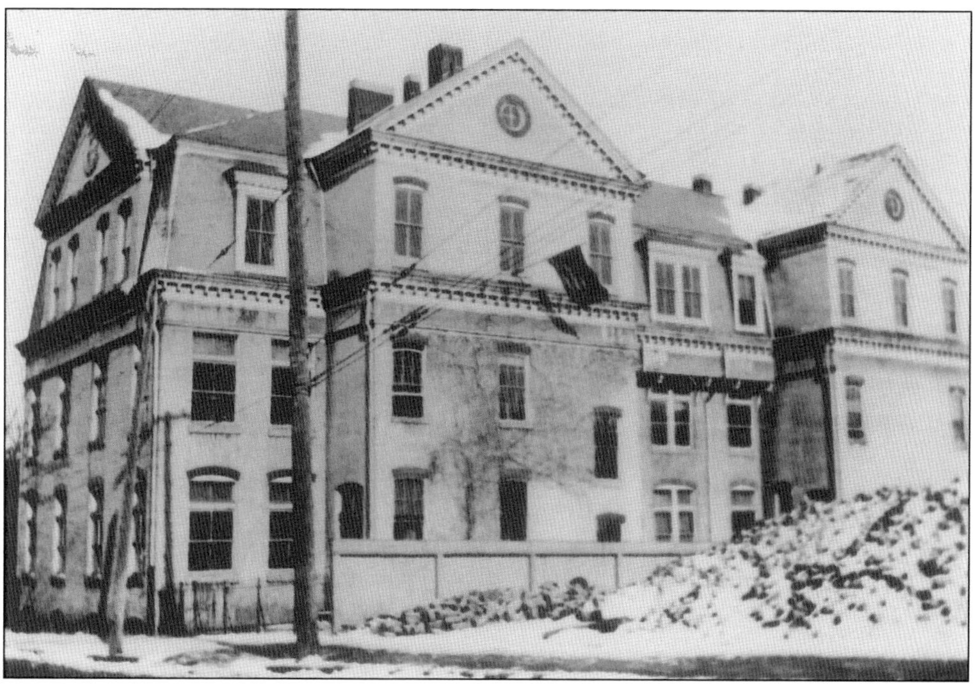

The Old Howard High School. *(Courtesy of the HSD.)*

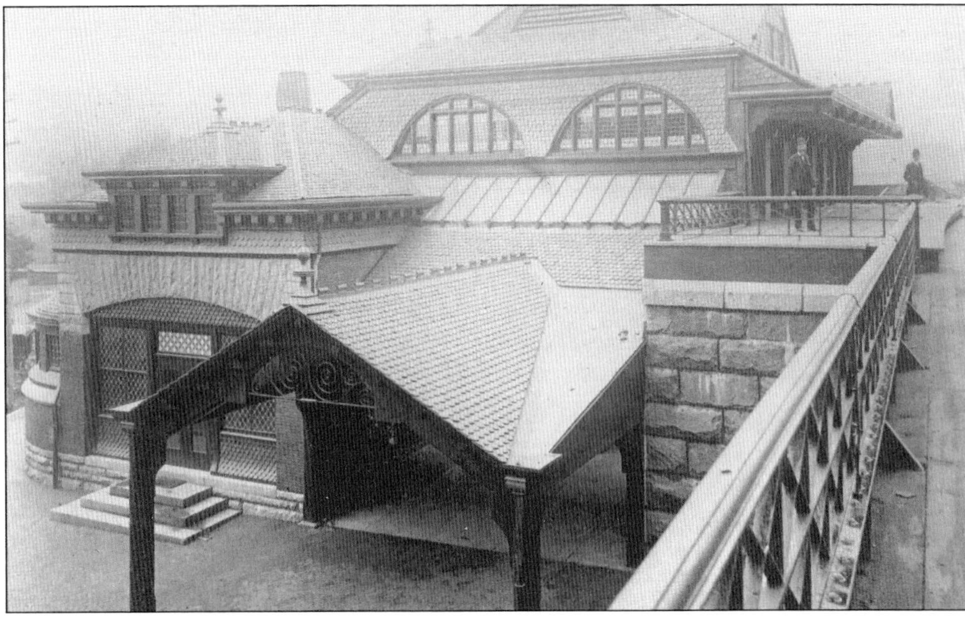

The B&O Train Station at Dupont Street.

then going into Wilmington, I guess the guys there were a little slick, too. But all the while I survived. I played football for one year while I was at Howard High School because they didn't have football I guess for the first two years I was going there. The third and fourth year I played for Howard.

We'd live in first one house and then another. There was a fellow by the name of Fred Buehler, bought a little farm down below us and he was living in the person's house where he worked—Mitchell's house. And he decided he could live in Mitchell's house and rent this place he bought, to Dad. So that's what he did and that's when we sort of stretched out and we had a cow and a horse. He bought a horse and wagon. He had a big place where he could have a big garden. And of course when the boys got big enough, Abe and I got big enough—we had to take care of the garden and pull weeds and such things as that.

My mother was active in the church. Dad was active in the school. He was one of the trustees in the school. And of course, the teachers had to come by him before they could get the job. And he would interview them. We couldn't listen in on it. We'd have to go out and play and such stuff as that. But he was active in the community. They had some type of organization out in Hockessin. And he was part of it. He was one of the colored ones that was part of this little organization that they had. I guess the only thing they were interested in was politics. They would have this meeting and decide who they were going to vote for—who they were going to root for as far as politics was concerned. And they would always have a big parade at that time. So we used to (after they made their suggestions of what they were going to do) go out in the evening and watch the parade.

Hockessin, I guess everybody knew everyone else. Everyone was friendly. I was working for the Mitchell's farm. Mitchell's were Quakers, and we had no trouble. We didn't know anything about race relations or anything like that. We knew that if we were going to eat, we would eat in the kitchen. My sister was working there too. We would go in the kitchen to eat and of course they would go in the dining room and eat. Well, I paid no attention to that. But race relations were very good at the time. I know one time there was a man who was hung. I think it was up somewhere around Hockessin. Of course there was an uproar about that. A [white] fellow was bragging about one of the toes. He had a "nigger toe." They found out he was bragging about it and the blacks were going to kill him. And he had to hide and leave Hockessin for a while. But other than that, didn't have any trouble.

They had two stores. Gephardt's, you could go there of course and buy anything you wanted, so far as I know. We didn't have any movies or anything like that there. We just had those two stores there. And if you wanted to go to a movie, you had to go to Kennett Square or Wilmington, Delaware.

Yes, I remember my grandmother on my father's side. That's probably the only one I can remember because she lived with us for a while. And poor woman, my brother and I tormented that woman to death. She'd always have an apron on and she liked to make what she called "Maryland biscuits." And we'd come home and mother would have put up some blackberries and she'd have a lot of juice in them. And we'd get this juice and drink it and eat these round biscuits, and I know my grandmother was saying, "Don't eat them all. Don't eat all those biscuits. I didn't make those biscuits for you." And we were the only ones—she had made them for us. Poor Granny, she always had this apron on and a nice bow in the back. And we would come along and pull the strings, and of course the bow would come out. After awhile the apron would drop down. "I guess I didn't tie it tight." Poor woman she had a time. She liked us boys. She would say, "No don't do this, don't do that." But she was alright!

Eliza Jane Peterson

When Dad stopped working on the farm, he went to the National Volcanized Rubber Company. He worked down there and then he would come home. We always had cows, pigs, chickens, and so forth. I would sometimes have the cow milked, so he didn't have to do that after he came home from work, because he drove home and by the time he got home it was dark because he worked in the stock until 5:00. But I was to make sure that things were pretty well on the way and sometimes gotten before he got there. And in the summer ... I think we lived on a 3-acre ground and he raised his own hay. He would cut the hay and then pitch it up on the wagon and I would pull it back, so he wouldn't have too many loads to make. So he always said that I was working more than two boys together. But my brothers and I got along fine although I was the one that bossed everybody all the time. But we got along fine. My oldest brother always said I was his second mother.

There was a place called the quarry because that was where they used to get lime and clay. Most of the colored people worked in the quarry. There were more colored people around here than there were white at the time. Oh, I guess there are still six colored families that originally lived here that are still here.

Jean Elizabeth Bolden Fleming

I was born February 4, 1933, in Hockessin, Delaware. The house is still standing on Grant Avenue. It's 615, I think Grant, and it's the only house standing. As a child growing up in Hockessin, I lived with my grandmother, Mary Bolden. There were houses all along Grant Avenue. The church was on the corner and Mrs. Stella Bantum lived next to the church. There was Miss Rachael Nelson who lived in the double house and on the other side was Joseph Thomas and then came James Jamison because we lived in the double house at the time. We lived next door to him. We called him "Tank" and we lived next door to Tank and then there was another house on the other side of us which Mr. William Skinner lived there. We were segregated, you know. I went to #107 Colored School which was right in my back yard. I was never late for school or missed a day unless it snowed. Because you had no reason to be late. You had to get over there when Miss Beaujohn would come out from Wilmington and ring the school bell. All the children would run from the houses and go to school. And during the summer, when we became eight or nine years old, we were allowed to go down to Golden Pit, which is where we used to swim. I learned to swim down there because of course we didn't have any swimming pools. Nobody, blacks didn't have swimming pools. There was a swimming pool in Yorklyn. Now that was for the Volcanized Rubber people. There were some black families that lived in Yorklyn but they were not allowed to swim in the pool. So, there were clay pits. They used to dig clay out of these pits long ago. I didn't know anything about that. But those pits filled up with water, so therefore we were allowed to go down there. We'd take a couple of jelly sandwiches. A couple of kids rallied around the neighborhood, because most of the people that I grew up with, some are still here. I know Clifford Poindexter has moved to Wilmington but still he has a home out there. Grew up with Ruby Copper, Charles Miller, which they call him "Chick" Miller. Isaiah and Beatrice Waters stayed down here. The Knotts' family lived out here. I'll get back to the story. We used to go down there to swim. I never learned to swim properly because I learned the doggie paddle. That's the only thing I can do and I can swim underwater but I can't stroke. We picked blackberries after we finished swimming and we walked down the railroad track to Yorklyn. There was a store down there. It was Gregg's Store, which was where they housed the post office also. And we'd walk all the way down there. And as we were walking down the railroad track, there used to be some houses along there. So we would sell these blackberries to the white people and they would come and give us 30¢ or something for this little container of blackberries. Then we used to go to Gregg's Store and buy ice cream cones. According to how many of us it was, you know. It was 5¢ a cone. So each of us would get a cone and then we would walk off. But we were allowed to do that. And nobody ever got in trouble. There were people, you, know, kids would have scraps, little fights—but nothing serious. We all played together. This used to be our summer thing. But then in the fall we would go back to school.

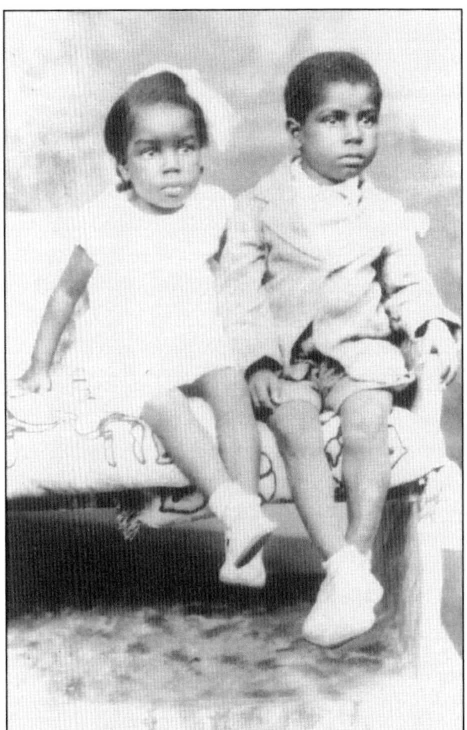

Jean Elizabeth Bolden Fleming and Her Brother William Bolden.

Chapter 7
Newark

Allan O. Wilson, D.D.S.

I was born in Newark, Delaware, in March of 1920. I was one of 12 children and I was number 11. I had a mother and dad who had maybe two years of schooling. My mother, Laura, never worked. They were married in 1902 or something like that. My dad, Charles, was just a handyman working for two white families, the Barnums and the Johnsons—very nice people. My dad worked 8 hours a day at 40¢ an hour. So you can figure that was not a lot of money. But they were very conscientious people. If I were to ask my mother, "Mom, do you think I could do this?" "Son, I don't know but, but I know this. If somebody else's son can, so can you." My mother and dad could hardly read or write. My dad was born in 1879. My mother was born in 1886. We ended up with one physician, one dentist, one nurse, and two social workers. My oldest brother was born in 1902 and my youngest sister was born in 1925. So it was sort of like two families. My mother lived to see my baby sister reach 11 years old. Of course I was 16. She died August 31, 1936. There is a cemetery there on Rose Street which is adjacent to my family home. She and my dad are both buried in a common grave. When my mother died he had them go down 9 feet. When he passed 9 years later, they opened the grave 6 feet.

My mother and dad couldn't read or write and my mother in particular. My father got so that he could count money and write his name and whatnot. They eventually went to night school. When my older brothers and sisters went to school my mother learned along with them. They taught her and she got to be so she was literate.

I went to Vernon Avenue Public School. Of course it was segregated. This was a new building that they built after having this little one-room school. The school they had for blacks. Well, I don't know whether it was indoctrination but the Dupont's in their way were very nice people. They built all these schools all over the state of Delaware for blacks.

So, I think that's the best thing to say. They weren't as nice as the white schools because the state was building them. But you know I came to high school here in Wilmington and I had to walk by the high school in Newark and couldn't attend. Catch a bus at 6 o'clock in the morning and come to Howard High School. I played football while I was in high school. I use to have to hitchhike home at night because that was the only way I could get home. It was usually 7 or 8 o'clock at night. I'm one who never missed a day in school. My mother had an unusual psychology. I wouldn't want to wake up. I wouldn't want to get out of bed, you know. And so I'm sick. She would simply say something like, "Well, you know if you are sick now at 3:30, you'll still be sick." So out of bed I got.

Well, without flattery, my family was very respected in the town. In a remote sort of way white people had a kind of respect for us. My dad could hardly read or write but he was a man of integrity. I remember it was so difficult for blacks to use the bank and what not. My dad signed a lot of notes for $100 dollars so some could get money. One hundred dollars a note. My dad was treasurer of this little church. And they had what was called a missionary box they passed during service. You'd put your little nickels or dimes or what ever it was in this. And this was used as a missionary fund to help. I'll never forget in 1927 we had a fire. My dad kept this money, the missionary money in a little tin box. All the people's money was burnt. Someone told my dad not to disturb it. That if he took it to the bank, the bank had a way of recognizing ashes of money and they would redeem it. I can remember this just as a little kid but never knew the difference until I was an adult in retrospect. And I know just because of the reputation of who my dad was, the president said, "Well, Charlie," (you know they called all black folk by their first names) "how much was in there?" and he said, "One hundred fifty to two hundred dollars." And when they took it and came back, they said, "Charlie that

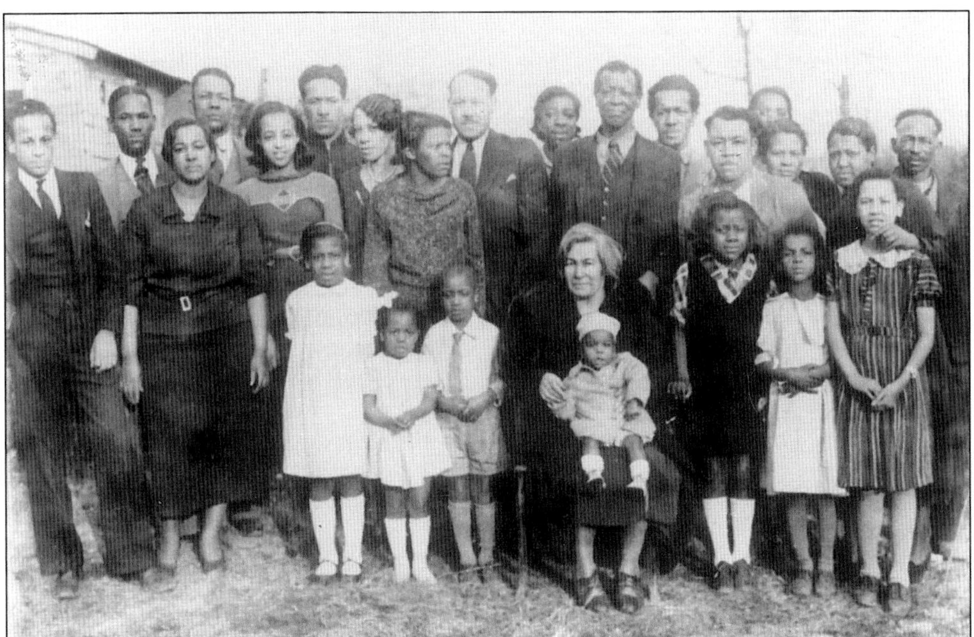

***Allan O. Wilson and His Parents and Siblings.** Allan is partially pictured to the far left in the three-piece navy suit.*

was right." And gave him the money. This was the type of reputation that my dad had.

I can remember some little things and didn't recognize them until I became an adult. My dad worked for a white family as a handyman and they had about a half acre beside the house. My dad said to him one day, "Mr. Barnum, why don't you build a garden here? I know how to grow a lot of nice vegetables and whatnot." And he said, "Go ahead!" You know what my dad had in mind—that he'd get some groceries. He did this and the man gave him everything he wanted. He had white squash, corn, bell squash. My dad would come home with a wheel barrow full and spread it throughout the community. The man knew he was not stealing. All the man wanted was what he needed. And the man knew my father was doing this to help people. And that's what he did. Every day practically he spread this food along the black community.

As I said, my dad worked for two white families. At least two times they bought him a car. And I'll never forget this. One of them said. They called him by his first name, then. "Charlie, I don't want those boys driving your car!" And you know what my dad told him? "You keep your car," he said. "Your children drive your's, so mine will drive mine!" That's what he told them. And you know what they told him, "Charlie, if you feel like that about it, go ahead and take this car." And my dad could hardly read or write. That's right! We had a 1939 6-horsepower Ford. They bought him two or three cars. But he told them, "My kids can have anything your kids can have, if I work for it!"

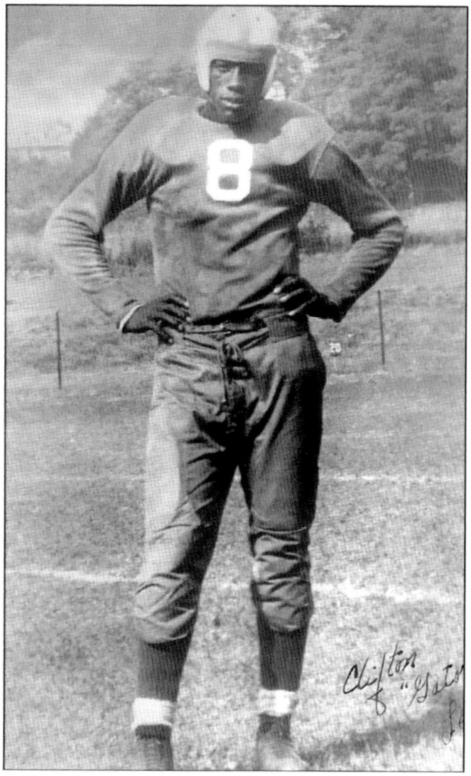

CLIFTON LEWIS.

CLIFTON ALVIN LEWIS

I was born March 7, 1929. I'm a split family. My father's name was Delbert Lewis and my mother's name was Catherine Lewis. Mama was born in Newark and father was born in Elkton, Maryland. I guess by the time I was born, I had three brothers and sisters. Got a whole lot of half brothers and sisters because he married two or three times. But my sister Violet who is still living, she's the oldest. My brother James died two years ago, three years ago. And myself. We stayed in Newark with my grandparents David Lewis and Carolyn Lewis. My grandfather was a farmer, primarily, and a laborer and grandma was a housewife. She didn't do anything but stay home. We lived 115 College Avenue. It's now part of the University of Delaware campus. When my grandfather and grandmother died the house and property was left to my Aunt Mary and my mother with a survivor's clause. My mother lived longer than any of the rest of them so we took all the property. None of us wanted it, so we decided to sell it to the University of Delaware. We didn't have running

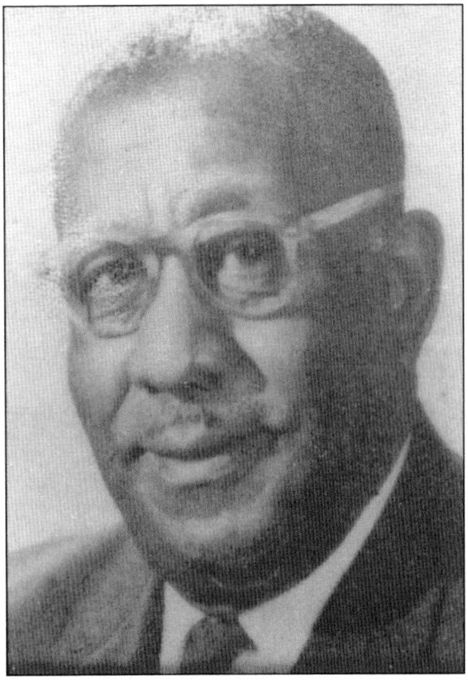

Clifton Lewis's father, Delbert Lewis.

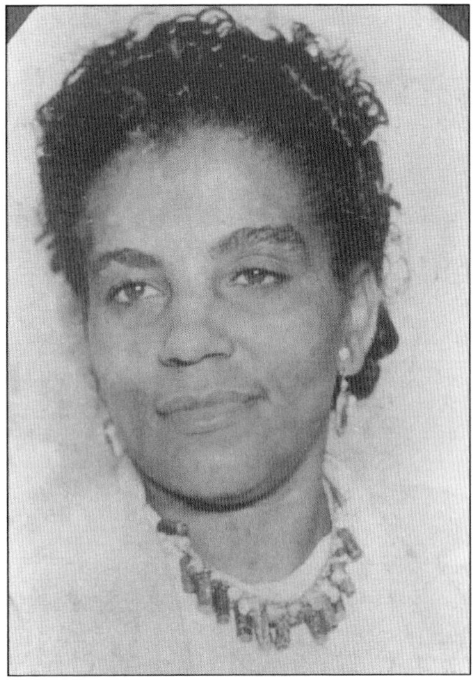

Clifton Lewis's mother, Catherine Lewis.

water—we had a pump. We had a junk stove in the kitchen, a pot-bellied stove in the living room and that's what you got for heat. We had those kinds of stoves that she had downstairs in the bedrooms, so in the morning, in order to get ready for school and work and all, you had to run downstairs and you'd pump some water in a little pan. Then you took it upstairs and put it on top of the stove, so by the time you got dressed it was hot. Alright, it was quaint. But my grandfather, let's see, he had a big garden at home and he used to raise hogs and chickens. Everybody at that time raised chickens and he was a hog man.

Where will lived was on North College Avenue and below that was an Italian village. We played with them and when I went to school, it was a couple of boys who lived down on what we called Kennedy's Corner. That's North College Avenue and Cleveland. We lived right on the corner. I played with them, baseball and everything. But when school time came, they went this way. I had the opportunity to be the first black boy in the University of Delaware on a scholarship and I didn't want that. I wanted to get away from home. My mother used to work for Perkins, who was the president. He tried to get her to send me to the university before blacks were even thought about inviting. I just wanted to get away from home. I was lucky. I mean I had a lot of good things happening in my life. I was the first black to play American Legion baseball.

That was two black guys and one white guy that did that. That was Bob Saunders, and George Wilson, we called him "Inkie." And the man who owned the team, Hamilton, "Pop" Hamilton, he came up to Bobbie and Inkie and told them he wanted to do something about this color line in the American Legion Baseball in Delaware. And asked if they had any young man up there they could recommend. He would have to take a lot of stuff. And they recommended me. Of course I had to go to school. I was told

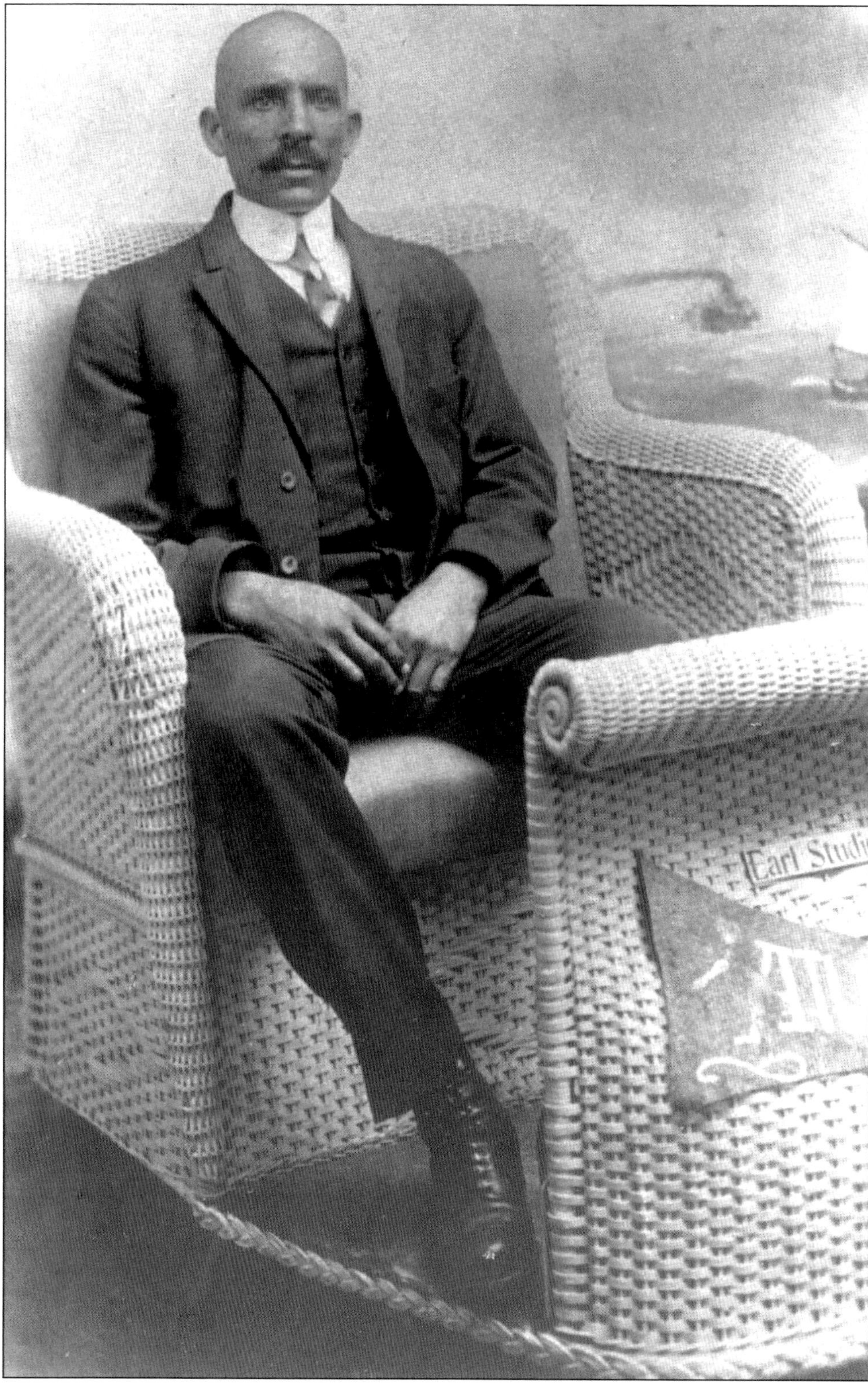

David Lewis, Clifton's Grandfather.

what I had to do when I got there from Bobbie and Inkie. I couldn't blow up when somebody called me a "Nigger." So, yeah, I came to be the first black to play American Legion Baseball. I was about 13, or 14. With the guys in Newark, it was no problem, 'cause many of them I knew. There was a white boy from New Castle, a boy names Sutton, who became a good friend of mine, so I didn't have any problems with them. I had problems when I went out to Conrad and played. I had trouble with some of the teams from downstate, when I played against them. An interesting thing was when we had the banquet, at the end of the season. They always had this big banquet in Dover and I was sitting with my teammates and Sutton had left his team and came over to sit beside me. Black boys from Delaware State were waiting tables. I'm the only black sittin' at the tables so one of the boys from Delaware State cruised by me and whispered, "I you want anything else to eat, hold your plate and I'll pick it up." I said, "What about my friend?" And he said, "Him, too." Until that point, I don't think any of the other white kids in there, other than the ones I knew, had anything to do with me—'til they found out we were getting more food. And they came running, slapped me on the back and everything. And Sutton told them, "You Suckers, get away from here!" But I didn't have to say anything. I didn't have to fight for myself. The Gregg boys (who lived not far from me), mother, a short Irish woman, she follows every game. I remember we were playing Conrad and I came up to bat. I got, "Nigger this and nigger that." All this you know while I'm trying to get my composure. And she came down out of the stands and grabbed two bats. She went up in the stands to this guy and said, "If you say anything else to him, I'm gonna hit you in the head with these bats. If I wanted to, I could turn him loose on you and he'd whip you but he's tryin' to do the right thing. But I'm gonna take up for him." She knew me when I was like this. It was a strange town. Newark was a strange town. The blacks lived here, the white lived there, but there was more harmony than it was anything else. I guess it might have been more harmony than in any small town in Delaware.

Chapter 8
Delaware City and Port Penn

Reverend Frank Gordon

It was early in my life that I moved from Hague, Virginia, to Delaware City, Delaware. Really, I was just about one year old. I came with my mother that winter, who had been working on the post in Delaware City. And due to the fact that the weather was very cold, Momma Lou and Papa Jake Sadler lived right where my mother passed with me in her arms and at one year old, during that cold winter, Momma Lou said to my mother, "Don't take that boy out in the cold. Leave him with us." Well that was it. I stayed with them in and out of their house for about five or six years. In the home of Momma Lou and Papa Jake was a daughter who had finished normal school and had begun to teach in a place called Kirkwood, Delaware. So it was her joy and delight always to try to teach me some of the academics, and most of all the courtesies that you should have as you grow up. In this home where we lived, where I lived most of my life, were these persons. One was a famous baseball player with the Delaware City Monarchs, and who later and in most recent years, had one of the stadiums in Delaware City named after him. His name was Bubby Sadler. There was Bubby Sadler at home; there was Phil Sadler at home and there was Frankie Sadler in the home. So being coddled by Hannah and this lovely family for many years, I had great inspiration on being something in life. They always encouraged me to do so. Let me say a word about this section of Delaware City where black people lived, because they wanted to live. They owned their own homes. There were seven families that lived very close together in Polktown, which they called it. In this section of Polktown where there were about seven families, there was an interesting church by the name of Mt. Salem UAME Church. The only church nearby. And there was a gentleman who was a Sunday School superintendent by the name of Mr. Alfred Miller. He took us all in to the Sunday school every Sunday—a wonderful, wonderful man.

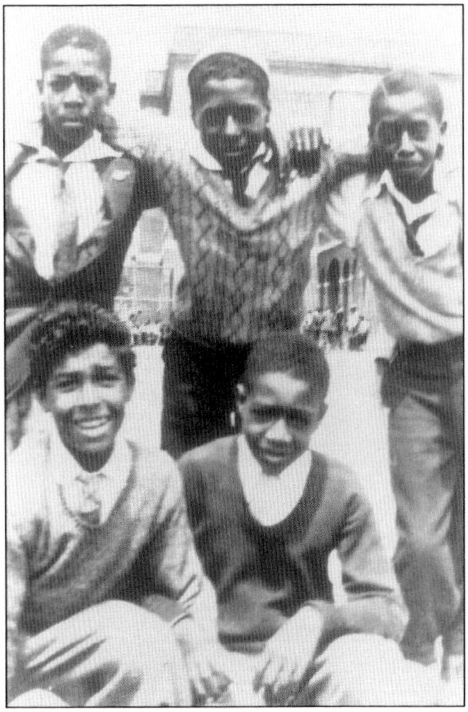

FRIENDS AT HOWARD HIGH SCHOOL. From left to right are (front row) Frank Gordon and Bill Washington; (back row) Philip Gooden, Zachary Scott, and Frankie Epps.

And he and his wife would often take us to their home. They had a nephew by the name of Alfred Miller who became a friend of mine after we graduated from school in Delaware City, and had gone to Wilmington to high school. Mr. Alfred Miller became a minister in the Union Church. And in later years when I would see him, I always thought if him as Mr. Alfred Miller, never as Reverend, and he never thought of me as anything but Frank. So we had a great comradeship between each other because I had respect for the kind of life he lived, and the kind of impressions he made upon me. Also, in this section of Delaware City where we lived were some interesting families whose names may not be recorded, yet they were unsung heroes. There was at the upper end of Polktown, a family by the name of Boyer. The head of the family was Mr. "Shady" Boyer. Now Mr. Shady Boyer must have had a link to the future. He was very interested in educating his children, and encouraged most of us. Mr. Shady, as I recall, had a wagon where he would go somewhere and bring back to the area where we were, groceries and fish and he sold them to the community. I think we call them hucksters. But whatever it was, he must have done well at it, because a large family with about ten children, most of them were college educated and became leaders in their own right. In this community were other names that I would like to mention, because they impressed me one way or another. There was an older fellow who had his arm cut off just above the elbow, and we called him "Uncle Tom." Uncle Tom was a fine man who would take time to talk to us, even play with us. And then there was also in this community of Papa Jake and Momma Lou, people who were mostly responsible for my whole life until the time that I went to Wilmington and to go to high school. And again, I say that there was in that family one person by the name of Bubby who became a very excellent baseball player. Now as you cross the bridge from Polktown into Delaware City, the main part of Delaware City, there was a path that went along the canal, the Delaware Chesapeake Canal, that connected the Chesapeake I think with the Delaware River. It was where the night boats would come through taking passengers from Philadelphia to Washington and then to Virginia. Quite often, my mother and I would take the boat and go back to Virginia where I was born and where most of the Gordons were at that time, many of the Gordons were. And along the tow path on the side where the Polktown people were these boats, we called them night boats, would come through there and the kids would gather 'round. They were hollering and waving at the people on the boats, and the people waved

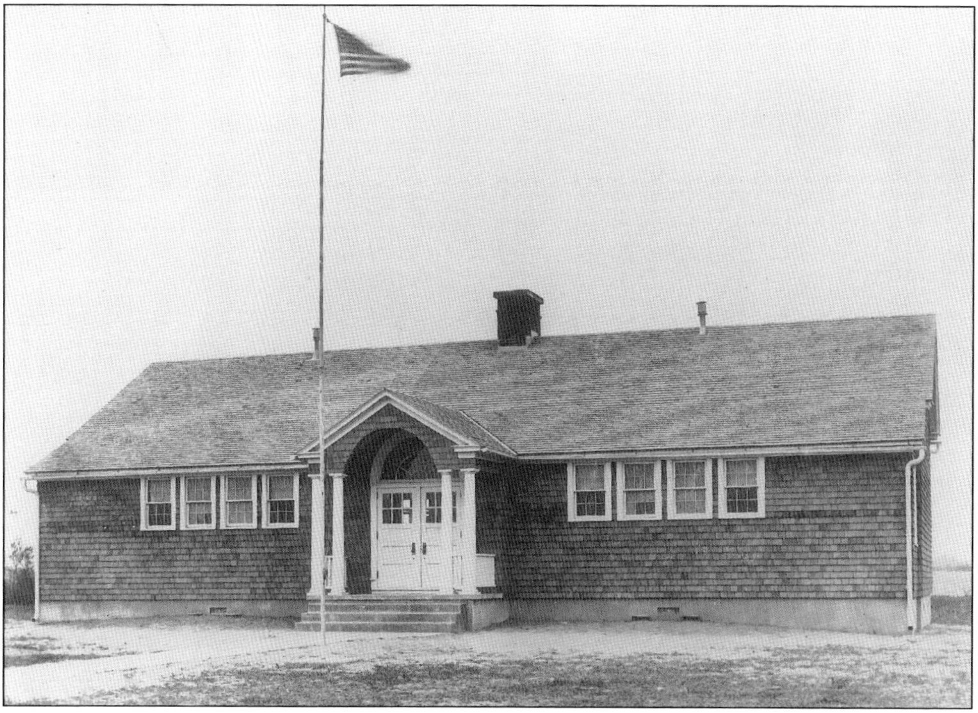

The Delaware City Colored School. (Courtesy of Hagley Museum and Library.)

back. And often times they would throw money at us on the ground and watch us scramble for the money that was thrown on the ground. This was quite interesting and memorable to me. But I spent the early part of the twenties in Polktown and I went to a two-room school. One room was the first to fourth grade, and in the other room was the fifth and sixth grade. After you finished that, then you could go to Howard High School. In the later years, they had buses that would take you. In the earlier years, if you had to go beyond that you either had to go by train to Wilmington or take residence in Wilmington in order to go to junior high and senior high school. So you see these were difficult times on order to get a good education. There was a man who devoted much of his life to education, by the name of Mr. Collins, who became principal of the two-room school. I think most people who might know anything about Delaware City will remember Professor Collins. Also from Delaware City we had a very famous baseball team by the name of the Delaware City Monarchs. This person who was in the Sadler home, Bubby was one of the stars, in fact, the main star on the baseball team. But other names that I remember were, and this son was a Delaware City citizen, and his name was Rogers. And then coming from New Castle, who played, was a pitcher, was a man by the name of Rick Lewis. So these are some of the memorable days that I had in Delaware City, especially in Polktown.

Jeanne Boyer Parler

I was born on June 30, 1923. My parents were Henrietta Jones Boyer and Shadrach Boyer. My father was a huckster. He would go to Philadelphia sometimes to get all kinds of vegetables and fruits. And I guess he went to Middletown and other places. And my mother stayed at

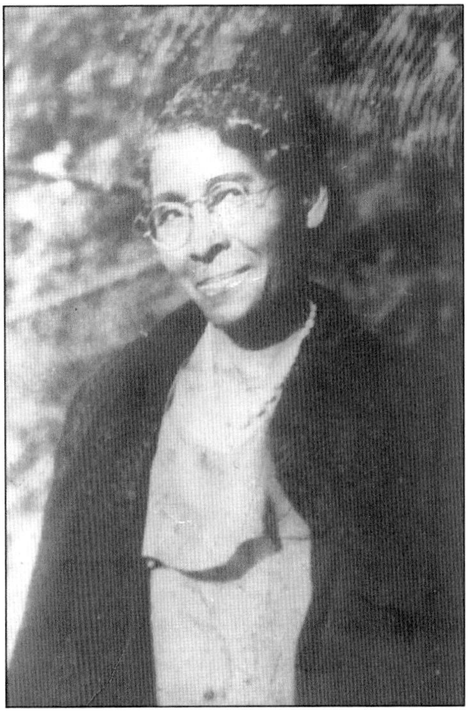

Jeanne's Mother, Henrietta Jones Boyer. *She owned real estate in Polktown.*

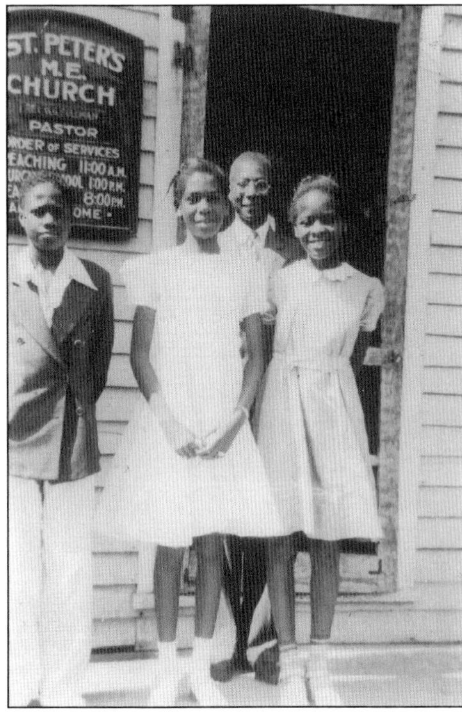

Some of the Members of the Methodist Youth Fellowship at St. Peter's Church.

home and reared the children most of the time. But there was a fort facility across the street, Fort Dupont. And the soldiers would bring their uniforms and she would wash and press them and sometimes she would go to the officers' homes and help them with work around the house. But most of the time she had to be home with her children because there were 11 of us. There was Pauline, Margaret, Louise, Shad, Samuel, and James, Madelyn, Marie, Henrietta, and Mildred.

My father was a rather easy going man—as sweet as he could be. Believed in buying my mother the best. He bought china. We had china from France and I still have some of the pieces. He bought her the piano because she wanted the children to take piano lessons. She was very fond of music. Oh, she loved music. She couldn't play the piano but she could always tell when we hit a wrong note. She wasn't in the room but she would yell from the kitchen, "That's wrong!" She had this woman, I think she was Irish, to come and teach us—just 50¢ a lesson. And Madelyn and I were taking them together at one time. But all of us had piano lessons except the boys. The boys didn't have them. This teacher would walk from Delaware City proper over to Polktown where we lived. She evidently thought the price was right because when she got near Polktown there were lots of rocks and stones and it wasn't paved that well. She had big bunions but she would come down to our house. She was very nice. She would call me "Now Sister" (I think she was Catholic) but any way she would always call me "Sister." "No, Sister." Madelyn was always so good. But I was laissez faire.

We went to church and we went to Sunday school. And we went to BYPU and we went to regular church. And of course that's where we had our social life because we would see our friends there. Sunday morning, Sunday afternoon and there was a night service or quartets or concerts from Wilmington or Roundabout, we'd always go to see that. We were teenagers then, my friend Sarah Taylor, Martha Taylor, and me.

Polktown was just a small little area. The Watson's lived there—Arthur Watson and his family. And my mother owned the two brick houses adjoining. She rented those out. I'm trying to remember who she rented them out to. Well, I can't. On the side of us my uncle, Wilson Jones, lived. They didn't have any children. But further down Naomi Jones, my cousin and her mother, Carrie, lived. And the Roberts family lived next to them. And there was an adjoining house and another set of Watsons, the older set—grandmother and grandfather, Thomas and Annie. And next to them was another one of our houses and my mother rented them out to another group of Watsons.

The most that I remember about Delaware City was we couldn't go to the library and I loved to read! We couldn't get books from the library located in the firehouse. So there was a good friend, she had been a teacher—Mrs. Ennis. And she had loads and loads of books. She let me and another one of my classmates, Ester Harmon, go into this room with all kinds of books. We would borrow those books and take them back and she'd give us more. Oh, she was a lovely person! Other things I remember about Delaware City were not that important. We didn't do much buying of goods down there. There wasn't what they called an American Store. People my sister's ages, older than we were, worked in the store. Sometimes we would go down with our older sisters and the white cashiers would carry on this

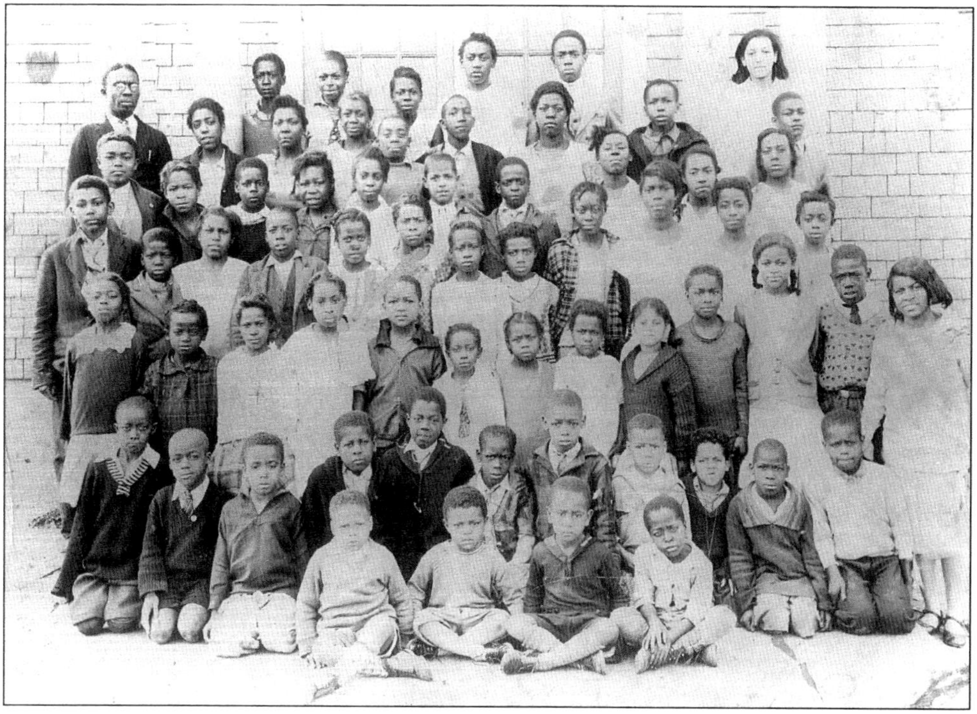

***The Delaware City Colored School with Mr. Collins, c. 1929.** Jeanne Parler is in the third row, sixth from the right. Her brother James is the first child in the second row. Her sister Marie is the last child in the fourth row, and her sister Madelyn is the fourth child from the right in the fourth row.*

great big conversation with my sisters. "And do you remember when..." And they would laugh and talk. And I would think to myself, "Well this is the way it's suppose to be. It should be like this all the time." But no, that was as far as it went. And of course we couldn't go into the ice cream parlor and eat. They would give us ice cream but we had to take it out with us. There really wasn't that much. There was a fabric store. My mother would buy fabric from there because she made a lot of the girls' dresses. But other than that Delaware City didn't hold that much for me.

There was a [white] high school girl whenever she would meet us (there usually were two or three of us black kids walking on the sidewalk) she would always smile and speak to us. Oh, my shoulders would go back and I would say, "Oh, she's so nice! She speaks to us." And we thought that was such a big thing. No, we never had white friends. Now some of the other girls that lived in Delaware City, maybe they had white acquaintances, not friends.

Robert George Harding

My date of birth is January 24, 1928. My parents were Perry Kenard Harding from Delaware City, and Mary Louise Harding, known as Madge, from Delaware City. Dad was a laborer up until he started working over at Governor Bacon, over at the Health Center at Fort Dupont. He was working there and Mr. Hart, who had a tailor shop, inquired if anyone was interested in learning to be a tailor and Dad agreed to it. So he started working with Mr. Hart at Fort Dupont as a tailor. And he did all the alterations basically when the soldiers wore pegs and things of this nature, you know. And also the state police, he did a lot of their work. Then he opened his own business at Sterling's Hotel, in the back of Sterling's Hotel. And he was there for I think five years. Then he bought two stores on Clinton Street. It was a haven. It was provisions for all of us to have everything we needed. The majority of things we wanted, we got because of Dad and Mom working at the shop. It was quite an experience. Never on the bread line. We played in and out of the tailor shop. In the yard upstairs. We lived over the tailor shop right there on Clinton Street for 29 years, I believe. We lived over the tailor shop and Dad was in business for 35 years. The majority of his work as far as tailoring went was with soldiers from Fort Dupont. They left Mr. Hart at Fort Dupont and come over to Dad because of his skills. Dad was an excellent tailor.

A lot of memories are concerning ... well I think we were looked at a little different than a lot of the others here because Dad was in business. It was a drug store here, Miss Larky had a drug store and she would always tell me that I could come in and have ice cream. But Ronny Portlock and my other cousins could never go in, so I would never go. But it was a case where it was segregated and they would not allow you to go. But because of Dad I could go to the store but I wouldn't go because the rest of them couldn't go. I'd gotten more grief from them than I did the other thing. Delaware City was very friendly. At a time when I was a youngster, if boys would come from New Castle and things like that, and if they started something with us, the white boys would run them out of town, you know. You basically had this kind of relationship. Kennard and I played ball with all the white boys whenever they had a game or something. They'd call Kennard and I to play ball with them. It was just a nice town. Everybody knew everyone. All the adults would correct the children, white or black it didn't matter, you know. So basically, it was a good town to grow up in.

I went to Delaware City 118 C from the first to the eighth grade. The teacher from

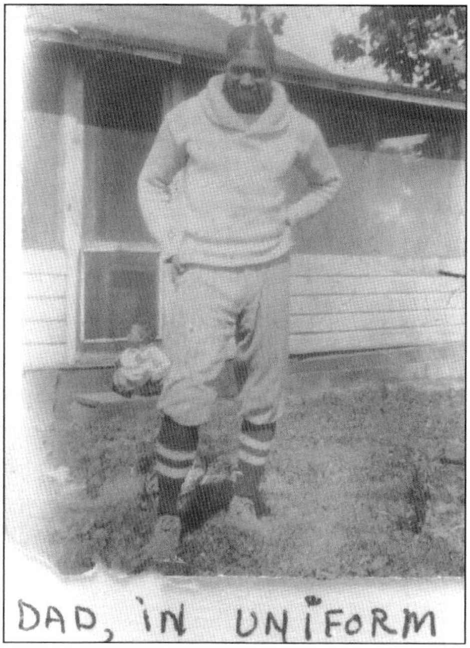

Perry Kenard Harding in His Early Years with the Delaware City Monarchs.

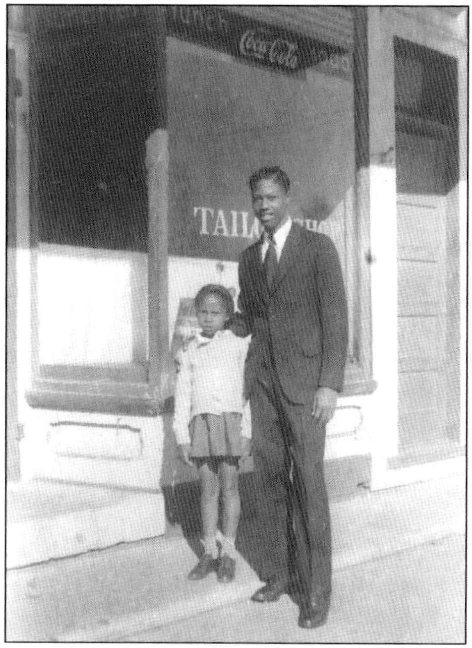

Robert Harding with His Sister Madge in front of Their Father's Tailor Shop.

one to four was Miss Carey Blackburn and from four to eight it was Mr. Clinton B. Collins. Then in the ninth grade we went to Howard High School. Well, I got a whippin every day for being mischievous either at school or home. I was always one who would always take a dare. "I bet you can't do somethin" and if I knew I could do it, I'd do it. Then I'd be in trouble. I remember one time I had done something in Miss Blackburn's room and the boys bet me that I wouldn't run from her. So I started runnin' from her and I'd get almost close enough for her to touch me and then I'd run a little faster. I would just keep her off. And I just got tired of runnin' and she got close to me, and I fell down on the floor, and she fell over me and fell off. The kids all laughed and I got two beatings that day. No, three... Mr. Collins, Miss Blackburn and Mama. You know that's what I mean mischievous things. I didn't think they were bad, but they were mischievous things, you know. Yeah, I did a lot of little things like that. I remember one time in school I did something and Mr. Collins was whipping me and I wouldn't cry and he beat me with the ... "black gentleman" he called it. Mr. Herb Brown has given him a horse ... a harness from a horse, a real thick leather strap that he used to double up. And he was whipping me and I wouldn't cry. I had welts all over my back and I sang "Home on the Range" 'cause he was beating me. And I just sang "Home on the Range" 'cause I wouldn't cry, you know. Then Mama and Dad both beat me for being so stubborn. And trying to show Mr. Collins up. Oh, boy, I'll tell you one incident there too. Pauline, a girl who Mr. Collins reared, was there and I had on a blue sock and a black sock. And Pauline said, "Oh, Bob's got mix matched socks on!" I thought she said Miss Madge's, and I went upside her head. And I got a terrible beating from Dad for fighting girls, you know. That's what I mean. That's the kind of things that I did. Yeah, I thought she said "Miss Madge's" and that was it.

The Delaware City Male Chorus was actually started by Mr. Jackie Watson and my dad. My dad was president, Mr. Jackie Watson was the secretary and treasurer. And we met every Tuesday night over the tailor shop. We used to have nice meetings. We used to practice every Tuesday and we sang from Connecticut down to Virginia all up and down. I was 14, so that would have been 1942 when we started. At one time there were 16 singers and Manny Brown was the piano player and Dad played piano, too. But Dad played by ear and Manny played by ear so the only one in the whole thing that knew any music was my brother Chester that played the guitar. So we had a fine time singing. We had a thing that nobody could have a drink coming to the meeting. Nobody could even have beer even on the breath. For years we used to travel. Like three car loads would go. Later we started hiring Mr. Earl Perry's bus and he used to take us different places. We paid him to take us. All we ever charged was 50/50 only of the offering they took in. We never set a price to anything.

Helen Marie Harding Powell

I was born December 26, 1930. My mother was, I thought she was a jack of all trades. She was the type of person who could do almost anything. She would paint. If something needed fixing, she would fix it. She was a very good mother, very nurturing. I was always under my mother's foot. Wherever she was, I was. I was always interested in cooking. So when I was a little tot, I would follow her. If she was making a pie, I would get a lid off a jar, and I would have to make my crust. Of course the crust would be so dirty sometimes nobody would eat it but it was my pie. I learned through her.

Most of the things we did were at home. After Daddy got finished working, then we would sit. We had this big living room and somebody would be playing pinochle. Somebody would be playing Chinese checkers. Somebody would play regular checkers. We'd have tables set up and all of us would get together, and

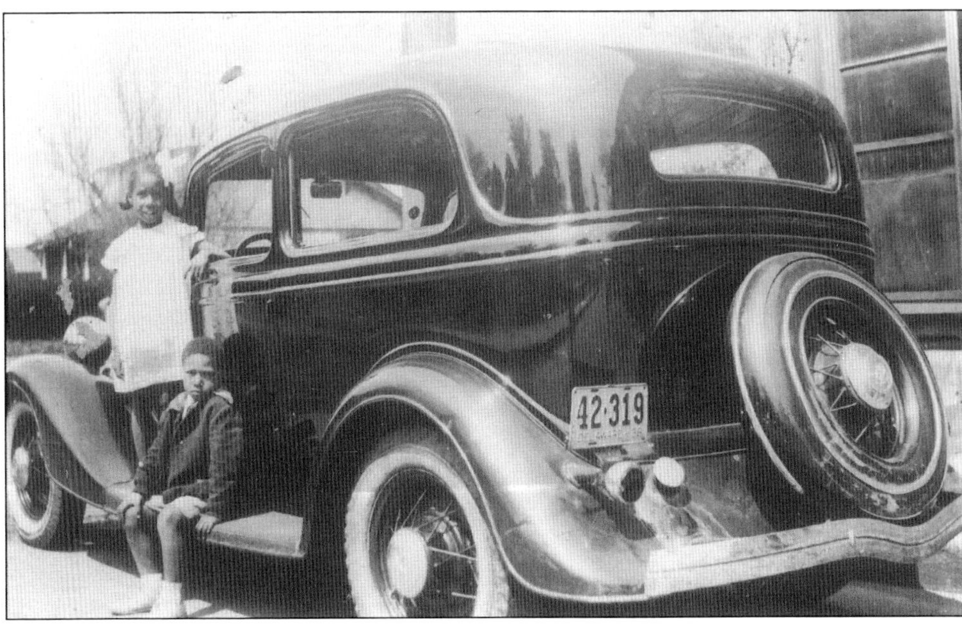

Helen Marie Harding Powell and Her Brother Chester Harding on the Running Board of Their Father's Car, c. 1935.

of course, if we had any friends, coming in, this is how we enjoyed ourselves as a family. We might play dominos. We played scrabble. We played all kinds of things. So we enjoyed it. We did every thing together as a family. And then we used to go as a family to wrestling matches. That's the armory in Wilmington. We did that every Thursday night. The was the outstanding thing for our family to do. We enjoyed that. I'll never forget one big wrestler, Indian wrestler, Jules Strongbow. I'll never forget his name. I was walking in there, one day not paying attention to where I was going, I bumped in to Jules Stongbow. I leaned over to my father and I said, "Oh, Daddy. Daddy!" "Don't tell me. What are you telling me for. He's too big for me." So naturally that tickled the wrestler, too. I guess that's why our parents, being relatively young, we did everything together. It really was a good childhood.

We had this car. And of course, I remember this car. The old cars would go uphill but the thing about it, you had to make sure you had enough gas in it. Because when you went up on an angle, if you didn't have enough gas in it, the gas wouldn't get to the accelerator to go. You would have to make sure you had gas or you can't go up a hill. And I remember one time, we were great for just taking a ride, just any place. There wasn't much to see then, but we would ride anyway. The car stops someplace along this farm road. And there is a bull in the field and he was ready to get loose. And the car stopped. Daddy got out. Daddy you know had to get out and crank the car from the front. Well, Daddy was out trying to crank this car, and the bull was there. We were scared to death. The bull didn't get out and of course he eventually got the car started.

Daddy used to played golf and of course years back, you weren't allowed on the golf course. He was very good at it. So what he would do is (he really didn't have a partner or anybody you know that lived in Delaware City) so what he would do is he would just go through the golf course in Pennsylvania. And so he would go to play golf and when he would go there sometimes they would tell him that he couldn't play because he was colored. He would always meet up with somebody else who was playing golf and they would invite him to go along and these would be white men. They would say, "Well you can play but he can't play." There would be some men that stood up. They said, "Well if he can't play, we can't play." They stood up for him. So they said, "Well, then he can play." They would let him play because he wanted to play golf so badly and he was good at it. But they did not want him to play golf.

Joseph Harmon

I was born in August 27, 1927. My family goes back to very early years in the 1800s. My grandfather's name was David

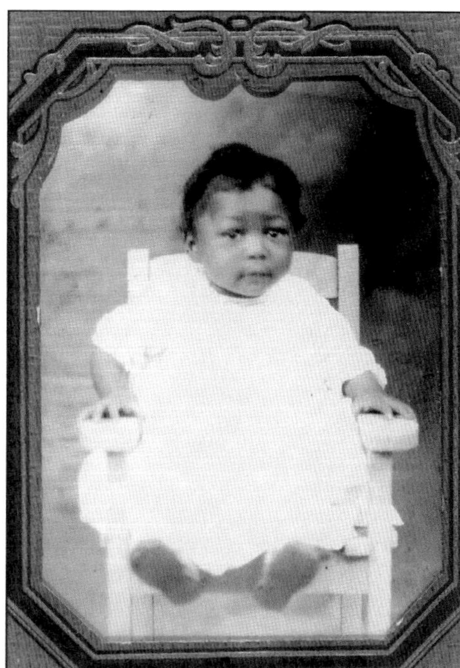

Joseph Harmon.

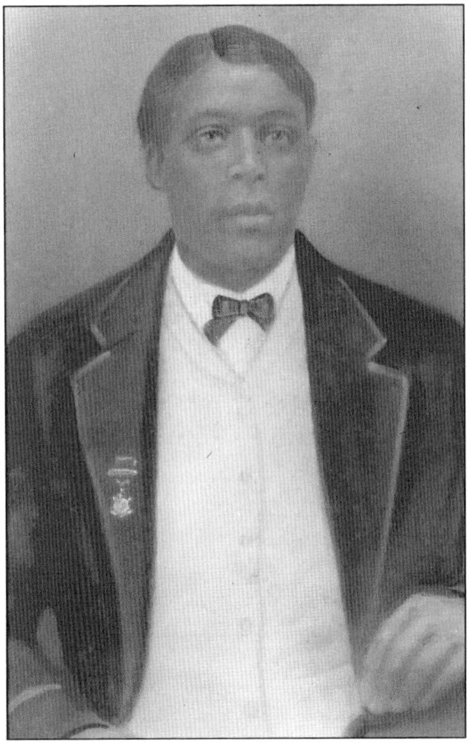

David Alexander Harmon.

Alexander Harmon. He fought in the Civil War, and he was in at least five battles and was wounded in the foot at Newmarket, Virginia. His wife was Margaret Congo and they lived outside of Port Penn, Delaware, which was called Congotown. My mother's father was named Samuel Lewis and he married Hester Money Lewis, who was my grandmother. My mother's name was Arlena Lewis and of course she married my father and became Harmon. She grew up in Odessa, Delaware. She was born in 1881. My father grew up in Congotown, which is a small community just outside of Port Penn. Mostly Congos lived there and the family home was the last standing building in Congotown. Many members of our family are buried in the Zion Cemetery, which is in Congotown. I was born in Wilmington, Delaware, but I grew up in Delaware City. I went to Delaware City Public School #118C and from there to Howard High School.

My father, while he lived in Delaware City, was the lawn man for H.P. Scott, who was a banker. H.P. Scott had a nine-hole golf course and many farm animals. That was a great estate which was located on what is now the refinery outside Delaware City. My mother did mostly housework. She worked at the Scott estate part-time. I had two sisters. My older sister was named Bernice and she was 12 years older than I. My younger sister's name was Ester, and she was 6 years older than I.

In the 1930s in Delaware City, which was during the era of the Depression, we were all poor. But there was enough work to keep most of the families employed. Delaware City was a community which of course was south of the Mason Dixon Line, so therefore some of the facilities were segregated. We managed to have at least a decent relationship with the white population. I don't remember any ugly incidents in town.One of the ironies of living in a place like that is that the school law prevented us from engaging in competitions, sports competitions with our white friends. However, on our own free time we used to go up to the school or on other diamonds and have competitions. We played with families by the name of Neal, Armstrong, and Higgins.

Well I guess it was exciting around Memorial Day. Near our home there were three different cemeteries. They were all in one block. And on Memorial Day, the soldiers from Fort Dupont would come over and fire over the graves of veterans in the cemeteries, which was pretty exciting for a young fellow. A lot of the activity and employment from Delaware City was centered around Fort Dupont, which was just across the canal from Delaware City.

Well, first I perhaps learned about my grandfather initially because every Memorial Day my father would get a flag and we would put it on his grave. I found out much later that he was in the 22nd Regiment Colored Troops and they were stationed down around Petersburg. And my grandfather used to tell my father (because my grandfather was dead before I was born) how they used to come up in files and load their rifles, fire them, and then they would fall back and someone else would step up and take their place. And this is how they managed most of the fighting in those days. They did not have automatic weapons.

At that time, there was a section which we called the "Y." It was named Y because the railroad used to come in and they would use two sections of track which would form a Y to switch their box cars around. But back in the other side of the railroad track was marsh and there was a beach that we would go swimming in. That's the Delaware River really. And at that time, I never knew of any lines drawn but we stayed to ourselves and the whites stayed to themselves. And it just seemed to be an invisible line that you didn't cross. But it was the same water, the same beach. But that was always free, particularly early in the summers, through June and July. Then we would stop swimming because people would say it was the dog days of August and you didn't go swimming then—for whatever reason.

William Jones Jackson

I was born in Philadelphia, to Minnie Jones, which was my real mother. She brought me to Wilmington, and I stayed with an aunt in Jone's Alley. My adopted father used to have a garage in that alley and he said he saw this little boy doing somersaults on the cobblestones and he thought that he was the greatest thing since kids were born. And he asked my mother, since she was partly blind and couldn't really do for me, if he could adopt me. She agreed and they went to Louis L. Redding. Lawyer Redding drew up the papers that were necessary to adopt a child back in those days. When we went before the judge (the judge was white) he said to me, "Your name (my name was suppose to have been William Arthur Jones) will no longer be William Arthur Jones. You'll be William Jones Jackson and will call these people mother and father for the rest of your life. And I just smiled and said, "Yes, sir."

My father was self-employed. He was a roofer. And he was one of a few that were self-employed back at that time. You know he came from a family of self-employed people. Mr. Hayman was a plumber and they owned several acres down in Port Penn next to our acreage. And he had a couple of sons. At one time the Haymans, I mean the Greens, which was my father's family that lived down in Port Penn, they owned all the land from Port Penn almost out to Route 13 at that time. They were free people. They weren't slaves in anyway. The Greens were very prominent down there. They were related to my dad. His mother was a Green and his father's name, believe it or not, was William J. Jackson. And when I saw it on a piece of paper, I liked to flip, 'cause by my being adopted, my name became William Jones Jackson.

I was fortunate enough about my mother being a schoolteacher and my father being self- employed that I had just about every toy in the world and the other kids down there didn't have roller skates. They didn't have bicycles. They didn't have none of that stuff. But I did. And I had a movie projector and they all wanted to come out to the house and see this movie projector to see the movies—the white and black kids and this is back in the 1930s. A guy named Clyde which was one of the white guys down there, he was my buddy. We used to go swimming every April and May. How cold the water was, down at the wharf in Port Penn. One day we decided to swim across to Jersey. So we got one of the fellows. And he got a little boat. And

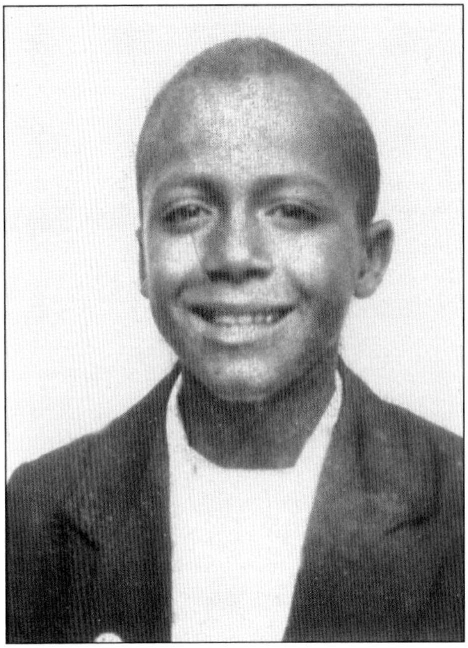

William Jones Jackson as a Boy.

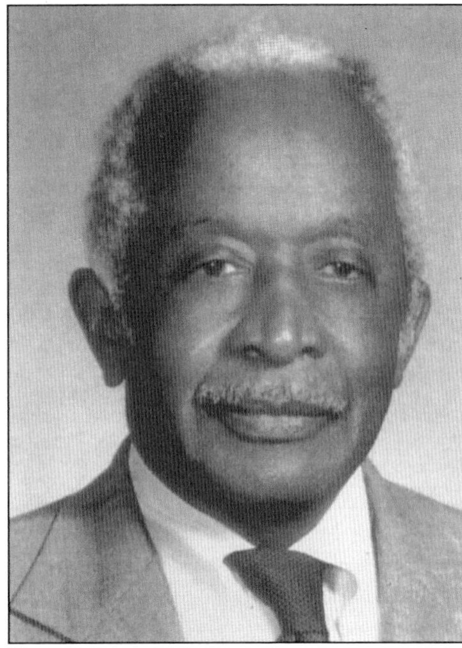

Lawyer Louis L. Redding.

Clyde and I and then an Italian, I can't remember his name now, but we swam on both sides of the boat. We had him along in case we got the cramps. The men from Port Penn, the fishermen (it was a fishing village) came out there in boats and got us and put us back in the boat because they said that two swimmers that lived in Port Penn drowned trying to do the same thing. But we used to do other things. We'd go down to the wharf and the people there would be crabbing. We used to dive down and take their baskets and tie them to the bottom of the pier. Then when they tried to pull it the string would break and when they'd leave, we'd have crab baskets. We had a good time. We played on the farm. I used to love to go around and watch when they had thrashing. We used to thrash wheat. All the farmers would help each other. So what I would like to do is to go on each farm when they were helping and work for nothing because they fed you. They had some good country meals there. We used to go ice skating. They had a pond down there. Carrie Jones, on her property, which had 250 acres and her name was Green. We used to go to her pond and take ice skates and skate on her pond.

My mother was Frances Jackson. They thought she was the best teacher in town. They did have very wonderful teachers in Howard School. You could not beat the teachers. They had so much dedication and so much concern for the children at that time. I have seen my mother hold my dad up and go down to Popular Street and buy shoes and clothes for the kids so they could come to school—out of her money. I've seen her do that plenty of times.